Camping
North Carolina

Help Us Keep This Guide Up to Date

Every effort has been made by the author and editors to make this guide as accurate and useful as possible. However, many things can change after a guide is published—campgrounds open and close, grow and contract; regulations change; facilities come under new management, and so forth.

We appreciate hearing from you concerning your experiences with this guide and how you feel it could be improved and kept up to date. While we may not be able to respond to all comments and suggestions, we'll take them to heart, and we'll also make certain to share them with the author. Please send your comments and suggestions to the following address:

Globe Pequot Press
Reader Response/Editorial Department
PO Box 480
Guilford, CT 06437

Or you may e-mail us at:

editorial@GlobePequot.com

Thanks for your input, and happy camping!

Camping
North Carolina

A Comprehensive Guide to Public Tent and RV Campgrounds

Melissa Watson

FALCONGUIDES

GUILFORD, CONNECTICUT
HELENA, MONTANA

To my siblings—
Maria Payton, Doug Watson, Sue Strazza
We've laughed, we've cried, and we've laughed some more.
You guys helped mold me into the woman I am today. Thank you!
I LOVE YOU!

Copyright © 2013 Rowman & Littlefield

FalconGuides is an imprint of Globe Pequot Press.

Falcon, FalconGuides, and Outfit Your Mind are registered trademarks of Rowman & Littlefield.

Maps by Design Maps Inc. © Rowman & Littlefield.
Interior photos by Melissa Watson unless otherwise noted.
Project Editor: David Legere
Layout Artist: Sue Murray

Library of Congress Cataloging-in-Publication Data is available on file.

ISBN 978-0-7627-4813-6

Printed in the United States of America

Distributed by NATIONAL BOOK NETWORK

Contents

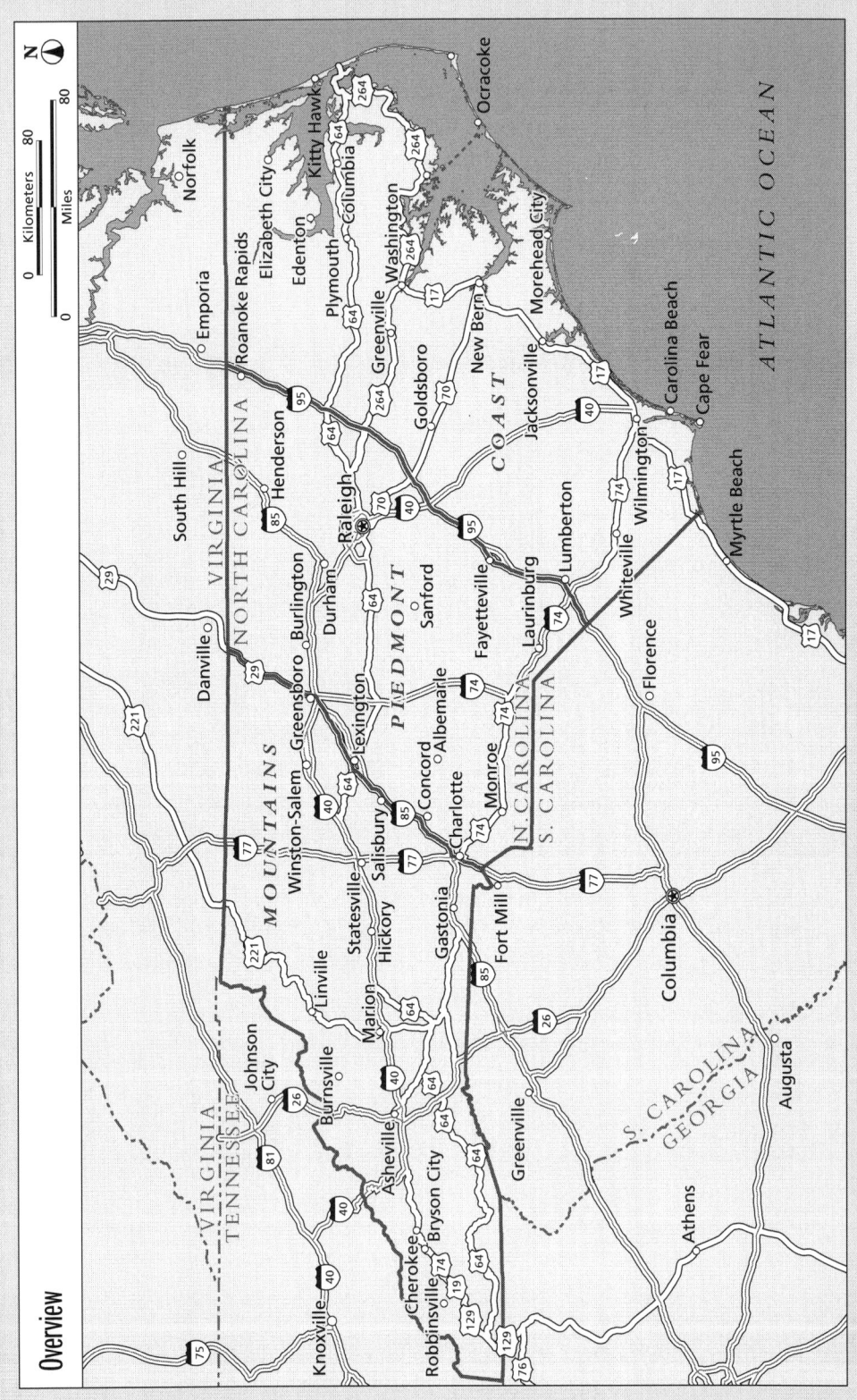

Overview

N

Kilometers
0   80
Miles
0   80

VIRGINIA

NORTH CAROLINA

TENNESSEE

VIRGINIA

S. CAROLINA

S. CAROLINA

GEORGIA

ATLANTIC OCEAN

COAST

PIEDMONT

MOUNTAINS

Ocracoke

Norfolk
Emporia
South Hill
Roanoke Rapids
Elizabeth City
Kitty Hawk
Edenton
Columbia
Plymouth
Washington
Greenville
Henderson
Danville
Goldsboro
New Bern
Morehead City
Jacksonville
Carolina Beach
Cape Fear
Wilmington
Whiteville
Lumberton
Myrtle Beach
Raleigh
Durham
Sanford
Fayetteville
Laurinburg
Florence
Burlington
Greensboro
Lexington
Albemarle
Monroe
Winston-Salem
Salisbury
Concord
Charlotte
Fort Mill
Columbia
Statesville
Hickory
Gastonia
Linville
Marion
Johnson City
Burnsville
Asheville
Greenville
Augusta
Athens
Knoxville
Cherokee
Bryson City
Robbinsville

75
81
26
40
40
19
129
129
76
64
64
64
221
221
29
29
85
77
40
64
85
77
26
95
74
74
74
74
85
77
40
70
95
64
647
264
264
264
264
264
17
117
117
117
40
95

Franklin

Highlands to Cashiers

Waynesville

Brevard to Asheville

Burnsville to Marion

Marion to Morganton

Roanoke Rapids

Laurinburg to Whiteville, Elizabethtown

Wilmington

Kenansville to Goldsboro

Jacksonville to Havelock

Beaufort to Harkers Island

Washington

Swanquarter to Nags Head/Outer Banks

Columbia to Plymouth

Edenton to Windsor

Hertford to Murfreesboro

Elizabeth City

Acknowledgments

First and foremost, my entire family has been so supportive in every way! Terri Sansonetti; Maria, Frazier, Christina, and Cory Payton; Doug Watson; Sue, Tom, Frank, Amy, Thomas, Joe, Kristen, Rebecca, Nathaniel, Katilee, Mark, Jonathon, Joshua, and Silas Strazza; Michelle, Roland, and Lucas Arisolo. I love you! Thank you ALL! To my "besties": Dawn McKinney, Shari Santos, Ixa Santos, Jenn Getter, Kristi Alsup, Cheryl Giovagnorio, Liz Martinez, Irene Freer, Terri Bennett—thanks for filling my downtime with laughter, love, and lots of FUN! My crew at Station 51 Craig Hatton, Chris Uzzo, Scott Barksdale, David Adams, Mike Osuna—as always, you have my back. My trusty pup Mikey, for keeping me company on the road, and keeping my tent warm.

And to the folks associated with the parks, you were an integral part of assuring accuracy: Jack Campbell, Dale Cagle, David Evans, Shelia Zuccaro, Brenda Arant, Ron Anundson, Theresa Savery, Deborah Walker, Terry Wood, Steve Godfrey, Jaime Osborne, Rebecca Montaldo, Brooke Ries, Heather Yanno, Jeremy Royster, Bryce Fleming, Toby Hall, Neill Lee, Shane Freeman, Patsy Hair, Kristen Woodruff, Erin Whitman, Steven Wilson, Dennis Foster, Wade Keeler, Kitty and Garry Marshall, David Tweedie, Steve Rogers, Debbie Leete, Roy Jenkins, and Jeff Turner. Thank you!

Introduction

Whatever your style of camping, whether you string a hammock between two trees and sleep under the stars or you prefer the comforts of an RV, North Carolina has a place for you.

The majestic mountains of the Blue Ridge beckon you with waterfalls galore and trail upon trail. Park your RV alongside one of several lakes in the Piedmont for spectacular sunsets bursting with color. Or head to the coast and pitch your tent on the shores of the Atlantic as the waves lap at the sand. No matter where you head, as you settle into your camp chair after a long day of hiking, or following a busy work week, the sounds of the crickets and frogs begin to lull you. Your tension eases as the glow of the flame flickers, mesmerizes. Then, as you rest at ease, you hear in the distance the rustle of a raccoon or a series of hoots from a great horned owl. This is why you're here. This is what you came for. Slowly you let go of your stress as the warm crackle of the fire begins to soothe your senses.

After spending months in a tent, six weeks at a time, with Mikey, my hundred-pound puppy, I was able to gather the information within these pages. Doing my homework, I drove thousands of miles visiting campground after campground, collecting information and enjoying as much of the experience as possible. The main focus of this book is campgrounds that you can drive right up to, put the car in park, and set up camp. I have, however, included a few campgrounds that require a very short walk and others that are "canoe-to" camping platforms that are prevalent in the coastal region. While I've done my best to provide as much information as possible, I recommend stopping by the ranger station or visitor center whenever possible prior to setting up camp. These folks are full of knowledge and are more than happy to share a wealth of information with you about the history of the area and the activities you can enjoy at their facility. Pack your gear, grab your camera, and get out and explore!

How to Use This Guide

As you thumb through the pages of this book, you will notice that it has been broken down into geographic regions. There are three major regions commonly designated in the state of North Carolina: the Mountains, the Piedmont, and the Coast (which includes the Outer Banks). To help you navigate and find the campground nearest your destination, I have broken it down even further into smaller geographic areas based on the nearest town. Maps are provided for each area, and tables provide a useful quick-reference tool to help you see if a campground suits your needs. For each entry I have provided essential information on certain common elements. Here's a brief explanation of each.

Location: If applicable, I have provided a physical address and the distance and direction from nearby towns to give you a general idea of where the campground is.

Season: While many of the campgrounds in the coastal region are open year-round, some on the Outer Banks, for example, and many in the mountain region are subject to extreme weather fluctuations and are open seasonally. I have listed the season dates, but some are subject to change. It's a good idea to call first and confirm that the campground is open and that campsites are available, especially in the winter months, November to March.

Sites: Here I have listed the number and type of campsites available. RV sites can accommodate RVs and may or may not have electric and water hookups. Tent sites are designed specifically for tent camping, but you can still drive right up to your site. Walk-in or canoe-to camping is tent only and is accessed either by a short walk or by boat. For those looking for a less-rustic experience, some of the campgrounds also offer cabin rentals.

Campgrounds listed as "dispersed" camping are not actual campgrounds but more a general area with designated campsites. Many forest roads, for example, offer well-groomed campsites right off the side of the road. Most of these sites have a tent pad, fire ring, and even a picnic table. These sites are designed for tents only and have no facilities whatsoever. You must bring all of your supplies, food, water, and even a shovel to dig a "cat hole" to dispose of bodily waste.

Group camps are typically reserved for nonprofit organizations, such as the Boy or Girl Scouts, or church groups, but campgrounds have been known to make exceptions. If you are planning a trip with seventeen of your closest friends, the logistics are much easier if you can stay in a group campsite, so it certainly doesn't hurt to ask.

Maximum length: This is the maximum-length RV the campground can accommodate. It's not to be confused with the maximum length of stay, which in most places is fourteen days. Most campgrounds in this book can accommodate RVs up to 40 feet; some can handle RVs as long as 148 feet.

Facilities: What's available at the campground? Here you'll find whether the bathhouse has flush or vault toilets or if you can expect a hot shower. I'll also tell you what amenities there are, such as a camp store.

Fee: I personally visited every campground in this book in 2012. The fees listed are per night, based on what the fee was at that time. As with anything in life, fees are subject to change. If cost might be an issue, call ahead.

$ = $0–$10
$$ = $10–$19
$$$ = $20 or more

If you see a range of fees, such as $$–$$$, assume that the tent sites are less and the RV sites are more. Many of the campgrounds have what's known as a self-pay station at the entrance, based on the honor system. Fill out an envelope, place the fee inside, drop the envelope in the safe box, and you are good to go. Keep in mind that you will need exact change unless you don't mind donating a few extra dollars to the forest service.

Management: I have gone to great lengths to try to include every public campground in the state. This section lists the agency—local, state, or federal—that maintains the park. In some cases the campgrounds may be located on federal land but run by a private concessioner.

Contact: Here I have listed the phone number and any pertinent websites where you can obtain more information. If a campground takes reservations, I have included that contact information as well. Keep in mind that many campgrounds fill up quickly, especially on weekends and holidays. It's a good idea to take advantage of the reservation system to ensure that you get a campsite.

Finding the campground: I've given my best effort to provide you with explicit driving directions, but there's nothing more valuable than a good map to help you navigate. I highly recommend the *DeLorme: North Carolina Atlas & Gazetteer*. I've been using this in conjunction with the National Geographic topographical maps for years. These maps have been an invaluable tool, helping me find my way around the mountains and back roads across the state. They include highways, state roads, and many forest service roads as well.

Today many people rely strongly on GPS units or on maps in their "smart" phones. While these devices do have value, I cannot stress enough that they also have limitations. A GPS is only as good as its satellite connection, and a smart phone is only useful when you have a signal. Please be aware that in many areas of the national parks and forests, and in remote parts of the state, you will not have cell phone service. So be sure to have a good map handy as a backup plan.

GPS coordinates: I have included GPS coordinates for each campground entry. For dispersed camping I have provided a general GPS coordinate of the forest road itself rather than a coordinate for each campsite.

About the campground: This is where I tell you a little bit about the campground and what to expect when you visit. Along with a description, you'll find out what kind of activities the campground offers, such as hiking and mountain biking. I also tried to alert you to any nearby attractions that might be worth a visit.

Key for Tables

Total sites
Hookup sites
Maximum RV: length in feet
Hookups: E = Electric, W = Water, S = Sewer
Toilets: F = Flush, V = Vault
Showers: Y or N
Drinking water: Y or N
Dump station: Y or N
Recreation:
    H = Hiking
    S = Swimming
    F = Fishing
    B = Boating
    L = Boat Launch
    R = Horseback riding/Bridle trails
    M = Mountain biking
    C = Cycling
    O = Off-road vehicle trails
    P = Picnicking
    T = Tubing
    ★ = Other activities
    Fee: $, $$, $$$
    Reservations: Y or N
    n/a = Not applicable

For Your Safety

Whenever you are planning a camping trip, whether in a tent or an RV, there are certain preparations that need to be made and important things to consider. Here are a few friendly reminders to help you enjoy your camping experience to the fullest.

Weather

The weather in North Carolina can range from hot, hot, hot on the coast in summer to snow on the mountaintops in winter. Do your homework before you head out. Dress in layers; this way you can be prepared for any fluctuations that Mother Nature may throw at you. And always have your rain gear handy just in case.

A few items I find very useful are zip-off pants and wool socks. The pants are great because they are thin but still keep you warm, and they double as shorts simply by zipping off the legs. And there's no better way to stay warm in a tent at night than a good pair (or two) of wool socks. There is some truth to the saying "cotton kills." Once cotton gets wet—from running, hiking, biking, or getting caught in the rain— it stays wet, keeping your body temperature dangerously low in cold weather. Wool, on the other hand, retains heat. The new quick-dry materials are fantastic for their moisture-wicking ability as well.

Gear

I don't care how experienced you are. Even if you've camped a thousand times, when it comes time to pack up your gear, you're bound to forget one thing or another. So follow Santa's practice of making a list and checking it twice—then check your gear twice too. There's nothing worse than craving a bowl of warm chili after a long day on the trail and discovering that you forgot a can opener or a lighter for your stove or campfire.

Here are a few items that are always good to bring along: A foldable camp chair for sitting and reading by the campfire is essential. A tarp for under your tent helps keep the dampness from the ground out. A tarp on top helps if you are in torrential downpours, even if you've sprayed your tent with "camp dry," or to give yourself a little shade in the heat of summer. The last item I really do not leave home without is a pack towel. These chamois-type towels are super lightweight, pack up to be very small, and dry in minutes by simply hanging them out or laying them on a rock for a few minutes in the sun. You can find them at local outfitters or in camping outlets like REI.

Many of the campgrounds in this guide are deep within the forest, in very remote areas that are far from towns, hospitals, and civilization. This may be part of why you came here in the first place. But there is some risk associated with this isolation. You may not have a cell phone signal, so it's a good idea to bring a first-aid kit and plenty of food and water. If you're in an RV, gas up when you can. Always give someone your itinerary before heading out, and let that person know when you expect to return as well.

Water

If you need to drink water from a stream or other watercourse, find a strong-flowing stream, and be sure to first chemically treat or filter the water. Many animals drink from these streams and at times use it as a restroom. Keep in mind that even the clearest creek or river still contains tiny bacteria and parasites.

Poison Ivy, Oak, and Sumac

All three of these plant irritants are common in the forests of North Carolina. If you do your homework and know how to identify them, you may save yourself some unpleasant itching. A nice little rule of thumb is "leaves of three, let it be," since poison ivy and poison oak both typically have three leaflets to a leaf.

Bugs, Bees, and Ticks

Whether you have known allergies or not, it's a *very* good idea to carry Benadryl with you at all times. Once while hiking deep in the forest with Mikey, we were viciously attacked by a swarm of angry bees. I had never been allergic to bees in my life, but the stings were so numerous that I literally started to feel a lump in my throat as my airway began to swell shut. I am a professional paramedic, and this is not an exaggeration. I truly believe that I might not be alive right now if I did not have Benadryl in my pack for both Mikey and myself. If you have known allergies, an EpiPen is essential.

As you move east into the Piedmont and the coast, mosquitoes and ticks become more prevalent. Insect repellent is sometimes a must to keep the bugs away, especially in the early-evening hours of the hot summer months. Repellent containing DEET seems to deter both mosquitoes and ticks.

As for ticks, these heat-seeking parasites are sneaky little buggers. It's a good idea to do a thorough "tick check" each night when you take a shower or before you go to bed. You may not even feel a tiny tick embedding itself under your skin. If you find a tick on you, tweezers work well for removing them.

Courtesy

People camp for the peace and quiet. They do not want to hear your favorite song blaring on the radio. Show your neighbors a little courtesy, and remember that campground quiet hours are typically from 10 p.m. to 6 a.m.

Pets

I'm a big fan of dogs and animals in general. As a matter of fact, my big dog Mikey spent the night in a tent with me at almost every campground in this book. But, as a person camping with a pet, you must be mindful. Not everyone loves your furry friend as much as you do. So keep them on a leash at all times. Again, be courteous if they are very vocal, and always pick up after them.

For Mother Nature's Safety

Wildlife

When you are out in the forest, you are a guest in the forest. Remember, many animals make their home here. Some you may not like, such as snakes and spiders; others, like otters and beavers, are cute and furry. No matter what you come across, whether it's a snow-white squirrel, a deer, or a bear, please DO NOT FEED WILDLIFE. Often these cuddly critters cannot digest people food, so you may be doing them more harm than good. More important, these animals learn to associate people with food. A bear that associates people with food often becomes a "nuisance" bear and may end up being euthanized to protect the public. As the saying goes, "A fed bear is a dead bear." Please do not contribute to this. Instead help keep wildlife wild.

Campfires

Campfires are one of the many reasons people enjoy camping. A campfire offers you a place to gather with your loved ones and roast marshmallows, tell scary ghost stories, or simply sit and enjoy the flicker of the flames as you listen to the sounds of nature.

Please be responsible with your fire. You don't need a massive bonfire to appreciate its warmth and beauty. Always make sure your campfire is completely out prior to vacating your campsite. Do not burn trash. If you collect wood from the forest, only collect felled wood. Never cut live trees or brush to use as firewood. For one thing you are killing the tree. Secondly, green wood does not burn, it smolders. All you will be doing is making an annoyingly smoky fire.

Many of the campgrounds in this guide sell firewood. I urge you to use the wood provided by the campground rather than bringing your own. You may inadvertently introduce a nonnative invasive species into the forest simply by bringing in your own firewood. For this reason, many campgrounds in state and national forests and parks now prohibit outside firewood.

Keep a Clean Camp

Keeping a clean camp is important for a number of reasons. First, plain and simple, littering is just bad. The next people to camp at your site do not want to have to pick up your cigarette butts or bottle caps. Use a trash bag, and be sure to carry out your trash if there's no receptacle available. Second, do not leave your trash out at night. Raccoons, opossums, and skunks love to rummage for food at night, and there's no easier target than some unsuspecting camper's trash.

Food Storage

Those same critters that like your trash *love* your food. I swear raccoons must have opposable thumbs. They can get into just about anything.

A handful of campgrounds provide bear-proof food storage containers. Black bears are prevalent in North Carolina, especially in the mountains and coastal region. If there are no food containers, store your food in your car or RV at night. If you are sleeping in a tent and do not have a car with you, string your food up between trees. Never bring food into your tent at night in bear country!

Dishes and Cat Holes

Wash dishes well away from any natural water source. On a similar and more important note, if no restrooms are provided and you must go in the forest, dig a cat hole to bury your waste *at least* 200 feet from any creek, lake, etc.

Leave No Trace

The last thing I'd like to share with you is a concept known as "no-trace" camping. Simply put: When you leave your campsite, it should be just as you arrived. "Take nothing but pictures, leave nothing but footprints."

You will hear me refer to "pack it in, pack it out." This means everything you bring into the forest you should also bring out—leaving no trace, no sign that you were ever there. This makes less impact on the environment and allows other campers to appreciate the natural beauty of their surroundings.

Author's Favorites

Map Legend

Transportation

Interstate Highway	══⟨40⟩══
US Highway	══⟨64⟩══
State Road	══⟨17⟩══
County/Forest Road	══[188]══
Railroad	┣━┿━┿━┫
Region Boundary	━━━━━

Hydrology

Body of Water	
River/Creek	
Intermittent River	

Symbols

Airport	✠
Campground	❶
Capital	✳
City	○
Ranger Station	⊞
Visitor Center	❓

Land Use

National Park/Forest/Preserve	
State Park/Forest	

Cliffside overlooks and breathtaking vistas greet you as you venture out to explore the mountain region of North Carolina. With two national parks and two national forests, this region really packs a punch! Whether you prefer a scenic drive along the Blue Ridge Parkway or wish to rappel down the face of Stone Mountain, you can do it here. Thousands of miles of hiking, mountain bike, bridle, and off-highway-vehicle (OHV) trails traverse the western part of the state. Wildlife ranges from elk to owls, beavers to bears. And hundreds of waterfalls await as creek after creek of crystal-clear water flows down the mountainsides. Watch a traditional Native American dance in Cherokee, hear some local live music in Asheville, go gem mining in Franklin, or see the white squirrels of Brevard. From natural landmarks to historic sites, the possibilities are endless.

Waterfalls are plentiful in the mountains of North Carolina.

Mountain Overview

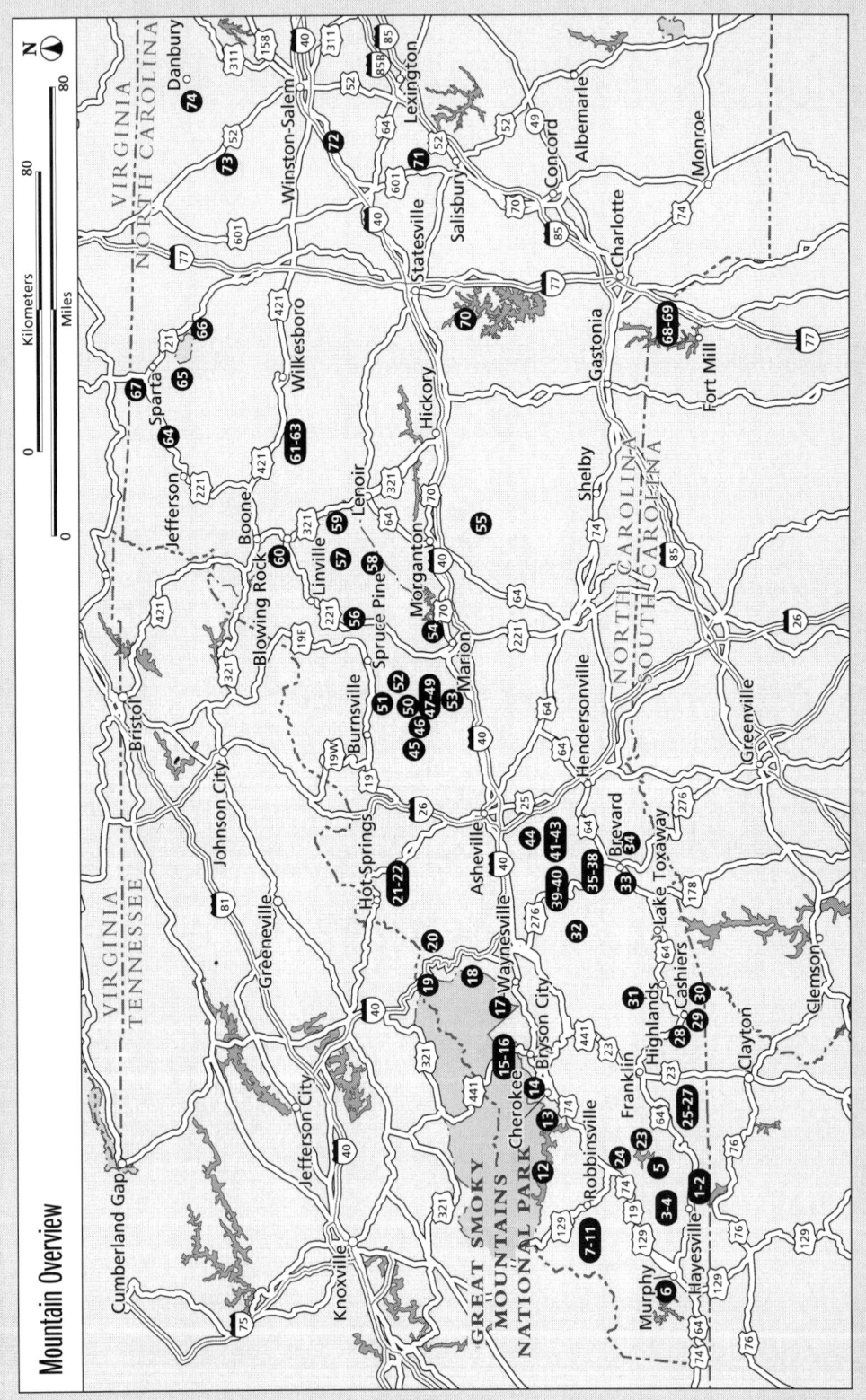

Murphy to Haysville

	Total Sites	Hookup Sites	Max. RV Length	Hookups	Toilets	Showers	Drinking Water	Dump Station	Recreation	Fee	Reservations
1 Jackrabbit Mountain	100	0	128'*	N	F	Y	Y	N	H, M, F, S, B, L	$$	Y
2 Clay County Park	99*	99	None	W, E	F	Y	Y	Y	S, F, B, L, P	$$	Y
3 Huskins Hole	9	0	n/a	N	V	N	N	N	H, F, R, P	No fee	N
4 Bristol Fields (Horse)	6	0	n/a	N	V	N	N	N	H, R, F	$	N
5 Bob Allison	*	0	n/a	N	N	N	N	N	H, F, R, P	No fee	N
6 Hanging Dog	51	0	32'	N	F, V	N	Y	Y	H, M, S F, B, L	$	Y

* See campground entry for specific information.

1 Jackrabbit Mountain Campground

Location: Off NC 175 on the east side of Lake Chatuge, about 6 miles southwest of Hayesville
Season: May 1–Sept 30
Sites: 100
Maximum length: 128 feet
Facilities: Flush toilets, hot showers, water spigots dispersed, fire rings, picnic tables, lantern holders, trash cans, dump station; pet friendly
Fee per night: $$
Management: Nantahala National Forest–Tusquitee Ranger District
Contact: (828) 837-5152; www.fs.usda.gov/recarea/nfsnc/recreation/camping-cabins/recarea/?recid=48912&actid=29. For reservations call (877) 444-6777 or visit www.recreation.gov.
Finding the campground: From the junction of NC 175 and US 64 near Hayesville, drive south on NC 175 for 0.9 mile. Veer to the right, head over the bridge, and continue to follow NC 175 until you've gone 3.4 miles. Turn right onto Jack Rabbit Road (SR 1155) at the sign for Jackrabbit Mountain Campground. Follow Jack Rabbit Road for 1.2 miles to a fork. Go left at the fork to get to the campground.

From the junction of NC 175 and the North Carolina–Georgia state line, drive north on NC 175 for 0.7 mile. Turn left onto Jack Rabbit Road (SR 1155) and follow directions above.
GPS coordinates: N35 00.586' /W83 46.116'
Maps: *DeLorme: North Carolina Atlas & Gazetteer:* Page 50 F4
About the campground: Resting comfortably on a peninsula alongside Lake Chatuge, Jackrabbit Mountain Campground has an ideal location. As you would expect, this campground is a great place to enjoy all that Lake Chatuge has to offer. With a swim beach and a boat launch, water activities are a highlight, but that's just a taste. Jackrabbit also has horseshoe pits, picnic shelters, and miles and miles of mountain bike and hiking trails.

Murphy to Haysville

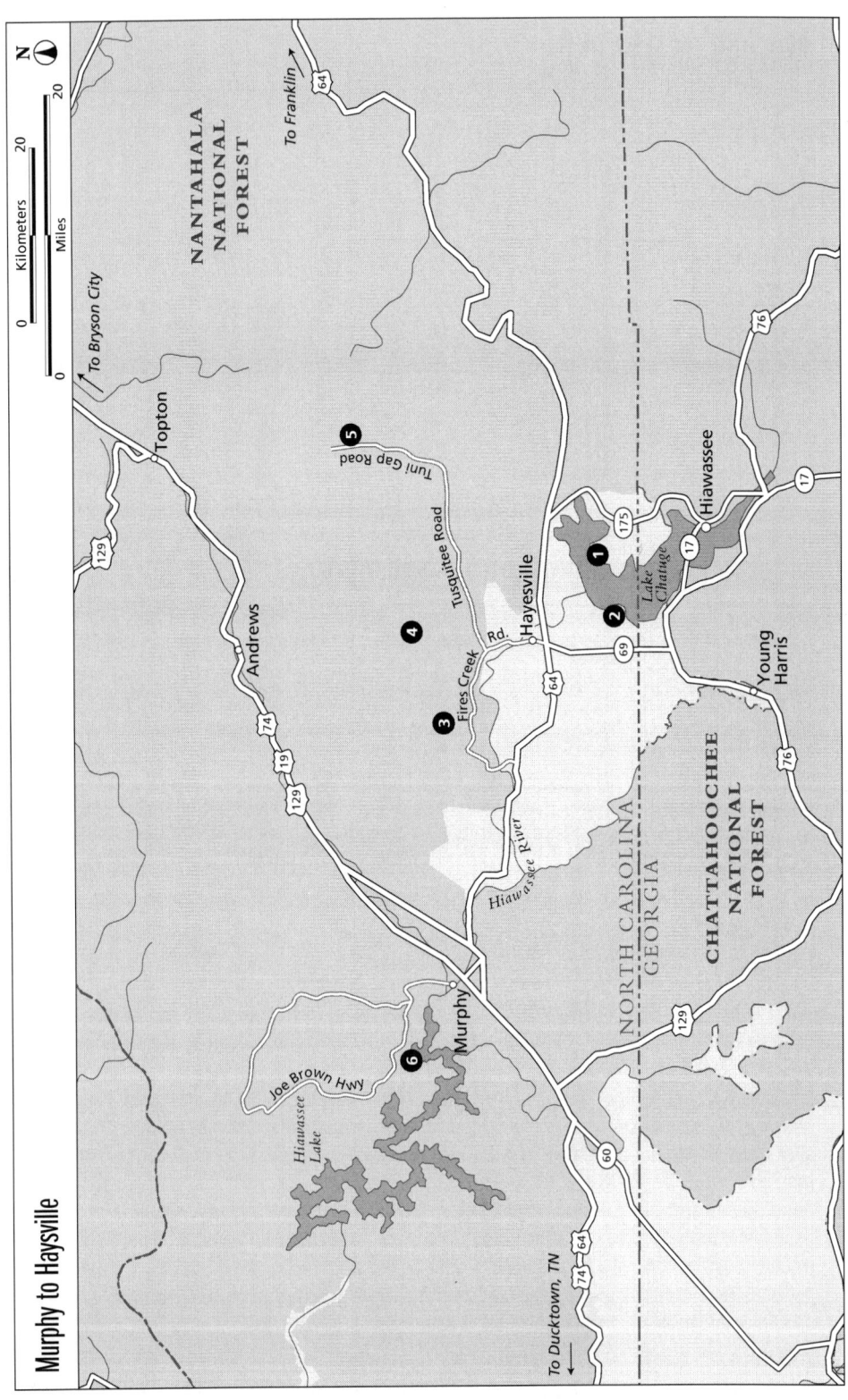

The stillness of Lake Chatuge can best be seen at dusk and dawn.

Whether you're a water child or prefer to stay on dry land, someone who's always on the go or content sitting lakeside with a good book, you are sure to enjoy this place. Many of the sites are surprisingly wooded, considering they are right along the lake's edge. Between the pristine location and the abundance of activities, this is easily one of my favorite places to camp within the mountain region.

2 Clay County Park Campground

Location: Myers Chapel Road, Hayesville; on the west side of Lake Chatuge, about 2.5 miles southwest of Hayesville
Season: Year-round
Sites: 99 RV sites, plus a large tent camping area with no set number of sites
Maximum length: None
Facilities: Flush toilets, hot showers, fire rings (RV sites only), picnic tables, lantern holders, water, electric, dump station; pet friendly

Fee per night: $$
Management: Clay County Parks and Recreation
Contact: (828) 389-3532
Finding the campground: From the junction of US 64 and NC 69 in Hayesville, drive east on US 64 for 0.6 mile. Turn right onto Myers Chapel Road (SR 1140) at the sign for CLAY COUNTY RECREATION DEPARTMENT, and continue for 2.2 miles, staying right at the fork. Turn left onto Clay Recreation Park Road. Follow the road to the office, pay the fee, and then continue into the campground.

From the junction of US 64 and NC 175 near Hayesville, drive west on US 64 for 4.1 miles. Turn left onto Myers Chapel Road, and follow directions above.

GPS coordinates: N35 00.391' / W83 47.821'
Maps: *DeLorme: North Carolina Atlas & Gazetteer:* Page 50 F3
About the campground: What this campground lacks in privacy, it more than makes up for with its lovely lakeside location. Many of the sites sit right on the edge of Lake Chatuge, and you can pull your boat right up to the lake's edge near your campsite. The campground has a swim area, a boat launch, and a very busy exercise trail that runs through the property and is used daily by many of the locals. A playground and several large picnic pavilions also sit right alongside this wonderful mountain lake.

There is a specific area designated for tent camping only. This area has tent pads and picnic tables, but the sites are on top of each other, and there are no fire rings. I would recommend Clay County Park for RV campers, especially if you have a boat. If you're a tent camper, head to the east side of Lake Chatuge and stay at Jackrabbit Mountain Campground for a bit more privacy.

3 Huskins Hole Campground

Location: Off FR 340, about 7 miles north of Hayesville and about 15 miles east of Murphy
Season: Year-round
Sites: 9
Maximum length: n/a; not recommended for RVs
Facilities: Vault toilets, primitive fire rings; pet friendly
Fee per night: None
Management: Nantahala National Forest–Tusquitee Ranger District
Contact: (828) 837-5152; www.fs.usda.gov/recarea/nfsnc/recreation/camping-cabins/recarea/?recid=48916&actid=34
Finding the campground: From the junction of NC 69 and US 64 in Hayesville, drive north on NC 69/Business 64 through downtown Hayesville. At 0.8 mile come to a four-way stop sign. Continue straight on NC 69 (Main Street) for 0.1 mile to another stop sign. Turn left here onto Tusquittee Road (SR 1307) and travel for 0.9 mile. Turn left onto Fires Creek Road (SR 1300), and continue for 4.5 miles. Turn right onto Fires Creek Wildlife Road (SR 1344) at the sign for BRISTOL FIELD HORSE CAMP, immediately after crossing the bridge over Fires Creek. Continue on Fires Creek Wildlife Road for 1 mile to Huskins Hole Campground on your left.

From the junction of US 64 and NC 141 near Murphy, drive east on US 64 for 4.6 miles. Turn left onto the unmarked Fires Creek Road (SR 1300), next to Hill's Store. Follow Fires Creek Road for 3.8 miles. Turn right onto Fires Creek Wildlife Road (SR 1344), and follow directions above.

Black bears are common throughout the mountains of North Carolina.

GPS coordinates: N35 05.227' / W83 52.004'
Maps: *DeLorme: North Carolina Atlas & Gazetteer:* Page 50 E3
About the campground: What used to be known as Fires Creek Campground, Huskins Hole is a small, primitive campground tucked just inside the Fires Creek Recreation Area of the Nantahala National Forest. A small creek runs through the property, adding to its ambience, but be prepared. This campground has the bare minimum when it comes to facilities. The upside: The Fires Creek area contains miles of hiking trails, bridle trails, and some of the best trout fishing in the region.

4 Bristol Fields Horse Camp

Location: Off FR 340, about 12 miles north of Hayesville and about 20 miles east of Murphy
Season: Year-round
Sites: 6
Maximum length: 50 feet
Facilities: Vault toilets, fire rings, picnic tables, lantern holders, tent pads; pet friendly
Fee per night: $
Management: Nantahala National Forest—Tusquitee Ranger District
Contact: (828) 837-5152; www.fs.usda.gov/recarea/nfsnc/recreation/horseriding-camping/recarea/?recid=49168&actid=30
Finding the campground: From the junction of NC 69 and US 64 in Hayesville, drive north on NC 69/Business 64 through downtown Hayesville. At 0.8 mile come to a four-way stop sign. Continue straight on NC 69 (Main Street) for 0.1 mile to another stop sign. Turn left here onto Tusquittee Road (SR 1307) and travel for 0.9 mile. Turn left onto Fires Creek Road (SR 1300), and continue for 4.5 miles. Turn right onto Fires Creek Wildlife Road (SR 1344) at the sign for Bristol Field Horse Camp, immediately after crossing the bridge over Fires Creek. Fires Creek Wildlife Road becomes FR 340 after 1.6 miles. Continue to follow FR 340, coming to a fork at 3.6 miles. Bear right, staying on FR 340 (the left is FR 340A) until you have gone a total of 5.7 miles from Fires Creek Road. Bristol Fields Horse Camp will be on your right at the sign for Bristol Fields Horse Camp.

From the junction of US 64 and NC 141 near Murphy, drive east on US 64 for 4.6 miles. Turn left onto unmarked Fires Creek Road (SR 1300), next to Hill's Store. Follow Fires Creek Road for 3.8 miles; turn right onto Fires Creek Wildlife Road (SR 1344), and follow directions above.
GPS coordinates: N35 06.395' / W83 48.763'
Maps: *DeLorme: North Carolina Atlas & Gazetteer:* Page 50 E3
About the campground: Although there are only six sites, they are well groomed, well maintained, and big enough for large RVs or a horse trailer. The campground has a community fire pit with benches around it. The sites sit all in a row, so don't expect much privacy during your stay. The Fires Creek Recreation Area that surrounds Bristol Fields contains miles of hiking trails, bridle trails, and fantastic fishing. There's a large open field at the end of the campground, so bring a Frisbee or a football to toss around on your downtime.

5 Bob Allison Campground

Location: Off FR 440, about 9 miles northeast of Hayesville
Season: Year-round
Sites: Open field; no set number of designated campsites
Maximum length: n/a; not recommended for RVs
Facilities: A handful of primitive fire rings and picnic tables scattered about the loop
Fee per night: None

Management: Nantahala National Forest—Tusquitee Ranger District

Contact: (828) 837-5152

Finding the campground: From the junction of NC 69 and US 64 in Hayesville, drive north on NC 69/Business 64 through downtown Hayesville. At 0.8 mile come to a four-way stop sign. Continue straight on NC 69 (Main Street) for 0.1 mile to another stop sign. Turn left here onto Tusquittee Road (SR 1307) and continue for 8.6 miles. Turn left onto Tuni Gap Road. Tuni Gap Road almost immediately becomes unpaved and after 0.4 mile becomes FR 440. Follow FR 440 for 4.3 miles to Bob Allison Campground on your right.

GPS coordinates: N35 08.371' / W83 41.427'

Maps: *DeLorme: North Carolina Atlas & Gazetteer:* Page 50 E4

About the campground: Isolated—in a word, Bob Allison Campground is just that. This is as rustic as it gets. There is no restroom, not even a vault toilet, so come prepared; and remember that cat holes must be dug *at least* 200 feet from any water source. There are a few primitive fire rings and picnic tables scattered about the "campground," but no designated sites.

CAUTION: The small loop "road" that heads through the campground is very rocky. It is imperative that you have a high-clearance vehicle to enter the campground, or you will probably end up doing some serious damage to your car.

With this in mind, I would categorize this as a tent-only campground—and I use the term "campground" very loosely.

6 Hanging Dog Campground

Location: Located on Hiawassee Lake, about 5 miles northwest of Murphy

Season: May 1–Sept 30

Sites: 51

Maximum length: 32 feet

Facilities: Flush toilets, fire rings, picnic tables, lantern holders, water spigots dispersed, dump station, *no* showers; pet friendly

Fee per night: $

Management: Nantahala National Forest—Tusquitee Ranger District

Contact: (828) 837-5152; www.fs.usda.gov/recarea/nfsnc/recreation/camping-cabins/recarea/?recid=48914&actid=29. For reservations call (877) 444-6777 or visit www.recreation.gov.

Finding the campground: From the junction of US 74/US 19 and US 64 on the east side of Murphy, drive east and up the hill on US 64. As you go through downtown Murphy, US 64 becomes Peachtree Street. Follow it past the courthouse, after which Peachtree Street becomes Tennessee Street. Follow this west. After leaving town, Tennessee Street becomes Joe Brown Highway (SR 1326). Follow Joe Brown Highway west for approximately 5 miles to the entrance to the Hanging Dog Recreation Area on your left. Follow the road through the recreation area for 1 mile to the campground.

GPS coordinates: N35 06.336' / W84 04.939'

Maps: *DeLorme: North Carolina Atlas & Gazetteer:* Page 50 E1

Horses graze in a field on the way to Hanging Dog.

About the campground: Hanging Dog sits right on the edge of Hiawassee Lake, but don't expect lakeside camping here. While you can see the water from some of the sites, none of them are right on the lakeshore. There's a boat launch nearby and an exceptional mountain bike trail system right down the road. Only a few miles from downtown Murphy, this is a great location, just don't expect a hot shower at the end of the day. There are no shower facilities on the property.

Robbinsville

	Total Sites	Hookup Sites	Max. RV Length	Hookups	Toilets	Showers	Drinking Water	Dump Station	Recreation	Fee	Reservations
7 Pine Ridge and Santeetlah Lake (Dispersed)	48	0	n/a	N	N	N	N	N	H, R, F, B, L, P	No fee	N
8 Santeetlah Creek (Dispersed)	18	0	n/a	N	N	N	N	N	H, R, F, P	No fee	N
9 Rattler Ford (Group)	4	0	n/a	N	F	Y	Y	N	H, F	$$$	Y
10 Horse Cove	18	0	30'	N	F, V	N	Y	N	H, F, L*	$$	N
11 Cheoah Point	23	6	40'	E, W	F	Y	Y	N	H, S, F, B, L, P	$$-$$$	Y
12 Cable Cove	26	0	40'	N	V	N	Y	N	H, F, B, L, P	$$	N
13 Tsali	42	0	40'	N	F	Y	Y	N	H, M, R, F, B, L, P	$$	N

* See campground entry for specific information.

7 Pine Ridge and Santeetlah Lake Dispersed Camping

Location: Alongside Santeetlah Lake, about 6 miles north of Robbinsville
Season: Year-round
Sites: 48
Maximum length: n/a; tents only
Facilities: Fire rings, picnic tables, lantern holders; pet friendly
Fee per night: None
Management: Nantahala National Forest–Cheoah Ranger District
Contact: (828) 479-6431; www.fs.usda.gov/activity/nfsnc/recreation/camping-cabins/?recid=48112&actid=34
Finding the campground: From the junction of NC 143 (Santeetlah Road) and US 129 in Robbinsville, drive southwest on NC 143 for 1 mile to the Cheoah District Ranger Station on your right.
Maps: DeLorme: North Carolina Atlas & Gazetteer: Page 50 B3
About the campground: The dispersed camping in this part of the Cheoah Ranger District is some of the best primitive camping around. The sites are located all around Lake Santeetlah and literally sit right along the banks of the lake, giving you wonderful waterfront views. The only downside is that the sites are right alongside the road as well, so you have the occasional car passing close by. These campsites are available on a first-come, first-served basis.

With so many dispersed campsites within the district, I've provided driving directions to the ranger station, where you can obtain maps and more information. There are hiking trails and a boat launch within the area, and you can fish right from many of the sites. But make sure you have a North Carolina state fishing license before casting your line.

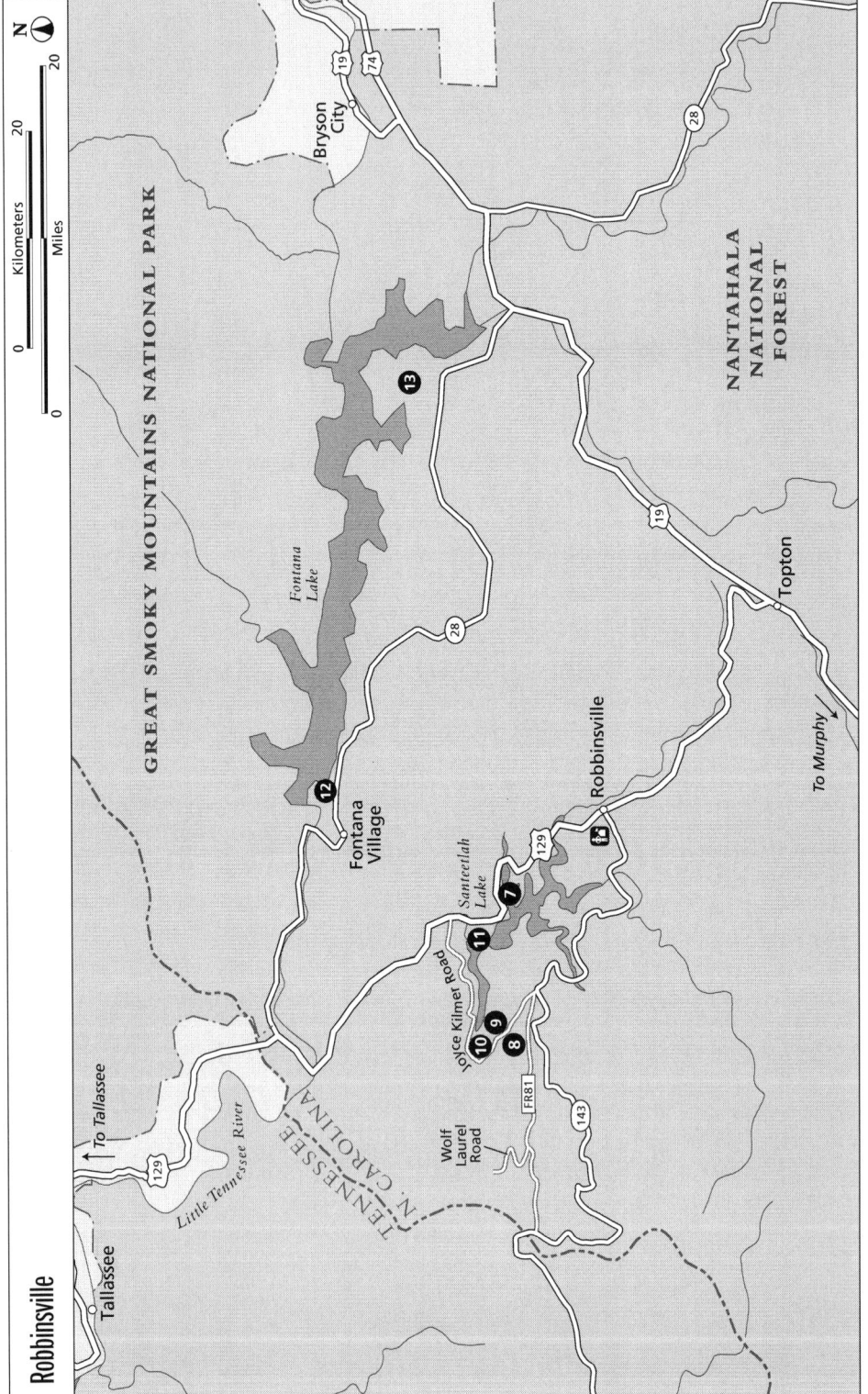

8 Santeetlah Creek Dispersed Camping

Location: Off FR 81, about 11 miles west of Robbinsville
Season: Year-round
Sites: 18
Maximum length: n/a; tents only
Facilities: Fire rings, picnic tables, lantern holders; pet friendly
Fee per night: None
Management: Nantahala National Forest—Cheoah Ranger District
Contact: (828) 479-6431; www.fs.usda.gov/activity/nfsnc/recreation/camping-cabins/ ?recid=48112&actid=34
Finding the campground: From the junction of NC 143 (Santeetlah Road) and US 129 in Robbinsville, drive southwest on NC 143 for 1 mile to the Cheoah District Ranger Station on your right.
Maps: *DeLorme: North Carolina Atlas & Gazetteer:* Page 50 B2
About the campground: The Santeetlah Creek dispersed campsites sit deep within the Nantahala National Forest off FR 81. The sites are nicely placed alongside Santeetlah Creek, which is stocked with trout from the local fish hatchery. Aside from fishing, you will find miles of hiking and bridle trails within easy reach. I also recommend hiking in the nearby Joyce Kilmer Memorial Forest to see some of the national forest's most spectacular trees.

Campsites are on a first-come, first-served basis. I've provided driving directions to the ranger station, where you can obtain maps and more information.

9 Rattler Ford Group Camp

Location: About 11 miles west of Robbinsville
Season: Apr 1–Oct 31
Sites: 4; up to 25 people per site
Maximum length: n/a; tents only
Facilities: Flush toilets, hot showers, fire rings, picnic tables; pet friendly
Fee per night: $$$
Management: Nantahala National Forest—Cheoah Ranger District
Contact: (828) 479-6431; www.fs.usda.gov/recarea/nfsnc/recreation/camping-cabins/ recarea/?recid=48926&actid=33. For reservations call (877) 444-6777 or visit www .recreation.gov.
Finding the campground: From the junction of NC 143 (Santeetlah Road) and US 129 in Robbinsville, drive west on NC 143 for 6.8 miles. Turn right onto Rattler Ford Campground Road (SR 1159) at the sign for the Joyce Kilmer Wilderness, and continue 1.9 miles to the campground on your left.
GPS coordinates: N35 21.668' / W83 54.928'
Maps: *DeLorme: North Carolina Atlas & Gazetteer:* Page 50 C2
About the campground: Four large, wooded, and private group camping areas await you at Rattler Ford Group Camp. With a creek passing right through the property, a volleyball court, and horseshoe pits, this is one of my favorite places for group camping in the mountain region.

10 Horse Cove Campground

Location: On FR 409, about 13 miles northwest of Robbinsville
Season: Apr 15–Oct 31; a few sites open year-round
Sites: 18
Maximum length: 30 feet
Facilities: Flush toilets, vault toilets (winter months), fire rings, charcoal grills, picnic tables, lantern holders, water spigots dispersed, trash cans, *no* showers; pet friendly
Fee per night: $$
Management: Nantahala National Forest–Cheoah Ranger District
Contact: (828) 479-6431; www.fs.usda.gov/recarea/nfsnc/recreation/camping-cabins/recarea/?recid=48924&actid=29
Finding the campground: From the junction of NC 143 (Santeetlah Road) and US 129 in Robbinsville, drive west on NC 143 for 6.8 miles. Turn right onto Rattler Ford Campground Road (SR 1159) at the sign for the Joyce Kilmer Wilderness, and continue 2.2 miles. Turn right onto Joyce Kilmer Road (SR 1134) and travel for 0.2 mile. Turn left onto FR 409 and into the campground.

From the junction of US 129 (Tapaco Road) and Joyce Kilmer Road (SR 1134), drive west on Joyce Kilmer Road for 5.5 miles. Turn right onto FR 409 and into the campground.
GPS coordinates: N35 21.902' / W83 55.155'
Maps: *DeLorme: North Carolina Atlas & Gazetteer:* Page 50 B2
About the campground: You'll enjoy beautiful mountain lake views as you make your way to Horse Cove Campground. Once you arrive you'll find well-spaced sites that sit along the edge of a clear-running creek. The sounds of the creek and the privacy these campsites have to offer make this one of my favorite campgrounds, despite the fact that there are no shower facilities.

While you're here, be sure to take some time to explore the Joyce Kilmer Memorial Forest. It is home to more than one hundred different species of trees, many of which are over 100 feet tall. The sight of these champion trees is simply awe inspiring!

11 Cheoah Point Campground

Location: Alongside Santeetlah Lake, about 6 miles north of Robbinsville
Season: Apr 15–Oct 31
Sites: 23; cabin rentals also available
Maximum length: 40 feet
Facilities: Flush toilets, hot showers, water spigots dispersed, electric, fire rings, picnic tables; pet friendly
Fee per night: $$–$$$
Management: Nantahala National Forest–Cheoah Ranger District
Contact: (828) 479-6431; www.fs.usda.gov/recarea/nfsnc/recreation/camping-cabins/recarea/?recid=48928&actid=29. For reservations call (877) 444-6777 or visit www.recreation.gov.

Fog rises above the Santeetlah Dam.

Finding the campground: From the junction of US 129 and NC 143 in Robbinsville, drive north on US 129 for 5.6 miles. Turn left onto Santeetlah Dam Road (SR 1146), and continue for 0.1 mile. Make a hard left turn onto Thunderbird Mountain Road, and travel 0.6 mile to the campground on your right.

From the junction of US 129 and NC 28 near Tapoco, drive south on US 129 for approximately 10.75 miles. Turn right onto Santeetlah Dam Road (SR 1146), and follow directions above.
GPS coordinates: N35 22.223' / W83 52.151'
Maps: *DeLorme: North Carolina Atlas & Gazetteer:* Page 50 B3
About the campground: Cheoah Point Campground sits on a little peninsula on Santeetlah Lake. The sites are rather open to one another so you don't get a ton of privacy here. The RV sites in particular are placed right on top of one another, but they do have electric and water hookups. The tent sites offer a bit more privacy. Some of them require a short walk down to the lake's edge to set up camp, giving you a prime waterfront camping experience.

Lake Santeetlah has island after island just waiting for you to explore. Whether in a boat, canoe, or kayak, the lake can be easily accessed via the nearby boat launch. If you prefer to enjoy the lake from the shoreline, the campground also offers a small beach with a swim area.

12 Cable Cove Campground

Location: About 15 miles northeast of Robbinsville and 3 miles from the Fontana Dam
Season: Apr 15–Oct 31
Sites: 26
Maximum length: 40 feet
Facilities: Vault toilets, water spigots dispersed, fire rings, picnic tables, lantern holders, barbecue grills at some sites, trash cans; pet friendly
Fee per night: $$
Management: Nantahala National Forest—Cheoah Ranger District
Contact: (828) 479-6431; www.fs.usda.gov/recarea/nfsnc/recreation/camping-cabins/recarea/?recid=48932&actid=29
Finding the campground: From the junction of NC 28 and NC 143 near Robbinsville, drive west on NC 28 for 6.1 miles. Turn right onto the unmarked road (SR 1287) at the sign for CABLE COVE CAMPGROUND, and continue 1 mile to the campground on your right.

From the junction of NC 28 and US 129 near Tapoco, drive east on NC 28 for approximately 13.8 miles. Turn left onto the unmarked road (SR 1287) at the sign for CABLE COVE CAMPGROUND, and follow directions above.
GPS coordinates: N35 25.905'/ W83 45.239'
Maps: *DeLorme: North Carolina Atlas & Gazetteer:* Page 50 A4
About the campground: If you look at most maps, Cable Cove Campground appears to be right on Fontana Lake, but in reality it's not, so don't be fooled. There is, however, a small, slow-moving creek that runs through the property with some campsites right beside it. So you *can* get a water-front camping experience here, just not the one you might be expecting. The sites are wooded and very well spaced.

A nearby boat ramp affords easy access to Fontana Lake, and the area offers miles of hiking trails. One thing to keep in mind: The area tends to stay damp. So if you are tent camping, be sure to bring a tarp to place underneath it as a barrier from the wet ground, no matter what time of year it is.

13 Tsali Campground

Location: Off NC 28, about 17 miles northwest of Robbinsville and 5 miles north of Almond
Season: Apr 15–Oct 31
Sites: 42
Maximum length: 40 feet
Facilities: Flush toilets, hot showers, water spigots dispersed, fire rings, picnic tables, lantern holders, charcoal grills, trash cans; pet friendly
Fee per night: $$
Management: Nantahala National Forest—Cheoah Ranger District
Contact: (828) 479-6431; www.fs.usda.gov/recarea/nfsnc/recreation/camping-cabins/recarea/?recid=48922&actid=29

Finding the campground: From the junction of NC 28 and NC 143 near Robbinsville, drive east on NC 28 for 7.8 miles. Turn left onto SR 1286 at the easy-to-miss sign for TSALI RECREATION AREA AND LEMMONS BEACH BOAT ACCESS. Follow SR 1286 for 1.5 miles, and turn left into the campground.

From the junction of NC 28 and US 19 South near Almond, drive west on NC 28 for approximately 3.6 miles. Turn right onto SR 1286, and follow directions above.

GPS coordinates: N35 24.375' / W83 35.146'

Maps: *DeLorme: North Carolina Atlas & Gazetteer:* Page 51 B5

About the campground: Simply put, the Tsali area is a mountain bike mecca. Known throughout the country as a favorite mountain biking destination, Tsali offers bike-in/bike-out capability. But Tsali is not limited to just that. The trail system alternates on a regular basis from mountain biking to equestrian, and hikers are always welcome. The trails run alongside Lake Fontana, affording spectacular lake views as you enjoy the fresh mountain air. With opportunities for fishing and boating as well, it's no wonder this place is so popular.

Now for the bad news. Tsali seems to have been designed to fit as many people as possible. With the amount of "traffic" in this area, the goal here is to get out and play. If you're looking for peace and quiet and privacy, I suggest heading down the road to Cable Cove. If you want easy access to a great trail system and don't mind a little crowding, then Tsali's your best bet.

Great Smoky Mountains National Park

	Total Sites	Hookup Sites	Max. RV Length	Hookups	Toilets	Showers	Drinking Water	Dump Station	Recreation	Fee	Reservations
14 Deep Creek	92	0	26'	N	F	N	Y	Y	H, R, F, P	$$	N
14 Deep Creek (Group)	3	0	n/a	N	F	N	Y	Y	H, R, F, P	$$$	Y
15 Smokemont	142	0	40'	N	F	N	Y	Y	H, R, F, P	$$-$$$	Y
15 Smokemont (Group)	3	0	n/a	N	F	N	Y	Y	H, R, F, P	$$$	Y
16 Tow String (Horse)	2	0	35'	N	V	N	Y	N	H, R, F, P	$$$	Y
17 Balsam Mountain	46	0	30'	N	F	N	Y	N	H, P*	$$	N
18 Cataloochee	27	0	31'	N	V	N	Y	N	H, R, F	$$$	Y*
18 Cataloochee (Group)	3	0	n/a	N	V	N	Y	N	H, R, F	$$$	Y
18 Cataloochee (Horse)	7	0	30'	N	V	N	Y	N	H, R, F	$$$	Y
19 Big Creek	12	0	n/a	N	F	N	Y	N	H, R, F, P	$$	N
19 Big Creek (Group)	1	0	n/a	N	F	N	Y	N	H, R, F, P	$$$	Y
19 Big Creek (Horse)	5	0	35'	N	F	N	Y	N	H, R, F, P	$$$	Y

* See campground entry for specific information.

14 Great Smoky Mountains National Park: Deep Creek Campground

Location: About 2.5 miles north of Bryson City and 10 miles west of Cherokee

Season: Apr 1–Oct 31

Sites: 92; also 3 group campsites (advance reservations required) that can accommodate up to 20 people each

Maximum length: 26 feet

Facilities: Flush toilets, water spigots dispersed, fire rings, picnic tables, lantern holders, dump station, *no* showers; pet friendly (Pets are allowed in campgrounds but are not permitted on any of the trails within the park.)

Fee per night: $$-$$$

Management: National Park Service–Great Smoky Mountains National Park

Contact: www.nps.gov/grsm/planyourvisit/frontcountry-camping.htm. For group camping reservations call (877) 444-6777 or visit www.recreation.gov.

Finding the campground: From the junction of US 19 and US 441 South, drive south on US 19 for 9.55 miles to a right turn onto Everett Street. After turning onto Everett Street, travel through downtown for 0.2 mile. Turn right onto Depot Street (immediately after the railroad tracks), and continue 0.2 mile to a stop sign at unsigned Ramseur Street. Turn left here and follow Ramseur

Great Smoky Mountains National Park

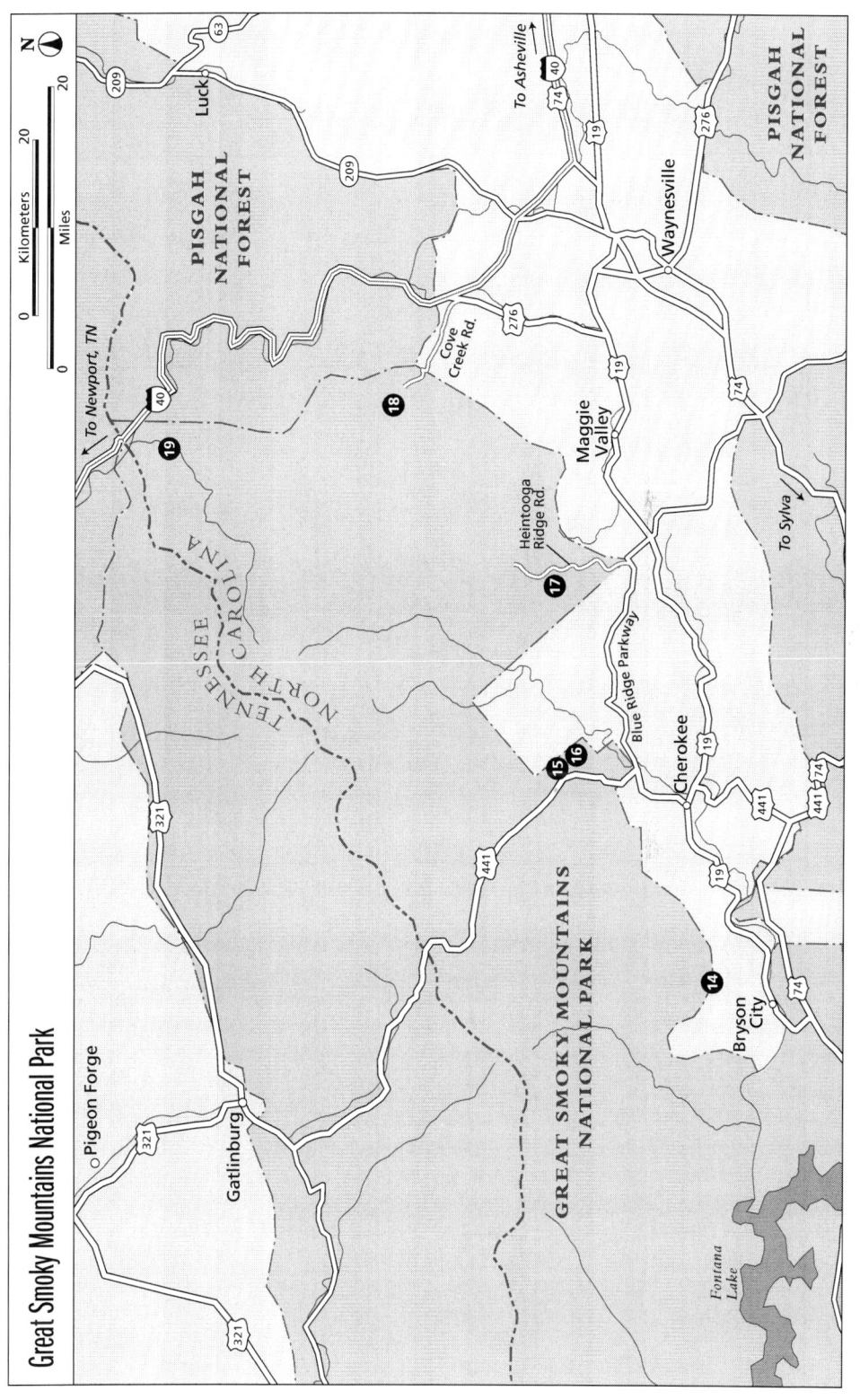

The Great Smoky Mountain Railroad departs daily for a scenic mountain ride.

Street, which soon becomes Deep Creek Road. Follow Deep Creek Road for 0.3 mile to a fork at West Deep Creek Road (SR 1337). Bear left at the fork, following West Deep Creek Road for approximately 2.5 miles to the campground entrance on your right.

From the junction of US 74 / US 19 (Great Smoky Mountains Parkway) and NC 28 near Lauada, drive east for approximately 2.2 miles. Take exit 64 (this is where US 74 and US 19 split), and follow US 19 north toward Bryson City for 3 miles. Turn left onto Everett Street, and follow directions above.

GPS coordinates: N35 27.585' / W83 26.181'

Maps: *DeLorme: North Carolina Atlas & Gazetteer:* Page 51 A7

About the campground: The National Park Service sure did it right at Deep Creek—at least for those camping in the RV section. Here, beautiful, wooded, and well-spaced campsites offer lots of privacy. Unfortunately the tent camping area is the exact opposite. This section of the campground is more like a giant checkerboard of tent pads right on top of one another. As with all campgrounds within Great Smoky Mountains National Park, there are no shower facilities, so plan accordingly. Although Deep Creek runs through the property, none of the campsites are beside it. Don't be disappointed, though. In the quiet hours of the night, you can hear the sturdy flow of the creek as it rushes by.

Three waterfalls can easily be accessed via the hiking trails located within the Deep Creek area. Along with hiking the area offers equestrian trails and fishing. Several tube rentals stands are located just outside the gates of the park. Just a few miles away, the quaint, touristy town of Bryson City offers kayak rentals and great shopping and is home to the Great Smoky Mountains Railroad, which departs daily for a scenic mountain train ride. All aboard!

Three group camping areas are available within the Deep Creek Campground, and each can accommodate up to twenty people. With all that Deep Creek has to offer, this is a great choice for your nonprofit organization. Advanced reservations are required.

15 Great Smoky Mountains National Park: Smokemont Campground

Location: Off US 441, about 4 miles north of Cherokee and about 27 miles south of Gatlinburg, Tennessee

Season: Year-round; group camp open May 15–Oct 31

Sites: 142; also 3 group campsites (advance reservations required) that can accommodate up to 20 people each

Maximum length: 40 feet

Facilities: Flush toilets, water spigots dispersed, fire rings, picnic tables, lantern holders, dump station, *no* showers; ice and firewood for sale nearby; pet friendly (Pets are allowed in camp-grounds but are not permitted on any of the trails within the park.)

Fee per night: $$–$$$

Management: National Park Service–Great Smoky Mountains National Park

Contact: (828) 497-9270; www.nps.gov/grsm/planyourvisit/frontcountry-camping.htm. For group camping reservations call (877) 444-6777 (828-497-1940 off-season) or visit www.recreation.gov.

Finding the campground: From the junction of US 441 and the Blue Ridge Parkway near Cherokee, drive north on US 441 for 3.8 miles. Turn right at the sign for SMOKEMONT, cross a small bridge, and immediately turn left. Travel less than 0.25 mile to the Smokemont Campground.

From the junction of US 441 and the North Carolina–Tennessee state line, drive south on US 441 for approximately 12.3 miles. Turn left at the sign for SMOKEMONT, and follow directions above.

NOTE: US 441 becomes Newfound Gap Road.

GPS coordinates: N35 33.323' / W83 18.682'

Maps: *DeLorme: North Carolina Atlas & Gazetteer:* Page 29 F8

About the campground: Sadly, Smokemont seems designed to fit as many people in as possible. I guess that allows more people to enjoy the beauty of the Great Smoky Mountains, but it certainly detracts from your camping experience. Most of the sites are shaded, and a few of the loops do not allow generators, which helps a little bit. Five-amp electric hookups are available at a few sites for use only by those with medical needs.

Hiking trails, bridle trails, horse rentals, wagon rides, and fishing can all be enjoyed within the Smokemont area. The town of Cherokee is just a few miles down the road. While you're in the

Painted bears can be seen throughout the town of Cherokee.

area, be sure to take note of the painted bears scattered throughout town, pan for gold, or visit the Oconaluftee Indian Village to see some traditional Native American dancing.

16 Great Smoky Mountains National Park: Tow String Horse Camp

Location: Off US 441, about 3 miles north of Cherokee and about 28 miles south of Gatlinburg, Tennessee
Season: Apr 1–Oct 31
Sites: 2 (reservations required)
Maximum length: 35 feet
Facilities: Vault toilets, water spigots dispersed, fire rings, picnic tables, lantern holders, trash cans, primitive horse stalls; ice and firewood for sale nearby; pet friendly (Pets are allowed in campgrounds but are not permitted on any of the trails within the park.)
Fee per night: $$$

Management: National Park Service—Great Smoky Mountains National Park

Contact: www.nps.gov/grsm/planyourvisit/horsecamps.htm. For reservations call (877) 444-6777 or visit www.recreation.gov.

Finding the campground: From the junction of US 441 and the Blue Ridge Parkway near Cherokee, drive north on US 441 for 2.8 miles. Turn right into the Tow String area, and travel 0.1 mile to a T. Turn left at the T and continue another 0.1 mile to the Tow String Horse Camp.

From the junction of US 441 and the North Carolina–Tennessee state line, drive south on US 441 for approximately 13.3 miles. Turn left into the Tow String area, and follow directions above.

NOTE: US 441 becomes Newfound Gap Road.

GPS coordinates: N35 32.546' / W83 17.850'

Maps: *DeLorme: North Carolina Atlas & Gazetteer:* Page 29 F8

About the campground: There are only two campsites available, but they sit alongside a swift-moving creek, making this quite a nice location. Far more primitive than the neighboring Smokemont Campground, Tow String is designed for campers who bring their own horses along to enjoy the miles of bridle trails available nearby. Rustic horse "stalls" are provided as hitching posts, so "Mr. Ed" can enjoy the sounds of the creek as well.

17 Great Smoky Mountains National Park: Balsam Mountain Campground

Location: North of the Blue Ridge Parkway off Heintooga Ridge Road, about 20 miles northeast of Cherokee and about 11 miles northwest of Maggie Valley

Season: May–Oct (Specific dates vary each year.)

Sites: 46

Maximum length: 30 feet

Facilities: Flush toilets, water spigots dispersed, fire rings, picnic tables, lantern holders, bear-proof food containers (on tent campsites only), *no* showers; pet friendly (Pets are allowed in the campgrounds but are not permitted on any of the trails within the park.)

Fee per night: $$

Management: National Park Service—Great Smoky Mountains National Park

Contact: www.nps.gov/grsm/planyourvisit/frontcountry-camping.htm

Finding the campground: From the junction of the Blue Ridge Parkway (BRP) and US 441 near Cherokee, drive north on the BRP for 10.9 miles. Turn left onto Heintooga Ridge Road at the sign for BALSAM MOUNTAIN CAMPGROUND, and continue 8.3 miles to the campground on your left.

From the junction of the BRP and US 19 near Maggie Valley, drive south on the BRP for approximately 2.5 miles. Turn right onto Heintooga Ridge Road at the sign for BALSAM MOUNTAIN CAMPGROUND, and follow directions above.

GPS coordinates: N35 34.112' / W83 10.459'

Maps: *DeLorme: North Carolina Atlas & Gazetteer:* Page 30 F1

About the campground: Sitting high on a spur, Balsam Mountain affords amazing long-range mountain views from just about anywhere within this small but wonderful campground.

The views are just a taste of why this is one of my favorite places to camp. The sites offer lots of privacy and the bathrooms are clean, as is the drinking water. There's a wonderful picnic area

The elk population is slowly growing in the Great Smoky Mountains.

0.5 mile up the road with stone tables that look like they were snatched right out of a *Flintstone* cartoon. And for the absolute highlight of them all, there's wildlife galore. The dedicated tent camping area has bear-proof food containers, you may see some wild turkey, and the elk population is growing at a healthy rate. I was lucky enough to see both a juvenile male and his mother on my last visit to Balsam Mountain Campground.

Although it's well off the beaten path, if you're in the Maggie Valley area and looking for a place to camp, this is it!

18 Great Smoky Mountains National Park: Cataloochee Campground

Location: About 20 miles north of Waynesville
Season: Mar 9–Oct 31
Sites: 27; also 3 group campsites (advance reservations required) that can accommodate up to 25 people each

Maximum length: 31 feet

Facilities: Vault toilets, water spigots dispersed, fire rings, picnic tables, lantern holders, trash cans, *no* showers; pet friendly (Pets are allowed in the campgrounds but are not permitted on any of the trails within the park.)

Fee per night: $$$

Management: National Park Service—Great Smoky Mountains National Park

Contact: (828) 497-1930; www.nps.gov/grsm/planyourvisit/frontcountry-camping.htm. For reservations call (877) 444-6777 or visit www.recreation.gov.

Finding the campground: From the junction of US 276 and US 19 near Lake Junaluska, drive north on US 276 for 5.5 miles. Turn left onto Cove Creek Road (SR 1395) at the sign for Smoky Mountains National Park Cataloochee Area. Follow Cove Creek Road for 7.4 miles to an intersection where you can go straight to Cosby and Big Creek or left to Cataloochee. Go left, following the now-paved road for another 3.1 miles to the Cataloochee Campground on your left.

From I-40 take exit 20 and drive south on US 276 for approximately 0.25 mile. Turn right onto Cove Creek Road (SR 1395), and follow directions above.

NOTE: As you travel along Cove Creek Road, the pavement ends after 4.6 miles; you enter the national park at 5.7 miles.

GPS coordinates: N35 37.915' / W83 04.892'

Maps: *DeLorme: North Carolina Atlas & Gazetteer:* Page 30 E2

About the campground: The most important thing to know about the Cataloochee Campground is that you *must* make a reservation ahead of time. There are no first-come, first-served campsites whatsoever in the Cataloochee area. What makes this even more important to know is that Cataloochee is very remote. If you forget to make a reservation in advance, and think to yourself, *Well, no big deal, I'll just call from there and make one,* think again! There is no cell phone service that deep within the park. You will find yourself backtracking on a very slow-moving, winding gravel road back toward civilization in hopes of finding a cell phone signal. Save yourself the trouble and make your reservation well in advance, especially since Cataloochee is a relatively small campground that tends to fill up quickly.

Cataloochee Campground is not only remote but also very primitive. It has vault toilets and no showers, yet the area still draws quite a lot of people on a regular basis. The campground hosts asked that I specifically pass on the information that there is no camp store and no ice or firewood for sale at (or near, for that matter) the campground. Apparently some literature has misinformed the public about this in the past, and people are still surprised to find out they can't ice down there cooler when they arrive.

Miles of hiking trails and bridle trails grace the area, and the campground itself is home to the headwaters of the Cataloochee River, which flows right by.

Cataloochee Horse Camp

Location: Approximately 0.5 mile past the Cataloochee Campground, about 20 miles north of Waynesville

Season: Apr–Nov

Sites: 7 (advance reservations required)

Maximum length: 30 feet

Facilities: Vault toilets, fire rings, picnic tables, *no* showers and *no* drinking water; pet friendly (Pets are allowed in the campgrounds but are not permitted on any of the trails within the park.)

Fee per night: $$$

GPS coordinates: N35 37.688' / W83 04.693'

About the campground: Seven well-groomed campsites are located within the Cataloochee Horse Camp. Located deep in the North Carolina portion of the Great Smoky Mountains, this area is home to some of the best bridle trails in the park. Each site has four primitive "stalls"/hitching posts for your equestrian friends, but be forewarned: There is no potable water within the campground, so you must bring enough water for both you and your animals.

You should also be aware that the road to the campground is a very narrow, winding gravel road with steep drop-offs. Use extreme caution when driving in, especially if you're pulling a horse trailer.

19 Great Smoky Mountains National Park: Big Creek Campground

Location: 16 miles east of Newport, Tennessee, and about 3 miles south of the North Carolina–Tennessee state line, just south of the town of Waterville

Season: Apr 1–Oct 31

Sites: 12; also 1 group campsite available that can accommodate up to 25 people

Maximum length: n/a; tents only

Facilities: Flush toilets, water spigots dispersed, tent pads, fire rings, picnic tables, lantern holders, *no* showers; pet friendly (Pets are allowed in the campgrounds but are not permitted on any of the trails within the park.)

Fee per night: $$–$$$

Management: National Park Service–Great Smoky Mountains National Park

Contact: (828) 486-5910; www.nps.gov/grsm/planyourvisit/frontcountry-camping.htm. For group and horse camp reservations, call (877) 444-6777 or visit www.recreation.gov.

Finding the campground: From the junction of US 276 and US 19, drive north on US 276 for 5.9 miles to where US 276 becomes I-40 West. Take I-40 West for 20.5 miles into Tennessee to exit 451 (Waterville Road). Turn left off the exit ramp onto Waterville Road (SR 1332), and travel for 2.3 miles to a stop sign. Continue straight at the stop sign, and enter the Great Smoky Mountains National Park. Follow this road for 0.9 mile to where it dead-ends at the campground.

GPS coordinates: N35 45.059' / W83 06.581'

Maps: *DeLorme: North Carolina Atlas & Gazetteer:* Page 30 D2

About the campground: Just minutes from the Tennessee state line, this small, well-designed campground is one of the best I've seen for tent camping. And it was made for just that—tents only. There is a designated parking area in the middle of the loop near the bathhouse, and each site requires a short walk with your gear to set up camp. The sites are well spaced, and Big Creek is within earshot of every site in the campground. As you rest upon your pillow, you are lulled to sleep by the sounds of the creek rushing by.

Be sure to hike the Big Creek Trail on your visit. The trailhead is just outside the campground. The trail itself follows Big Creek for miles, leading you to two wonderful waterfalls along the way. This trail is popular among equestrians as well, so as you enjoy the lively flow and brilliant colors of the creek, be sure to watch where you step.

Midnight Hole is one of two wonderful waterfalls you can hike to on the Big Creek Trail.

Big Creek Horse Camp

Location: About 0.5 mile before reaching the Big Creek Campground on your left; 16 miles east of Newport, Tennessee, and about 3 miles south of the North Carolina-Tennessee state line, just south of the town of Waterville
Season: Apr 1-Oct 31
Sites: 5 (reservations required)
Maximum length: 35 feet
Facilities: Flush toilets, water spigots dispersed, fire rings, horse stalls, *no* showers; pet friendly (Pets are allowed in the campgrounds but are not permitted on any of the trails within the park.)
Fee per night: $$$
GPS coordinates: N35 45.423' / W83 06.326'
About the campground: Five sites form a small loop, with a large community area of horse stalls/hitching posts in the center. With miles of bridle and hiking trails within walking distance of the horse camp, this is a great place to saddle up and hit the trail.

Hot Springs

	Total Sites	Hookup Sites	Max. RV Length	Hookups	Toilets	Showers	Drinking Water	Dump Station	Recreation	Fee	Reservations
20 Harmon Den (Dispersed)	3	0	n/a	N	N	N	N	N	H, R, F, P	No fee	N
20 Harmon Den (Horse)	10	0	30'	N	V	N	Y	N	H, R, F	$$	Y
21 Rocky Bluff	30	0	50'	N	F	N	Y	N	H, F, P	$	N
22 Silvermine (Group)	1	0	n/a	N	V	N	Y	N	H	$$$	Y

20 Harmon Den

Dispersed Camping

Location: Off FR 148, about 19 miles southwest of Hot Springs and about 24 miles northeast of Waynesville
Season: Year-round
Sites: 3
Maximum length: n/a; tents only
Facilities: Fire rings, picnic tables; pet friendly
Fee per night: $$
Management: Pisgah National Forest—Appalachian Ranger District
Contact: (828) 675-5616; www.fs.usda.gov/recarea/nfsnc/recreation/camping-cabins/recarea/?recid=70836&actid=34. For reservations call (877) 444-6777 or visit www.recreation.gov.
Finding the campground: Take exit 7 off I-40, and follow Cold Springs Creek Road (FR 148) northeast for 1 mile to the first primitive campsite. Continue on FR 148 for another 1 mile to the next campsite, and then another 1 mile from there to the next campsite.

From the junction of NC 209 and US 25 North/US 70 West in Hot Springs, drive south on NC 209 for 7.1 miles. Turn right onto Meadowfork Road (SR 1175), and continue 5.2 miles. Turn right onto Little Creek Road, and travel 3.5 miles. Turn left onto Max Patch Road, and continue 0.2 mile to a right turn onto Cold Springs Creek Road (FR 148). Follow Cold Springs Creek Road for 2.6 miles to the first primitive campsite. Continue traveling another 1 mile to the next campsite, and then another 1 mile from there to the next campsite.

GPS coordinates: Primitive campsites are dispersed alongside FR 148.
Maps: DeLorme: North Carolina Atlas & Gazetteer: Page 30 C3–D3
About the campground: Dispersed campsites are found alongside many of the forest roads throughout the national forest system. Even if an area appears to be suitable for camping, please camp there *only* if you see a placard with a camping symbol on it, indicating that it is

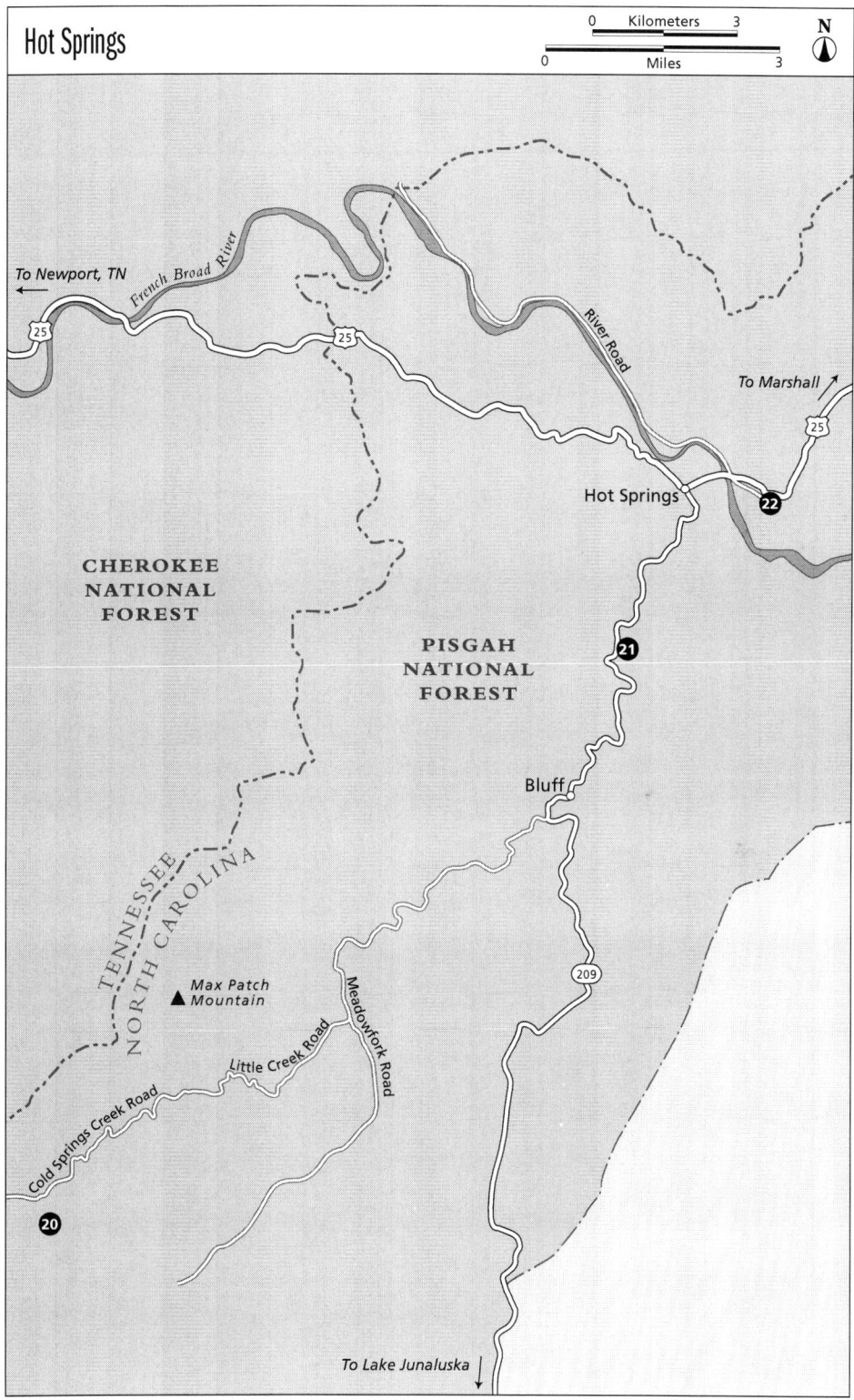

Hot Springs

0 Kilometers 3
0 Miles 3

N

To Newport, TN

French Broad River

25

25

River Road

To Marshall

25

Hot Springs

22

CHEROKEE
NATIONAL
FOREST

PISGAH
NATIONAL
FOREST

21

Bluff

TENNESSEE
NORTH CAROLINA

Max Patch
Mountain

Meadowfork Road

209

Little Creek Road

Cold Springs Creek Road

20

To Lake Junaluska

Several trails run across the top of Max Patch.

one of the designated roadside campsites. By camping in designated sites only, you lessen the impact on the land and help preserve it for years to come. The Harmon Den area has three designated sites, and they are absolutely beautiful! Each is strategically placed along the edge of Cold Springs Creek.

If you are looking for a true primitive camping experience, this is it. Be sure to remember to practice no-trace camping: Pack it in, pack it out. Let's keep the Harmon Den Area as untouched and natural as we can.

Harmon Den Horse Camp

Location: Off FR 3526, about 19 miles southwest of Hot Springs and about 24 miles northeast of Waynesville
Season: May 1–Oct 31
Sites: 10
Maximum length: 30 feet
Facilities: Vault toilets, water spigots dispersed, fire rings, picnic tables; pet friendly
Fee per night: $$
Finding the campground: Take exit 7 off I-40, and follow Cold Springs Creek Road (FR 148) northeast for 3.1 miles to a fork. Bear right at the fork (the left is FR 148A), continuing to follow FR 148 for another 0.5 mile to an intersection. The left (FR 148) leads to Max Patch. Turn right onto FR 3526, and continue 0.3 mile to the campground on your left.

From the junction of NC 209 and US 25 North/US 70 West in Hot Springs, drive south on NC 209 for 7.1 miles. Turn right onto Meadowfork Road (SR 1175) and travel for 5.2 miles. Turn right onto Little Creek Road, and continue for 3.5 miles. Turn left onto Max Patch Road, and travel 0.2 mile to a right onto Cold Springs Creek Road. Follow Cold Springs Creek Road for 2.5 miles. Turn left onto FR 3526, and travel 0.3 mile to the campground on your left.
GPS coordinates: N35 45.489' / W82 58.620'
About the campground: As with most horse camps, there are picnic tables and fire pits here. But unlike many other horse camps, this one has designated, numbered campsites and is not just a large open field to be shared by all. While you are in the middle of horse country, remember: All the bridle trails are also hiking trails, so you are likely to come across some hikers as you navigate your way along the trails.

Beautiful views abound. While you're in the area, I highly recommend a visit to nearby Max Patch Mountain, home to many trails, including the North Carolina Birding Trail. Unlike any other mountaintop in the region, Max Patch is like a grassy bald. You are sure to be wowed at the sight of it.

21 Rocky Bluff Campground

Location: Off NC 209, about 3 miles south of Hot Springs and 31 miles north of Lake Junaluska
Season: May 1–Oct 1
Sites: 30
Maximum length: 30 feet

Facilities: Flush toilets, water spigots dispersed, fire rings, picnic tables, lantern holders; pet friendly
Fee per night: $
Management: Pisgah National Forest—Appalachian Ranger District
Contact: (828) 682-6146; www.fs.usda.gov/recarea/nfsnc/recreation/camping-cabins/recarea/?recid=48602&actid=29
Finding the campground: From the junction of NC 209 and Meadowfork Road (SR 1175) in Bluff, drive north on NC 209 for 4 miles to the Rocky Bluff Campground on your right.

From the junction of NC 209 and US 25 North/US 70 West in Hot Springs, drive south on NC 209 for 3.1 miles to the Rocky Bluff campground on your left.
GPS coordinates: N35 51.758' / W82 50.827'
Maps: *DeLorme: North Carolina Atlas & Gazetteer:* Page 30 B4
About the campground: Rock on! Rocky Bluff is a marvel to see. Hand-laid stone wall after stone wall creates a layered look and make this campground one of a kind. It's no wonder that this is one of my favorites. The campground is made up of two loops. I prefer the upper loop to the lower loop; it seems to offer a bit more privacy.

There are hiking trails, a scenic overlook, an old-time cemetery, and an excellent trout stream all within the property. The town of Hot Springs is just a few miles up the road, giving you easy access to restock your provisions. NC 209 offers some of the best scenic views in the state.

22 Silvermine Group Camp

Location: About 0.5 mile east of the town of Hot Springs
Season: May 1–Oct 31
Sites: 1 site that can accommodate up to 50 people
Maximum length: n/a; tents only
Facilities: Vault toilets, water spigot, fire rings, picnic shelter; pet friendly
Fee per night: $$$
Management: Pisgah National Forest—Appalachian Ranger District
Contact: (828) 675-5616; www.fs.usda.gov/recarea/nfsnc/recreation/camping-cabins/recarea/?recid=48608&actid=33. For reservations call (877) 444-6777 or visit www.recreation.gov.
Finding the campground: From the junction of US 70/25 and NC 209 in Hot Springs, drive east on US 70/25 for 0.5 mile. Turn left onto River Road (SR 1304) immediately after crossing the bridge over the French Broad River. Follow River Road for less than 0.1 mile, and cross under the US 70/US 25 bridge. Drive another 0.4 mile to the gated entrance to Silvermine Group Camp. The road continues another 0.2 mile to where it dead-ends at the campground.

From the junction of US 70/25 and NC 208 in Hurricane, drive west on US 70/25 for 4.6 miles. Turn right onto River Road immediately before crossing the bridge over the French Broad River, and follow directions above.
GPS coordinates: N35 53.356' / W82 48.711'
Maps: *DeLorme: North Carolina Atlas & Gazetteer:* Page 31 B5

About the campground: Surprisingly well maintained, this wonderful group camp has a group fire ring, paved paths, a large picnic shelter, and hiking trailheads right on the property. Its short distance from downtown Hot Springs makes this a convenient location, just in case you forget to bring the marshmallows or graham crackers to make some s'mores.

After a long weekend overseeing the Scouts, treat yourself to a massage, or take a dip in water from the hot springs at the Hot Springs Resort and Spa. Be advised, however, that you won't actually be in the spring itself. The resort pipes natural mineral water from the hot springs up the river into man-made hot tubs.

Franklin

	Total Sites	Hookup Sites	Max. RV Length	Hookups	Toilets	Showers	Drinking Water	Dump Station	Recreation	Fee	Reservations
23 Wine Spring (Horse)	6	0	None	N	V	N	N	N	H, R, F	No fee	N
24 Appletree (Group)	4	0	n/a	N	F	Y	Y	N	H, M, F	$$$	Y
25 Standing Indian	78	0	50'	N	F	Y	Y	N	H, R, F, P	$$-$$$	Y
26 Kimsey Creek (Group)	3	0	n/a	N	V	N	Y	N	H, R, F, P	$$$	Y
27 Hurricane Creek	*	0	n/a	N	V	N	N	N	H, R, F	$	N
27 Hurricane Creek (Horse)	*	0	None	N	V	N	N	N	H, R, F	$	N

* See campground entry for specific information.

23 Wine Spring Horse Camp

Location: Off FR 711, about 19 miles northwest of Franklin and about 10 miles northeast of Andrews
Season: Year-round
Sites: 6 (reservations required)
Maximum length: None
Facilities: Vault toilets, fire rings, lantern holder, picnic tables; pet friendly
Fee per night: None
Management: Nantahala National Forest–Nantahala Ranger District
Contact: (828) 524-6441; www.fs.usda.gov/recarea/nfsnc/recreation/horseriding-camping/recarea/?recid=48676&actid=30
Finding the campground: From the junction of US 64 and US 441 Business in Franklin, drive west on US 64 for 3.7 miles. Turn right onto Old Murphy Road (SR 1142) at the sign for WAYAH BALD, and travel for 0.2 mile. Just before Old Murphy Road bends to the right, turn left onto Wayah Road (SR 1310). Continue on Wayah Road for 10.6 miles, and turn right onto FR 711 at the sign for HORSE CAMP AND SHOOTING RANGE. Follow FR 711 for 4.7 miles to the campground on your right at the large stone sign for WINE SPRING HORSE CAMP.

From the junction of US 64 and NC 175, drive east on US 64 for 24.2 miles. Turn left onto Old Murphy Road (at the sign for WAYAH BALD), and follow directions above.

From the junction of US 19 and US 129 North in Topton, drive north on US 19 for 2.1 miles. Turn right onto Wayah Road (SR 1310), and travel for 17.3 miles. Turn left onto FR 711, and continue 4.7 miles to the campground on your right at the large stone sign for WINE SPRING HORSE CAMP.

From the junction of US 19 and NC 28 North, drive south on US 19 for 11.9 miles. Turn left onto Wayah Road (SR 1310), and follow directions above.

Franklin

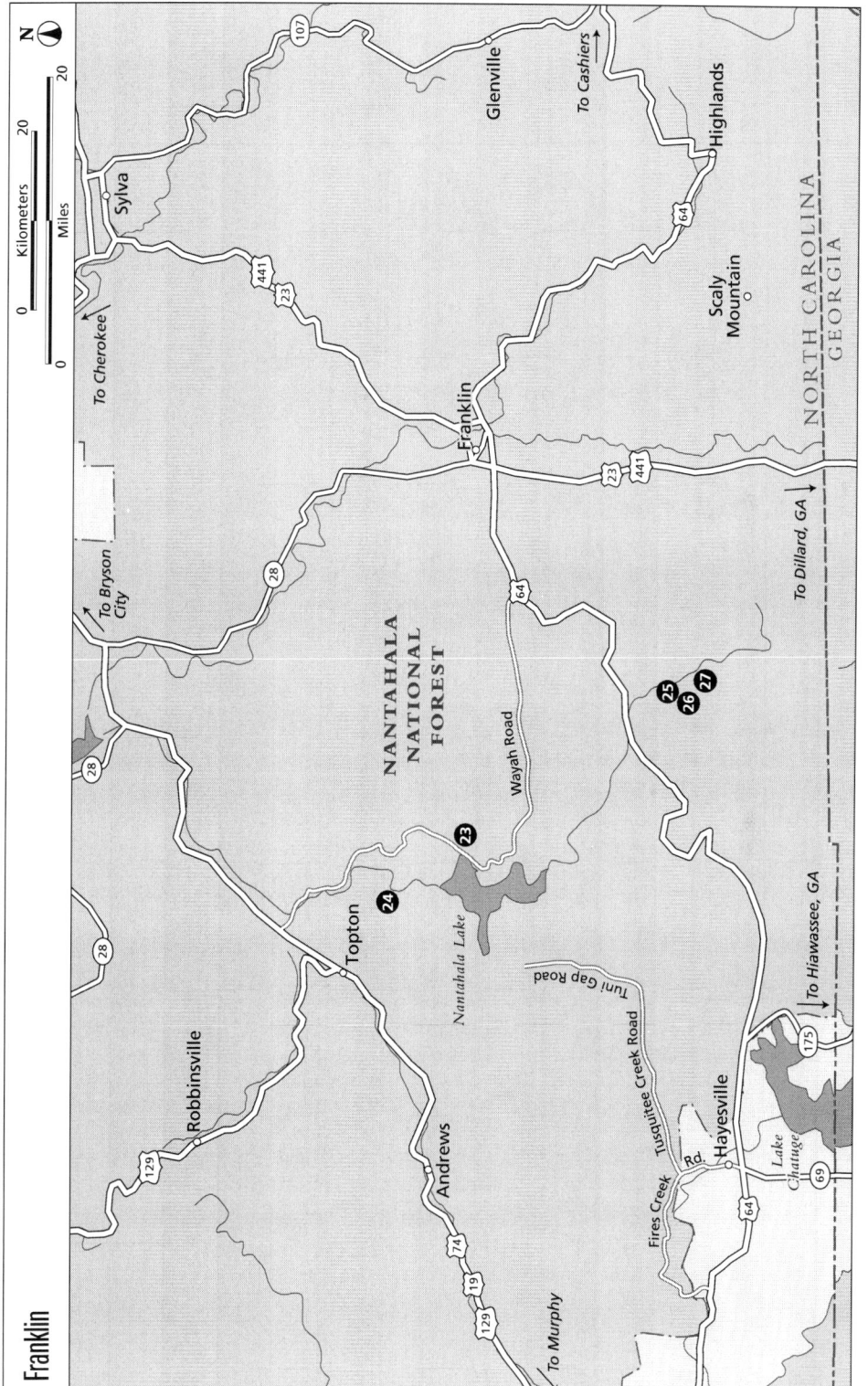

You never know what you'll come across in the forest.

GPS coordinates: N35 10.649' / W83 36.825'

Maps: *DeLorme: North Carolina Atlas & Gazetteer:* Page 51 D5

About the campground: With miles and miles of bridle/hiking trails at your fingertips, Wine Spring is an ideal location for a long weekend or an extended camping trip. The campground has more than ample parking for your horse trailer, and the road through the campground makes a small loop off FR 711, giving you pull-through convenience for your horse trailer.

There is no fee to camp at Wine Spring, but advance reservations are required. The campground entrance is locked with a combination lock at the gate; you get the combination when you make your reservation. Please use the designated areas to tether your horse, and do not tether horses to the trees. This damages the bark and over time kills the tree. It's all part of the no-trace/minimal-impact philosophy that all campers should follow.

24 Appletree Group Camp

Location: On FR 377, about 12 miles southwest of Andrews and about 30 miles west northwest of Franklin

Season: Apr 1–Oct 31

Sites: 4; 2 that can accommodate up to 25 people each and 2 that can accommodate up to 50 people each (reservations required)

Maximum length: n/a; tents only

Facilities: Flush toilets, hot showers, water spigots, fire rings, picnic tables; pet friendly

Fee per night: $$$

Management: Nantahala National Forest—Nantahala Ranger District

Contact: (828) 524-6441; www.fs.usda.gov/recarea/nfsnc/recreation/camping-cabins/recarea/?recid=48642&actid=33

Finding the campground: From the junction of US 19 and US 129 North near Topton, drive north on US 19 for 2.1 miles. Turn right onto Wayah Road (SR 1310), and travel for 4.1 miles. Turn right onto Old River Road, and continue for 3.2 miles. Turn right onto Junaluska Road (SR 1505), and travel 0.1 mile to a right turn onto FR 377, which leads to the Appletree Group Campground.

From the junction of US 19 Business and US 74 in Andrews, drive north on US 19 Business for 2 miles. Veer right onto Junaluska Road (SR 1505), and continue for 10.3 miles to a left onto FR 377, which leads to the Appletree Group Campground.

From the junction of US 64 and US 441 Business in Franklin, drive west on US 64 for 3.7 miles. Turn right onto Old Murphy Road at the sign for Wayah Bald, and travel for 0.2 mile. Just before Old Murphy Road bends to the right, turn left onto Wayah Road (SR 1310). Continue on Wayah Road for 23.8 miles. Turn left onto Old River Road and follow it for 3.2 miles. Turn right onto Junaluska Road (SR 1505), and continue for 0.1 mile to a right turn onto FR 377, which leads to the Appletree Group Campground.

GPS coordinates: N35 13.367' / W83 39.618'

Maps: *DeLorme: North Carolina Atlas & Gazetteer:* Page 51 D5

About the campground: Although Appletree is a bit off the beaten path, the surrounding Nantahala National Forest has trails galore. Whether your group likes to hike, mountain bike, or ride on horseback, you are sure to find a place to do it here. The icing on the cake: The Nantahala River passes nearby, so there is ample opportunity for whitewater rafting as well. Advance reservations are required.

25 Standing Indian Campground

Location: Off FR 67, about 13 miles southwest of Franklin and about 25 miles northeast of Hayesville
Season: Apr 1–Nov 30
Sites: 78
Maximum length: 50 feet
Facilities: Flush toilets, hot showers, water spigots dispersed, fire rings, picnic tables, lantern holders, trash cans, amphitheater, camp store; pet friendly
Fee per night: $$
Management: Nantahala National Forest—Nantahala Ranger District
Contact: (828) 524-6441; www.fs.usda.gov/recarea/nfsnc/recreation/camping-cabins/recarea/?recid=48668&actid=29. For reservations call (877) 444-6777 or visit www.recreation.gov.
Finding the campground: From the junction of US 64 and US 441 Business in Franklin, drive west on US 64 for 11.7 miles. Turn left onto West Old Murphy Road at the sign for WALLACE GAP, and travel for 1.8 miles. Turn right onto FR 67 at the sign for STANDING INDIAN CAMPGROUND, and continue 1.7 miles to the campground on your right. *NOTE:* Be sure to drive the full distance when heading west on US 64 to the westernmost West Old Murphy Road.

From the junction of US 64 and NC 175, drive east on US 64 for 16.2 miles. Turn right onto West Old Murphy Road at the sign for WALLACE GAP, and follow directions above.
GPS coordinates: N35 04.708' / W83 31.776'
Maps: *DeLorme: North Carolina Atlas & Gazetteer:* Page 51 E6
About the campground: This campground offers some of the best—and some of the worst—camping I've seen. Some of the sites are well spaced and wooded and sit right alongside the Nantahala River; others are out in an open field, right on top of one another, with no privacy whatsoever. Also, the campground is pretty big, and not very well marked, so be sure to grab a site map when you come in. One other word of warning: The campground is located in a flash-flood area, so use caution if you opt to camp during times of heavy rainfall.

Now for the good news. Trails galore, both hiking and equestrian, run throughout the area as well as the campground. Even the Appalachian Trail can be easily accessed from the Standing Indian Campground. Don your hiking boots or saddle your horse, and go see the forest.

26 Kimsey Creek Group Camp

Location: Within Standing Indian Campground off FR 67, about 13 miles southwest of Franklin and about 25 miles northeast of Hayesville
Season: Apr 1–Nov 30
Sites: 3 sites that can accommodate up to 25 people each (reservations required)
Maximum length: n/a; tents only
Facilities: Vault toilets, water spigots dispersed, fire rings, picnic tables, lantern holders, trash cans; pet friendly
Fee per night: $$$
Management: Nantahala National Forest–Nantahala Ranger District
Contact: (828) 524-6441; www.fs.usda.gov/recarea/nfsnc/recreation/camping-cabins/recarea/?recid=48674&actid=33. For reservations call (877) 444-6777 or visit www.recreation.gov.
Finding the campground: From the junction of US 64 and US 441 Business in Franklin, drive west on US 64 for 11.7 miles. Turn left onto West Old Murphy Road at the WALLACE GAP sign, and travel for 1.8 miles. Turn right onto FR 67 at the sign for STANDING INDIAN CAMPGROUND, and continue 1.7 miles to the Standing Indian Campground on your right. Kimsey Creek Group Camp is accessed between Campsites 37 and 38.

From the junction of US 64 and NC 175, drive east on US 64 for 16.2 miles. Turn right onto West Old Murphy Road at the WALLACE GAP sign, and follow directions above.
GPS coordinates: N35 04.279' / W83 31.917'
Maps: *DeLorme: North Carolina Atlas & Gazetteer:* Page 51 E6
About the campground: This is one of the best group camping areas I have ever seen. Three campsites sit in a cul-de-sac right alongside the river. Each site is limited to twenty-five people, keeping this pristine setting intact. Miles and miles of trails await, as does the Nantahala River, which is great for rafting or trying your hand at fly fishing. Be sure to get any applicable licenses prior to casting your line. Advance reservations are required.

27 Hurricane Creek Campground

Location: Off FR 67, about 15 miles southwest of Franklin and about 23 miles northeast of Hayesville
Season: Mar 15–Jan 1
Sites: Open field; no set number of designated campsites
Maximum length: None
Facilities: Vault toilet (next door at the Hurricane Creek Horse Camp), fire rings; pet friendly
Fee per night: $
Management: Nantahala National Forest–Nantahala Ranger District
Contact: (828) 524-6441; www.fs.usda.gov/recarea/nfsnc/recreation/horseriding-camping/recarea/?recid=48672&actid=30
Finding the campground: From the junction of US 64 and US 441 Business in Franklin, drive west on US 64 for 11.7 miles. Turn left onto West Old Murphy Road at the sign for WALLACE GAP, and

travel for 1.8 miles. Turn right onto FR 67 at the sign for Standing Indian Campground, and continue 4 miles to the campground on your left. *NOTE:* Be sure to drive the full distance when heading west on US 64 to the westernmost West Old Murphy Road.

From the junction of US 64 and NC 175, drive east on US 64 for 16.2 miles. Turn right onto West Old Murphy Road at the sign for Wallace Gap, and follow directions above.

GPS coordinates: N35 03.339' / W83 30.637'

Maps: *DeLorme: North Carolina Atlas & Gazetteer:* Page 51 F6

About the campground: While the neighboring horse camp is making strides toward improvement, the Hurricane Creek Primitive Campground is not. In fact, *primitive* is an understatement! There are no sites, no tent pads, no picnic tables, nary a fire ring. And to top it off, you have to walk next door to the horse camp if you want to use the vault toilet located there.

Unless you are looking for the bare minimum, bypass this one, and head up the road a few miles to the Standing Indian Campground instead.

Hurricane Creek Horse Camp

Location: Off FR 67 just past the Hurricane Creek Campground, about 15 miles southwest of Franklin and about 23 miles northeast of Hayesville

Season: Mar 15–Jan 1

Campers use the primitive stalls to house their horses at Hurricane Creek Horse Camp.

Sites: Open field; no set number of designated campsites
Maximum length: None
Facilities: Vault toilet, fire rings, trash cans; pet friendly
Fee per night: $
About the campground: Although the National Forest Service states there are five designated campsites here, there really are no designated sites. There is a large open, grassy field, with picnic tables dispersed on the outskirts and some fire rings as well. Many of those camping here simply drive their RV and horse trailers in and are ready to ride.

Some of the local horse clubs have been instrumental in making this horse camp what it is today. They petitioned to get the vault toilet installed, and they have volunteered their time and effort to building the "stables" that now stand in the corner of the campground. These hardworking locals even made a conscientious effort toward conservation by building the stables out of yellow locust, a native tree species whose lumber should last even longer than pressure-treated wood.

Highlands to Cashiers

	Total Sites	Hookup Sites	Max. RV Length	Hookups	Toilets	Showers	Drinking water	Dump station	Recreation	Fee	Reservations
28 Van Hook Glade	19	0	36'	N	F	Y	Y	N	H, S*	$$	Y
29 Blue Valley (Dispersed)	*	0	n/a	N	N	N	N	N	H	No fee	N
30 Ammons Branch	4	0	n/a	N	V	N	N	N	H	No fee	N
31 Ralph Andrews Park	36	29	50'	E, W	F	Y	Y	Y	S, F, B, L*, P	$$–$$$	N

* See campground entry for specific information.

28 Van Hook Glade Campground

Location: On the north side of US 64, about 8 miles east of Franklin and 4.5 miles west of Highlands
Season: Apr 1–Oct 31

Lake Sequoyah Dam creates one of many waterfalls near the town of Highlands.

Highlands to Cashiers

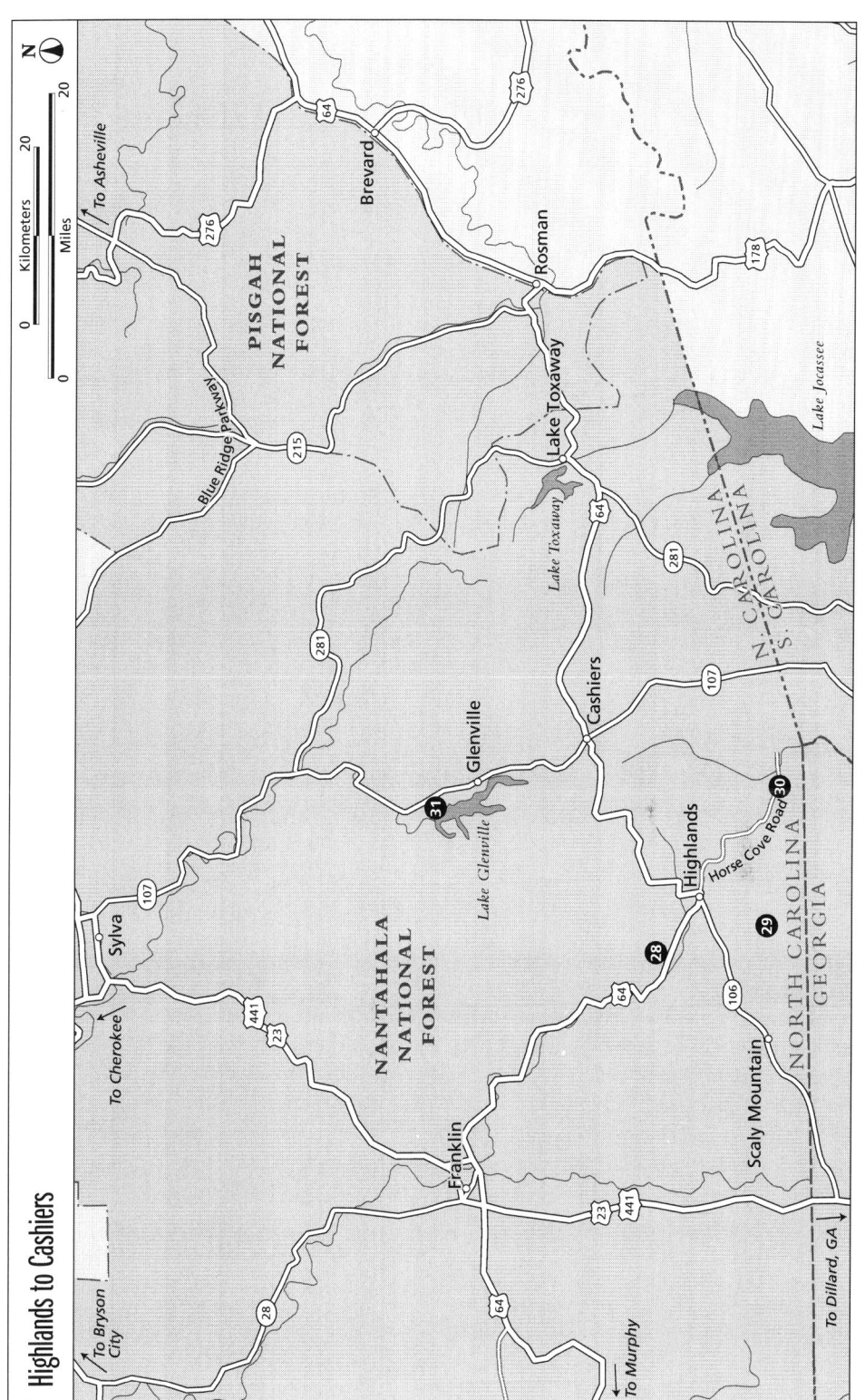

Sites: 18

Maximum length: 36 feet

Facilities: Flush toilets, hot showers, water spigots dispersed, fire rings, picnic tables, lantern holders; pet friendly

Fee per night: $$

Management: Nantahala National Forest—Nantahala Ranger District; run by private concessioner

Contact: (828) 526-5912; www.fs.usda.gov/recarea/nfsnc/recreation/camping-cabins/recarea/?recid=48652&actid=29. For reservations call (877) 444-6777 or visit www.recreation.gov.

Finding the campground: From the junction of US 64 and US 441 Bypass in Franklin, drive east on US 64 for 12.1 miles to the campground on your left.

From the junction of US 64 and NC 106 in Highlands, drive west on US 64 for 4.2 miles to the campground on your right.

GPS coordinates: N35 04.710' / W83 14.767'

Maps: *DeLorme: North Carolina Atlas & Gazetteer:* Page 52 E1

About the campground: Although you can hear the traffic going by on US 64, it's sparse at night, so this is still one of my favorite little hideaways, with private campsites tucked away in a great location just outside the town of Highlands. This stretch of US 64 is a great scenic drive and home to several waterfalls that can be easily accessed right off the roadside. There are miles of hiking, mountain bike, and bridle trails within easy reach. Or you can go for a quick dip in the neighboring Cliffside Lake. For a tamer time, try your hand at gem mining in Franklin, or visit the quaint little shops of Highlands. The options in this area are endless.

29 Blue Valley Dispersed Camping

Location: Dispersed off Blue Valley Road and FR 479C, about 6 miles south of Highlands

Season: Year-round

Sites: Camping allowed in marked sites dispersed along Blue Valley Road and FR 479C

Maximum length: n/a; tents only

Facilities: Picnic tables, lantern holders, primitive fire rings; pet friendly

Fee per night: None

Management: Nantahala National Forest—Nantahala Ranger District

Contact: (828) 524-6441; www.fs.usda.gov/recarea/nfsnc/recreation/camping-cabins/recarea/?recid=48640&actid=34

Finding the campground: From the junction of NC 28 and US 64 in Highlands, drive south on NC 28 for 5.9 miles. Turn right onto Blue Valley Road (SR 1618) at the BLUE VALLEY CAMPING sign, and travel 2.1 miles to where the dispersed campsites begin. Continue on Blue Valley Road to where it ends at a T at 3.6 miles. Turn right here onto FR 479C; more dispersed campsites begin immediately on your right.

NOTE: At 0.5 mile on Blue Valley Road, the paved Clear Creek Road (SR 1613) bends right. Be sure to veer left and continue following the unpaved Blue Valley Road.

GPS coordinates: N35 01.110' / W83 14.685'

Maps: *DeLorme: North Carolina Atlas & Gazetteer:* Page 52 F1

At 411 feet, Whitewater Falls is the tallest waterfall in North Carolina.

About the campground: The Blue Valley Experimental Forest contains approximately 1,400 acres of primarily white pine trees with hardwoods mixed in. Miles of hiking trails with breathtaking long-range views await as you explore the depths of this "road less traveled." Several waterfalls can be found within this area, and the Glen Falls Trail leads you to three of them—talk about a bang for your buck. Be sure to carry a map and compass or a great guidebook, such as *Hiking Waterfalls in North Carolina* (FalconGuides, 2011), before going too far off the beaten path.

30 Ammons Branch Campground

Location: About 5 miles south of Highlands
Season: Year-round
Sites: 4
Maximum length: n/a; tents only
Facilities: Vault toilet, fire rings, picnic tables, lantern holders; pet friendly
Fee per night: None
Management: Nantahala National Forest—Nantahala Ranger District
Contact: (828) 524-6441; www.fs.usda.gov/recarea/nfsnc/recreation/camping-cabins/recarea/?recid=48638&actid=34
Finding the campground: From the junction of NC 28 and US 64 (Main Street) in Highlands, drive east on Main Street, passing through the light at 5th Street. After approximately 0.2 mile, Main Street becomes Horse Cove Road (SR 1603). Follow Horse Cove Road for 4.4 miles (total mileage from the light at US 64 and SR 28), and turn right onto the gravel Bull Pen Road. Continue 1.2 miles to a right turn onto FR 441 at the sign and entrance into Ammons Branch Campground.
GPS coordinates: N35 01.298' / W83 08.679'
Maps: *DeLorme: North Carolina Atlas & Gazetteer:* Page 52 F1–F2
About the campground: This tiny, remote campground has just four campsites, each surrounded by the forest, giving you lots and lots of privacy. Although you are only a few miles from the town of Highlands, it feels as though you are deep within the forest and isolated from civilization.

The fact that there are no RVs allowed may contribute to the rustic ambience as you pitch your tent and enjoy the sounds of the wilderness around you.

31 Ralph Andrews Campground

Location: Pine Creek Road, Glenville; about 6 miles north of Cashiers and about 8 miles south of Tuckasegee
Season: Apr 15–Oct 31
Sites: 36; RV "cabin" rentals also available
Maximum length: 50 feet
Facilities: Flush toilets, hot showers, electric, water spigots dispersed, fire rings, picnic tables, lantern holders, dump station; pet friendly
Fee per night: $$–$$$
Management: Jackson County Department of Parks and Recreation

Fall colors burst around Lake Glenville and the entire mountain region.

Contact: (828) 743-3923

Finding the campground: From the junction of NC 107 and US 64 in Cashiers, drive north on NC 107 for 6.2 miles. Turn left onto Pine Creek Road, and travel for 1.1 miles to a left turn into Ralph Andrews Park.

From the junction of NC 107 and NC 281 in Tuckasegee, drive south on NC 107 for 8.3 miles. Turn right onto Pine Creek Road, and follow directions above.

GPS coordinates: N35 11.592' / W83 08.797'

Maps: *DeLorme: North Carolina Atlas & Gazetteer:* Page 52 D1

About the campground: Resting right above Lake Glenville, this campground has a great location for those who love the water. There's a boat launch just 0.2 mile down the road, a swim beach, playgrounds, a great picnic shelter, and views of the lake from many of the campsites. It's no wonder this place gets so crowded on the weekends.

If you plan on camping here on the weekend, try to arrive early. Some of the sites are more private than others, and you may end up smack dab in the middle of the masses if you're not the early bird.

Waynesville

	Total Sites	Hookup Sites	Max. RV Length	Hookups	Toilets	Showers	Drinking water	Dump station	Recreation	Fee	Reservations
32 Sunburst	10	0	30'	N	F	N	Y	N	H, M, F, P	$$	N

32 Sunburst Campground

Location: Off NC 215, about 9 miles south of Bethel and 13 miles north of Balsam Grove
Season: Early Apr–late Oct
Sites: 10
Maximum length: 30 feet
Facilities: Flush toilets, water spigots dispersed, fire rings, picnic tables, lantern holders, *no* showers; pet friendly
Fee per night: $$
Management: Pisgah National Forest—Pisgah Ranger District; run by private concessioner
Contact: (828) 648-7841; www.fs.usda.gov/recarea/nfsnc/recreation/camping-cabins/recarea/?recid=48160&actid=29
Finding the campground: From the junction of NC 215 and the Blue Ridge Parkway near Balsam Grove, drive north on NC 215 for 8.6 miles to the Sunburst Campground on the left.

From the junction of NC 215 and US 276 in Bethel, drive south on NC 215 for approximately 8.9 miles to the Sunburst Campground on the right.
GPS coordinates: N35 22.445' / W82 56.444'
Maps: *DeLorme: North Carolina Atlas & Gazetteer:* Page 52 B3
About the campground: Sunburst Campground is very small, and with only ten campsites, it tends to get pretty busy on the weekends. The campground sits right beside NC 215 and is openly exposed to it. That, combined with the fact that it's not wooded, adds to the lack of privacy at any campsite in this campground. If you keep this in mind before you head out, you won't be disappointed when you hear your neighbor coughing in the night. But if you visit during the week, you may be lucky enough to have the place to yourself. Under these circumstances it's quite pleasant as you are lulled to sleep by the sounds of the river rushing by in the distance.

Sunburst sits right between the Middle Prong and the Shining Rock Wilderness Areas. Be sure to make the best of it, and enjoy the Great Balsam Mountains that surround you. Whether you take a scenic drive along the Blue Ridge Parkway or make the strenuous hike up to the top of Cold Mountain, you are sure to be awed by the scenery these mountains have to offer. Spectacular view after view simply take your breath away.

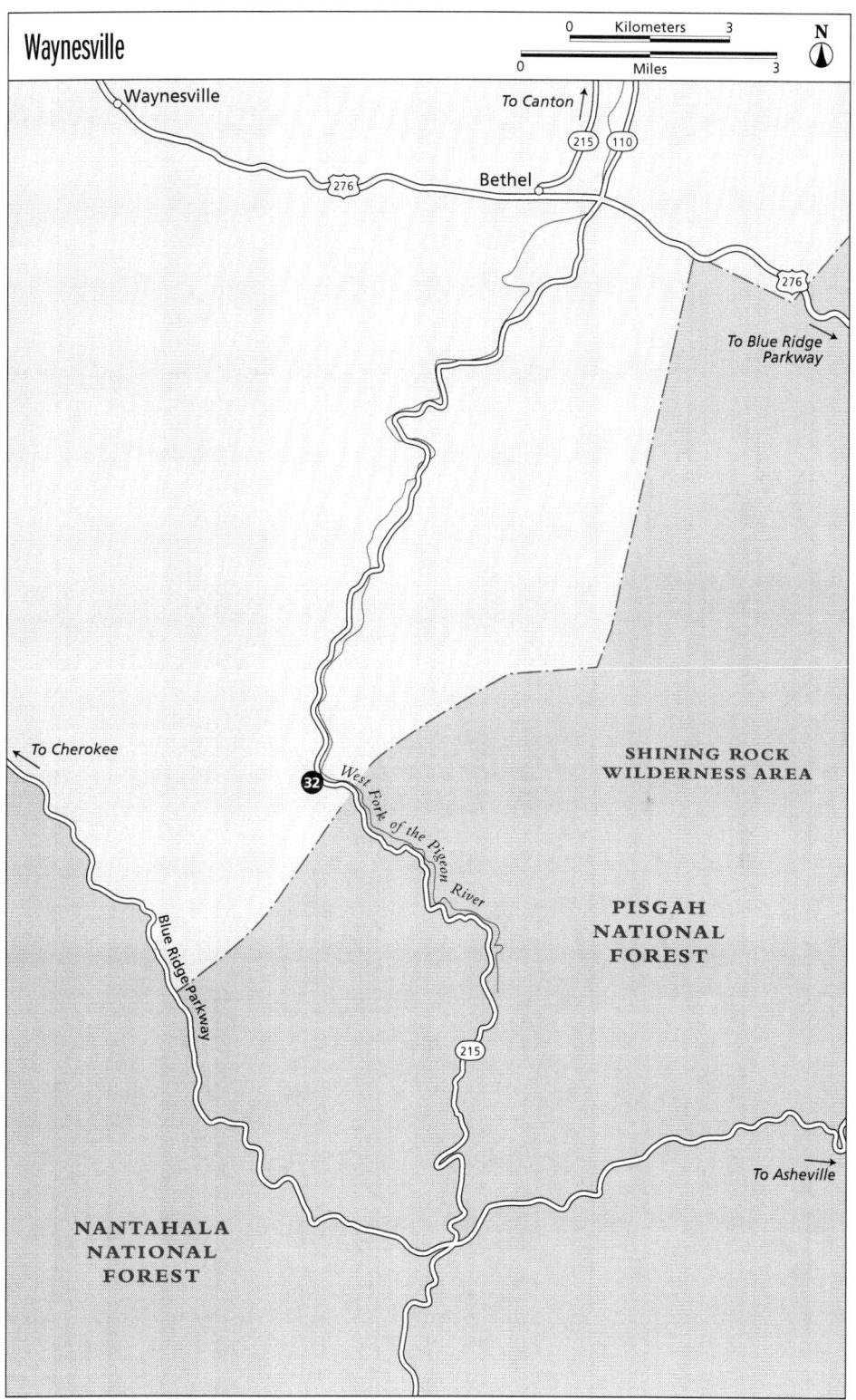

The West Fork of the Pigeon River flows under the High Arch Bridge, creating what kayakers call the "Garden of the Gods."

Brevard to Asheville

	Total Sites	Hookup Sites	Max. RV Length	Hookups	Toilets	Showers	Drinking water	Dump station	Recreation	Fee	Reservations
33 Kuykendal (Group)	1	0	n/a	N	V	N	Y	N	H, F	$$$	Y*
34 Cascade Lake	160	154	40'	E, W, Wi-Fi	F	Y	Y	Y	S, F, B	$$–$$$	Y
35 Davidson River	161	14	45'	E, W	F	Y	Y	Y	H, F, S, M, T, R*, P*	$$$	Y
36 White Pines (Group)	2	0	n/a	N	V	N	Y	N	H, R, M, F, P*	$$$	Y
37 FR 477 (Dispersed)	11	0	n/a	N	N	N	N	N	H, R, M, F, P	No fee	N
38 Cove Creek (Group)	2	0	n/a	N	V	N	Y	N	H, S, M, F, P	$$$	Y
39 FR 1206 (Dispersed)	14	0	n/a	N	N	N	N	N	H, M, R, F, P	No fee	N
40 Mount Pisgah	128	0	35'	N	F	Y	Y	Y	H, C, P	$$	Y
41 North Mills River	31	1	35'	E, W	F	Y	Y	Y	H, M, R, F, P	$$	Y
42 FR 5000 and FR 142 (Dispersed)	15	0	n/a	N	N	N	N	N	H, M, R, F, P	No fee	N
43 Wash Creek (Group)	1	0	n/a	N	V	N	N	N	H, M, R, F, P	$$$	Y
44 Lake Powhatan	85	12	50'	E, W	F	Y	Y	Y	H, M, S, F, P	$$$	Y

* See campground entry for specific information.

33 Kuykendall Group Camp

Location: On FR 2058, about 3 miles west of Brevard and 5 miles east of Rosman
Season: Year-round
Sites: 2 sites, each accommodating up to 100 people (reservations required)
Maximum length: 30 feet
Facilities: Vault toilet, drinking water, picnic tables, lantern posts, fire rings; pet friendly
Fee per night: $$$
Management: Pisgah National Forest—Pisgah Ranger District; run by private concessioner
Contact: (828) 862-5960; www.fs.usda.gov/recarea/nfsnc/recreation/camping-cabins/recarea/?recid=48134&actid=33. For reservations call (877) 444-6777 or visit www.recreation.gov.
Finding the campground: From the junction of US 64 and NC 215, drive east on US 64 for 5.4 miles. Turn left onto Cathey's Creek Road (SR 1401) at the sign for Kuykendall Camp, and then immediately turn left onto SR 1338. Follow SR 1338 for 1.4 miles to a right turn onto FR 2058 at the entrance to Kuykendall Group Campground. NOTE: SR 1338 becomes unpaved FR 471.

From the junction of US 64 and US 276 South, drive west on US 64 for 3.4 miles. Turn right onto Cathey's Creek Road (SR 1401) at the sign for Kuykendall Camp, and follow directions above.

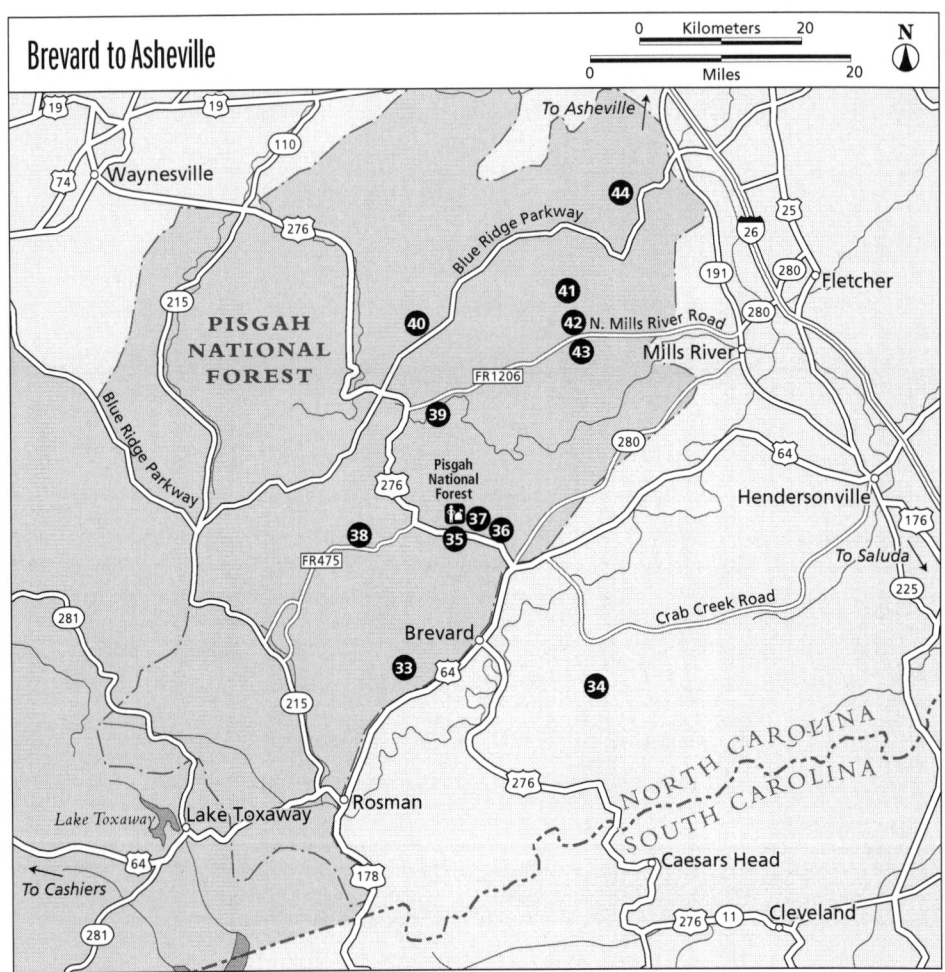

0   Kilometers   20

N

0   Miles   20

To Asheville

19   **19**

110

74   Waynesville

276

Blue Ridge Parkway

215

PISGAH
NATIONAL
FOREST

44

25

26

191   **280**   Fletcher

41

40   **42**   N. Mills River Road   **280**

43   Mills River

FR1206

39

280

64

Pisgah
National
Forest

276   **37**   **36**   Hendersonville   **176**

38   **35**

FR475   To Saluda

281   Crab Creek Road   **225**

Brevard

33   **64**   **34**

215

NORTH CAROLINA

SOUTH CAROLINA

276

Lake Toxaway   Lake Toxaway   Rosman

64   Caesars Head

To Cashiers   **178**

281   **276**   **11**   Cleveland

GPS coordinates: N35 12.825' / W82 47.151'

Maps: *DeLorme: North Carolina Atlas & Gazetteer:* Page 53 D5

About the campground: Resting on the outskirts of the Pisgah National Forest, you would think the Kuykendall Group Camp would be easy to reach. Geographically, yes, but be aware that you must drive across Kuykendall Creek to reach the camping area. High-clearance vehicles are recommended, especially during spring and summer, when it tends to rain a lot.

Once you get settled in, it's easy to let go of the stress and simply lose yourself in the refreshing sounds of the creek as it makes its way down the mountainside. Bring your fishing pole and cast a line as you unwind, or head a bit deeper into the forest to explore hundreds of miles of trails for hiking, mountain biking, or horseback riding.

This is a pack it in, pack it out facility, so bring plenty of trash bags and be sure to practice no-trace camping. Reservations are required and must be made at least four days in advance. Also, the forest service requests that you call (828) 862-5960 within five days of your arrival to receive the combination to the lock on the entrance gate. Make sure you have your reservation confirmation number handy.

34 Cascade Lake Campground

Location: 1679 Little River Campground Rd., Penrose; about 3 miles west of Brevard and 17 miles east of Hendersonville
Season: Apr 1–Oct 31
Sites: 160
Maximum length: 40 feet
Facilities: Flush toilets, hot showers, electric, water spigots, fire rings, picnic tables, lantern holders, dump station, camp store, small cafe, laundry, wireless Internet connection, ice and firewood for sale, boat rentals, boat ramp, swimming area; pet friendly
Fee per night: $$–$$$
Management: Pisgah National Forest–Pisgah Ranger District; run by private concessioner
Contact: (828) 877-4475; www.cascadelakerecreationarea.com/index.html
Finding the campground: From the junction of US 64 and US 276 North, drive east on US 64 for 3.6 miles. Turn right onto Crab Creek Road (SR 1127) at the sign for DuPont State Forest, and travel 2.3 miles. Turn right onto Cascade Lake Road (SR 1536). At 1.1 miles go left onto the now-gravel Cascade Lake Road, and continue for 0.7 mile. Turn left onto Little River Campground Road (SR 1570), and travel 1.6 miles to where it dead-ends at the entrance to the Cascade Lake Campground.

From the junction of US 64 and US 25 in Hendersonville, drive west on US 64 for 13.5 miles. Turn left onto Crab Creek Road, and follow directions above.
GPS coordinates: N35 12.941' / W82 37.842'
Maps: *DeLorme: North Carolina Atlas & Gazetteer:* Page 53 D6
About the campground: Even the drive through the beautiful Little River Valley is enjoyable as you make your way to the Cascade Lake Campground. The campground sits on a peninsula, adjacent to pristine Cascade Lake. As with most North Carolina mountain lakes, the views here are spectacular no matter what time of day. While some of the campsites seem to be packed together and crowded, others are nicely tucked away in a far more private setting.

The campground has a camp store, a small cafe, laundry facilities, and a free wireless Internet connection—all of which tend to draw in the RV crowd more than tent campers. The gate is open from 7 a.m. to 10 p.m., and no alcoholic beverages are allowed.

35 Davidson River Campground

Location: 1000 Pisgah Hwy., Pisgah Forest; about 2 miles north of Brevard and 20 miles south of Asheville
Season: Year-round
Sites: 161
Maximum length: 45 feet
Facilities: Flush toilets, hot showers, water spigots dispersed, fire rings, picnic tables, lantern holders, dump station, ice and firewood for sale, sandy beach, bicycle rentals; pet friendly
Fee per night: $$$
Management: Pisgah National Forest–Pisgah Ranger District; run by private concessioner

An old cemetery sits behind the Davidson River Campground off the North Slope Trail.

Contact: (828) 877-3265 or (828) 862-5960; www.fs.usda.gov/recarea/nfsnc/recreation/
camping-cabins/recarea/?recid=48130&actid=29. For reservations call (877) 444-6777 or visit
www.recreation.gov.

Finding the campground: From the junction of US 276 and US 64 in Brevard, drive north on US
276 for 1.2 miles. Turn left at the sign for DAVIDSON RIVER CAMPGROUND, and travel 0.1 mile to where
the road veers to the right at the campground entrance.

From the junction of US 276 and the Blue Ridge Parkway, drive south on US 276 for 13.4
miles. Turn right at the sign for the DAVIDSON RIVER CAMPGROUND, and follow directions above.

GPS coordinates: N35 16.877' / W82 43.375'

Maps: *DeLorme: North Carolina Atlas & Gazetteer:* Page 53 C5

About the campground: Davidson River sees a lot of traffic! This place is open year-round and
crowded year-round—for a very good reason. Located within the heart of the Pisgah National Forest, it is convenient to everything an outdoor enthusiast needs. Name your pleasure, and it's within
easy reach of this campground. Picnic grounds, waterfalls galore, hiking, mountain biking, road
cycling, horseback riding, rock climbing, swimming, fishing, tubing—the list goes on.

Despite the fact that most of the campsites do not have full hookups, Davidson River sees lots of RVs. But don't despair; some sites offer a little more privacy for those of us who prefer the simplicity of a tent. The "Poplar Loop" is designated as a generator-free area, affording a bit more tranquility.

36 White Pines Group Camp

Location: Off FR 477, about 3 miles north of Brevard
Season: Year-round
Sites: 2, each site accommodating up to 25 people (reservations required)
Maximum length: n/a; tents only
Facilities: Vault toilets, drinking water, picnic tables, lantern holders, fire rings; pet friendly
Fee per night: $$$
Management: Pisgah National Forest—Pisgah Ranger District; run by private concessioner
Contact: (828) 862-5960; www.fs.usda.gov/recarea/nfsnc/recreation/camping-cabins/recarea/?recid=48168&actid=33. For reservations call (877) 444-6777 or visit www.recreation.gov
Finding the campground: From the junction of US 276 North and US 64, drive north on US 276 for 2.1 miles. Turn right onto FR 477 at the Riding Stables sign and travel for 0.2 mile to FR 477C. Turn right onto FR 477C, which leads you to the White Pines Group Campsites both South and North.

From the junction of US 276 and the Blue Ridge Parkway, drive south on US 276 for 12.6 miles. Turn left onto FR 477 at the Riding Stables sign, and follow directions above.

NOTE: When coming from the north, you will pass one entrance to FR 477 at 4 miles. Continue past it to the second entrance as listed above.
GPS coordinates: N35 17.448' / W82 44.311'
Maps: *DeLorme: North Carolina Atlas & Gazetteer:* Page 53 C5
About the campground: Nestled away in the mountains of the Pisgah National Forest, White Pines Group Camp offers lots of opportunities for outdoor recreation. The group camping areas are walk-in only, so you must cart your gear about 0.25 mile from the gated entrance to the camping area. Once you are settled in, you'll see that the camping areas sit right beside Avery Creek. You don't even have to leave the property to dip your toes into the chilly mountain water or try your hand at a bit of fly fishing. You can obtain your fishing license just outside the pillared entrance to the forest at the Davidson River Outfitters.

If you want to take your group for a guided horseback ride, the Pisgah Riding Stables are just a bit farther up FR 477. The possibilities are endless! Stop by the ranger station and see which trails might be most suitable for your group. Reservations are required and must be made at least four days in advance. As with all the national forest group campgrounds, pack it in, pack it out.

37 FR 477 Dispersed Camping

Location: Campsites dispersed off FR 477, about 3 miles north of Brevard
Season: Year-round
Sites: Many designated primitive campsites available on a first-come, first-served basis
Maximum length: n/a; tents only
Facilities: None
Fee per night: None
Management: Pisgah National Forest—Pisgah Ranger District
Contact: (828) 862-5960; www.fs.usda.gov
Finding the campground: From the junction of US 276 North and US 64, drive north on US 276 for 2.1 miles. Turn right onto FR 477 at the RIDING STABLES sign. There are several primitive campsites dispersed along FR 477.

From the junction of US 276 and the Blue Ridge Parkway, drive south on US 276 for 12.6 miles. Turn left onto FR 477 at the RIDING STABLES sign. There are several primitive campsites dispersed along FR 477.

NOTE: When coming from the north, you will pass one entrance to FR 477 at 4 miles. The campsites are located all along FR 477 between both access points to the forest road.
GPS coordinates: N35 18.390' / W82 44.450'
Maps: *DeLorme: North Carolina Atlas & Gazetteer:* Page 53 C5
About the campground: As with all dispersed camping in national forests, be sure to set up camp in designated sites only. These sites are easily identified and clearly marked with a sign showing a tent symbol. As you travel up and down FR 477 looking for your perfect campsite, you will notice that just about every one is perfect. They are spaced out, so you have lots of privacy, and each has either a groomed tent pad or a nice flat area to pitch your tent. Best of all, almost every site off this forest road sits alongside Avery Creek. As the swift water of this clear mountain creek passes by, it not only serenades you but also brings a chill to the air that can only be felt sitting near a cool mountain stream.

The only negative about the roadside camping here is that FR 477 sees quite a bit of traffic. Between the riding stable and the popular mountain biking trailheads that stem from this road, the dust gets stirred up on a regular basis as cars go speeding by.

38 Cove Creek Group Camp

Location: 1 Davidson River Circle, Pisgah Forest; about 8 miles north of Brevard and 27 miles south of Asheville
Season: Year-round
Sites: 2, each site accommodating up to 100 people (reservations required)
Maximum length: None
Facilities: Vault toilet, drinking water, large picnic shelter, charcoal grills, fire rings; pet friendly
Fee per night: $$$
Management: Pisgah National Forest—Pisgah Ranger District; run by private concessioner

Looking Glass Falls is one of the most popular waterfalls in Transylvania County.

White squirrels, a unique variant of gray squirrel, can be found in the town of Brevard.

Contact: (828) 862-5960; www.fs.usda.gov/recarea/nfsnc/recreation/camping-cabins/recarea/?recid=48128&actid=33. For reservations call (877) 444-6777 or visit www.recreation.gov.

Finding the campground: From the junction of US 276 North and US 64, drive north on US 276 for 5.2 miles. Turn left onto FR 475 at the sign for Pisgah Fish Hatchery, and travel 3.1 miles to FR 809 on the right, at the sign for Cove Creek Group Camp. Follow FR 809 up the hill for 0.5 mile to reach the lower group camping area. The gravel road continues a few more tenths of a mile to the upper group camping area.

From the junction of US 276 and the Blue Ridge Parkway, drive south on US 276 for 9.6 miles. Turn right onto FR 475 at the sign for Pisgah Fish Hatchery, and follow directions above.

GPS coordinates: N35 16.994' / W82 49.025'

Maps: *DeLorme: North Carolina Atlas & Gazetteer: Page 53 C5*

About the campground: The Cove Creek group camping area itself is nothing special. It consists primarily of two large, open grassy fields, with a gravel road for easy access. A large picnic shelter with charcoal grills and a vault toilet are the extent of its amenities. However, Cove Creek passes right by, and two beautiful waterfalls are just a short walk away. A third and even more impressive waterfall lies within easy reach of the campground, as miles of hiking and mountain biking trails lead directly from the campsites out into the vast respite of the Pisgah National Forest.

Be forewarned that you must drive across a small creek to get to the camping areas, so you may want to bring high-clearance vehicles, especially during the wetter months of spring and summer. Reservations are required and must be made at least four days in advance.

39 FR 1206 Dispersed Camping

Location: Campsites dispersed off FR 1206, about 15 miles north of Brevard and about 10 miles west of Mills River
Season: Year-round
Sites: Several designated primitive campsites; available on a first-come, first-served basis
Maximum length: n/a; tents only
Facilities: None
Fee per night: None
Management: Pisgah National Forest—Pisgah Ranger District
Contact: (828) 862-5960; www.fs.usda.gov
Finding the campground: From the junction of US 276 North and US 64, drive north on US 276 for 11.5 miles. Turn right onto FR 1206 (Yellow Gap Road). There are several primitive campsites dispersed along FR 1206.

From the junction of US 276 and the Blue Ridge Parkway, drive south on US 276 for 3.2 miles. Turn left onto FR 1206 (Yellow Gap Road). There are several primitive campsites dispersed along FR 1206.

Alternate route: The dispersed campsites on FR 1206 can also be accessed from NC 191 in Mills River by driving west on North Mills River Road for approximately 8 miles. North Mills River Road becomes gravel FR 1206 after approximately 5.5 miles. *NOTE:* FR 1206 is a gated forest road, and portions of the road are subject to closure at times. Please contact the Pisgah Ranger District office to check on road closures before you visit.
GPS coordinates: N35 22.964' / W82 44.827'
Maps: *DeLorme: North Carolina Atlas & Gazetteer:* Page 53 B5–B6
About the campground: Deep within the Pisgah National Forest and well off the beaten path, you are likely to find peace and solitude here. FR 1206 is not nearly as busy as FR 477, so you can enjoy the sounds of the creek as it rushes by rather than the traffic. The price you pay for this privacy is that it takes a little bit of time to drive all the way up winding US 276 and then a few more miles in on FR 1206 before you finally arrive at your campsite. Yes, it is a beautiful scenic drive, but it can grow tedious after too many daily ice runs.

Several trailheads lead off FR 1206, so you won't be at a loss for outdoor things to do. The wonderful multiuse Mills River Trail runs alongside the river and is a great place to hike, bike, or ride on horseback. Pink Beds Picnic Area is within easy reach, as is the Blue Ridge Parkway if you want to head out for a scenic drive. Just keep in mind that if you're interested in spending time in the quaint mountain town of Brevard or want to pop up to Asheville to hear some live music, you may want to stay somewhere a bit closer to the main drag.

40 Blue Ridge Parkway: Mount Pisgah Campground

Location: Milepost 408 on the Blue Ridge Parkway, between US 276 and NC 191
Season: Mid-May–end of Oct
Sites: 128
Maximum length: 35 feet
Facilities: Flush toilets, fire rings, picnic tables, lantern holders, bear-proof food containers (tent sites only), dump station, camp store, firewood for sale, *no* showers; pet friendly. There's a restaurant across the Parkway at the Pisgah Inn.
Fee per night: $$
Management: National Park Service—Blue Ridge Parkway
Contact: (828) 298-0398; www.nps.gov/blri/planyourvisit/camping-on-the-blue-ridge-parkway .htm. For reservations call (877) 444-6777 or visit www.recreation.gov.
Finding the campground: Mount Pisgah Campground is located at Milepost 408 on the Blue Ridge Parkway, between US 276 and NC 191.
GPS coordinates: N35 24.169' / W82 45.400'
Maps: *DeLorme: North Carolina Atlas & Gazetteer:* Page 53 A5

Amazing views can be seen all along the Blue Ridge Parkway.

About the campground: A room with a view. As you travel along the Blue Ridge Parkway, that's exactly what you get—jaw dropping view after view. And when you arrive at the Mount Pisgah Campground, at nearly 5,000 feet of elevation, the awesome views continue. The campsites are well spaced, well groomed, and private. Two loops are designated for tents only, one for pop-ups and vans, and yet another for RVs and trailers. The National Park Service has left just the right amount of brush to keep the sites separated and private.

Across the Parkway are a camp store, a gift shop, and a restaurant with amazing views of the valley below. And if the weather turns nasty and you feel the need to seek solid shelter, the Pisgah Inn is just a stone's throw away and ready to comfort you.

41   North Mills River Campground

Location: 5289 North Mills River Rd., Mills River; about 12 miles south of Asheville and 10 miles north of Brevard
Season: Year-round; limited services Nov–Mar
Sites: 31
Maximum length: 35 feet
Facilities: Flush toilets, hot showers, water spigots dispersed, fire rings, picnic tables, lantern holders, dump station, ice and firewood for sale; pet friendly
Fee per night: $$
Management: Pisgah National Forest—Pisgah Ranger District; run by private concessioner
Contact: (828) 890-3284; www.fs.usda.gov/recarea/nfsnc/recreation/camping-cabins/recarea/?recid=48148&actid=29. For reservations call (877) 444-6777 or visit www.recreation.gov.
Finding the campground: From the junction of NC 191 and NC 280 East in Mills River, drive north on NC 191 for 0.8 mile. Turn left onto North Mills River Road at the sign for North Mills River Recreation Area, and travel for 5 miles to the entrance to the campground on both your left and right.

From the junction of NC 191 and NC 280, where they split, drive south on SR 191 for 0.2 mile. Turn right onto North Mills River Road at the sign for North Mills River Recreation Area, and follow directions above.

Alternate route: The Mills River Campground can also be accessed from US 276 by traveling east on FR 1206 for approximately 11.75 miles, but be advised that FR 1206 is a bumpy, gravel forest road that is subject to closure at times.
GPS coordinates: N35 24.387' / W82 38.664'
Maps: *DeLorme: North Carolina Atlas & Gazetteer:* Page 53 B6
About the campground: Riverside sites, double sites, group sites, hot showers, flush toilets, and ice and firewood for sale. Wow! The North Mills River Campground has come a long way over the years. You can go fishing without ever leaving the campground or head up the road a short distance for some of the best mountain biking in the area at the Trace Ridge Trailhead.

Hiking trails, bridle trails, waterfalls, picnicking, birding, wildlife viewing—whether you prefer passive or active, it is within easy reach at the North Mills River Campground. Take a scenic drive along the Blue Ridge Parkway, or visit the North Carolina Arboretum to view blossom after blossom. No matter which direction you go, this hidden gem has something to offer. One of the two campsite loops remains open year-round, but winter facilities are limited to vault toilets and no showers.

42 FR 5000 and FR 142 Dispersed Camping

Location: Off FR 5000 and FR 142, about 6 miles west of Mills River
Season: Year-round
Sites: Several designated primitive campsites, available on a first-come, first-served basis
Maximum length: n/a; tents only
Facilities: None
Fee per night: None
Management: Pisgah National Forest—Pisgah Ranger District
Contact: (828) 862-5960; www.fs.usda.gov
Finding the campground: From the junction of NC 191 and NC 280 East in Mills River, drive north on NC 191 for 0.8 mile. Turn left onto North Mills River Road at the sign for NORTH MILLS RIVER RECRE-ATION AREA, and travel 4.9 miles to a right turn onto Wash Creek Road (FR 5000). There are several

Barred owls are common throughout North Carolina.

primitive campsites dispersed along FR 5000. To reach FR 142, continue 2 miles on FR 5000 to a left turn onto FR 142.

From the junction of NC 191 and NC 280, where they split, drive south on SR 191 for 0.2 mile. Turn right onto North Mills River Road at the sign for NORTH MILLS RIVER RECREATION AREA, and follow directions above.

Alternate route: FR 5000 can also be accessed from US 276 by traveling east on FR 1206 for approximately 11.85 miles, but be advised that FR 1206 is a bumpy, gravel forest road that is subject to closure at times.

GPS coordinates: N35 18.390' / W82 44.450'

Maps: *DeLorme: North Carolina Atlas & Gazetteer:* Page 53 B6–A6

About the campground: As with most of the dispersed camping within the Pisgah National Forest, the campsites here are great for privacy, and some of them sit right beside Wash Creek. You should be prepared for some traffic though. FR 142 is home to Trace Ridge, one of the most popular mountain bike trailheads in the forest. Anglers, hunters, and hikers frequent the area as well.

Remember the principles of no-trace camping. Set your tent up at least 50 feet from the water's edge, and dig your cat hole at least four times that distance. These simple acts of preservation help ensure that we'll all enjoy the land for years to come.

43 Wash Creek Group Camp

Location: On FR 5000 directly across from FR 142, about 7 miles northwest of Mills River
Season: Year-round
Sites: 1 site accommodating up to 35 people and 15 vehicles
Maximum length: None
Facilities: Vault toilet
Fee per night: $$$
Management: Pisgah National Forest—Pisgah Ranger District
Contact: (828)877-3265; www.fs.usda.gov. For reservations call (877)444-6777 or visit www .recreation.gov.
Finding the campground: From the junction of NC 191 and NC 280 East in Mills River, drive north on SR 191 for 0.8 mile. Turn left onto North Mills River Road at the sign for NORTH MILLS RIVER REC-REATION AREA, and travel 4.9 miles. Turn right onto Wash Creek Road (FR 5000), and continue for 2 miles to the gated entrance to the group camp on the right (just across from FR 142).

From the junction of NC 191 and NC 280, where they split, drive south on SR 191 for 0.2 mile. Turn right onto North Mills River Road at the sign for NORTH MILLS RIVER RECREATION AREA, and follow directions above.

GPS coordinates: N35 25.599' / W82 39.072'

Maps: *DeLorme: North Carolina Atlas & Gazetteer:* Page 53 A6

About the campground: I love the Pisgah National Forest, but the forest service really dropped the ball on this one. A large grassy field with a gated entrance and a single vault toilet—that's it. That's all you get when you bring your group to stay at Wash Creek Group Camp. The one thing the site has going for it is a good location. It's close to both Asheville and Brevard. There are a handful of waterfalls close by, tons of places to have a picnic, and miles of trails surround you.

44 Lake Powhatan Campground

Location: 375 Wesley Branch Rd., Asheville; on the west side of Asheville
Season: Apr 1–Oct 31
Sites: 85
Maximum length: 50 feet
Facilities: Flush toilets, hot showers, water spigots dispersed, fire rings, picnic tables, lantern holders, dump station, fishing pier, swimming area; pet friendly
Fee per night: $$$
Management: Pisgah National Forest—Pisgah Ranger District; run by private concessioner
Contact: (828) 257-4200, www.fs.usda.gov/recarea/nfsnc/recreation/camping-cabins/recarea/?recid=48172&actid=29
Finding the campground: From the junction of NC 191 and NC 112, drive south on NC 191 for 1.4 miles. Turn right onto Bent Creek Ranch Road (SR 3480) at the sign for Lake Powhatan Recreational Area, and travel 0.2 mile to where the road bends left onto Wesley Branch Road (SR 3484). Follow Wesley Branch Road for 2.3 miles to a fork in the road. Bear left at the fork, and travel another 0.2 mile to the gatehouse at the entrance to Lake Powhatan Campground.

From the junction of NC 191 and the Blue Ridge Parkway, drive north on NC 191 for 0.6 mile. Turn left onto Bent Creek Ranch Road (SR 3480) at the sign for Lake Powhatan Recreational Area, and follow directions above.

GPS coordinates: N35 29.055' / W82 37.620'
Maps: *DeLorme: North Carolina Atlas & Gazetteer:* Page 53 A6
About the campground: Surrounded by miles of mountain bike trails, and mere minutes from the Blue Ridge Parkway, Lake Powhatan Campground is every cyclist's dream. With bike-in/bike-out access to the famous Bent Creek trail system, this place rivals North Carolina's own mountain bike mecca: Tsali.

If biking isn't your thing, the campground is built around Lake Powhatan, which has a designated swimming area, a fishing pier, and a small man-made waterfall. If that's not enough to entice you, the North Carolina Arboretum lies right around the bend, and the cultural offerings of downtown Asheville are just minutes away.

Burnsville to Marion

	Total Sites	Hookup Sites	Max. RV Length	Hookups	Toilets	Showers	Drinking water	Dump station	Recreation	Fee	Reservations
45 Big Ivy (Dispersed)	*	0	n/a	N	N	N	N	N	H, M, R, F, P	$	N
46 Mount Mitchell State Park	9	0	n/a	N	F	N	Y	N	H, P	$$–$$$	Y
47 Black Mountain	44	0	None	N	F	Y	Y	N	H, M, F	$$	N
48 Briar Bottom (Group)	6	0	n/a	N	F	Y*	Y	N	H, M, F	$$$	Y
49 South Toe River (Dispersed)	*	0	n/a	N	N	N	N	N	H, M, R, S, F, T, P	$	N
50 Carolina Hemlocks	37	0	50'	N	F	Y	Y	N	H, S, R, F, P	$$	N
51 Toe River Park	93	28	None	E, W, S	F	Y	Y	Y	H, S, F, P, *	$$$	Y
52 Crabtree Meadows	93	0	None	N	F	Y	Y	Y	H, P	$$	N
53 Curtis Creek	14	0	35'	N	V	N	Y	N	H, F	$	N

* See campground entry for specific information.

45 Big Ivy Dispersed Camping

Location: Off FR 74 in the remote Big Ivy area of Pisgah National Forest, about 5 miles southeast of Barnardsville

Season: Year-round

Sites: A handful of primitive campsites, available on a first-come, first-served basis

Maximum length: n/a; tents only

Facilities: None

Fee per night: None

Management: Pisgah National Forest—Appalachian Ranger District

Contact: (828) 682-6146; www.fs.usda.gov/recarea/nfsnc/recreation/camping-cabins/recarea/?recid=70825&actid=34

Finding the campground: From the junction of the Blue Ridge Parkway (BRP) and NC 128 (unmarked NC 128 is the road leading to Mount Mitchell State Park), drive south on the BRP for 12 miles. Turn right into the Craggy Gardens Picnic Ground, and go up the hill. After approximately 0.35 mile, make a hairpin turn to the left and head downhill on the unmarked gravel FR 63. Follow FR 63, being sure to ignore the road off to the left at 3.8 miles, which crosses the creek. Instead continue straight ahead at this junction. After 4.9 miles the gravel FR 63 becomes paved. Continue on the paved road for another 1.5 miles until you come to a stop sign at Dillingham Road. Be sure to note that the paved part of FR 63 was named Stoney Fork Road for your return trip. Turn right onto Dillingham Road, and travel approximately 1.3 miles. At this point Dillingham Road crosses a bridge and becomes dirt FR 74. The Big Ivy dispersed campsites are located along FR 74.

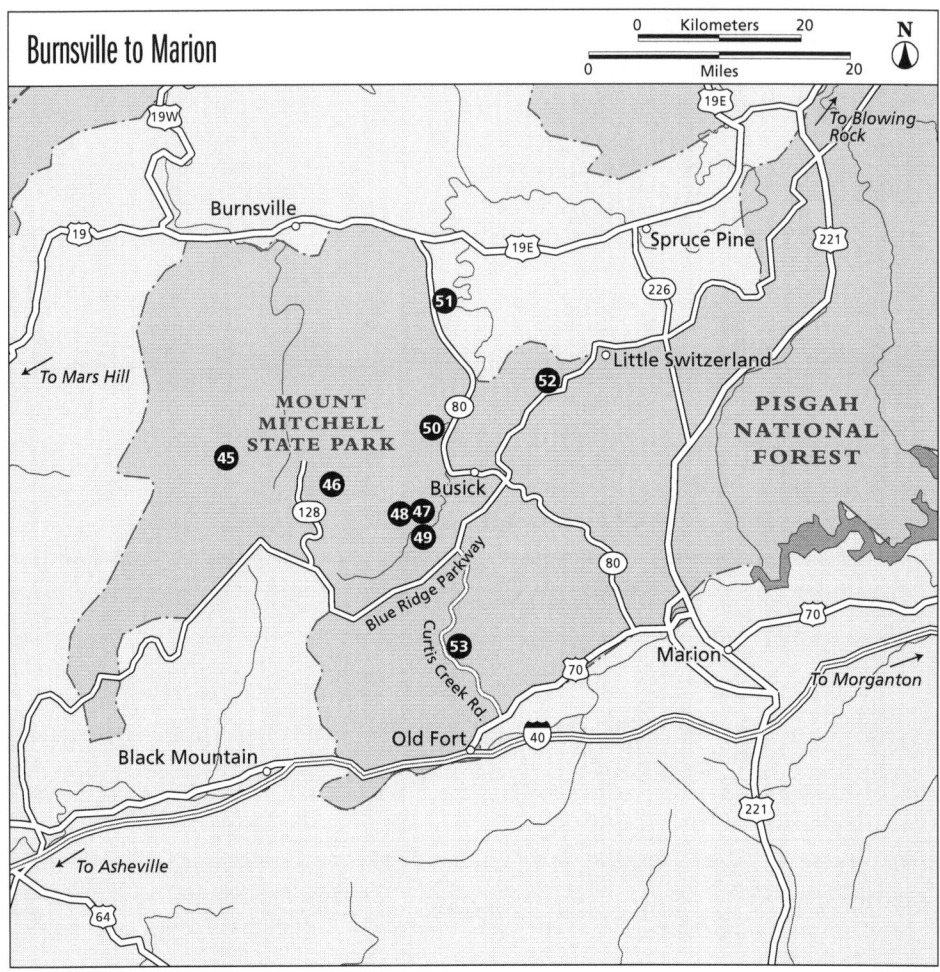

0   Kilometers   20

0   Miles   20

N

To Blowing Rock

19W

19E

Burnsville

Spruce Pine

221

19

19E

226

To Mars Hill

51

Little Switzerland

52

MOUNT
MITCHELL
STATE PARK

80

50

PISGAH
NATIONAL
FOREST

45

46

Busick

128

48 47

80

49

Blue Ridge Parkway

Curtis Creek Rd

53

70

Marion

70

To Morganton

Old Fort

40

Black Mountain

221

To Asheville

64

From the junction of the BRP and US 70, drive north on the BRP for 14.9 miles. Turn left into the Craggy Gardens Picnic Ground, and follow directions above.

NOTE: Craggy Gardens is located between Mileposts 367 and 368 on the Blue Ridge Parkway.
GPS coordinates: N35 46.129' / W82 21.707'
Maps: DeLorme: North Carolina Atlas & Gazetteer: Page 32 E1
About the campground: As you make your way to the Big Ivy area, be sure to take note of the Great Craggy Mountains that surround you. The high slopes of the "Craggies" are known for their heath balds, which are visible from the valley floor as you head down Dillingham Road. I thoroughly enjoy the view every time I pass by. Only a handful of primitive campsites are found off FR 74. This is an extremely remote portion of the Pisgah National Forest, so be sure to have all your provisions, including drinking water, before you head out.

Aside from the nearby Corner Rock Picnic Area, I highly recommend a visit to Douglas Falls. As you stand beneath the mammoth rock overhang, the cool mist of the falls refreshes both your

Christmas tree farms dot the countryside near the Big Ivy area.

body and spirit. But remember not to bathe in any of the creeks unless you are using biodegradable soap. In addition to a few short hiking trails, you will find several bridle trails running through this small section of the Great Craggy Mountains.

46 Mount Mitchell State Park

Location: 2388 State Highway 128, Burnsville; about 25 miles southwest of Little Switzerland and 33 miles north of Asheville
Season: Year-round; Closed Christmas Day
Sites: 9
Maximum length: n/a; tents only
Facilities: Flush toilets, water spigots, fire rings, picnic tables, lantern holders, tent pads, bear-proof food containers, *no* showers; pet friendly. During winter there is a vault toilet only and *no* water available.
Fee per night: $$–$$$
Management: North Carolina Department of Natural Resources
Contact: (828) 675-4611; www.ncparks.gov/Visit/parks/momi/main.php. For reservations call (877) 722-6762 or visit www.reserveamerica.com.
Finding the campground: From the junction of the Blue Ridge Parkway (BRP) and NC 128, drive north on NC 128 for 2.3 miles to the gate and entrance to Mount Mitchell State Park. From

The view from atop Mount Mitchell is spectacular.

the gate continue for another 1.2 miles to the tent camping area on the right. *NOTE:* NC 128 is unmarked, and is located between Mileposts 355 and 356 on the BRP.

GPS coordinates: N35 45.589' / W82 16.276'

Maps: *DeLorme: North Carolina Atlas & Gazetteer:* Page 32 D2

About the campground: Mount Mitchell is the king of the East. Standing at 6,684 feet, this is the highest peak east of the Mississippi River. And as you would expect, the campground is as lofty as the mountain itself. Sitting just over a mile by road below the summit, it offers some of the most stunning views around. The sites are what's known as walk-in sites and require a short uphill walk to get to. They are very well spread out and private, but the wind still whips through this small, cozy campground. Between the wind and the elevation, Mount Mitchell tends to be colder than most other campgrounds, so keep this in mind when you're packing your gear for this trip.

Caution: This is black bear country, and Mount Mitchell State Park has gone above and beyond by providing bear-proof food containers. But that's just a small step toward bear safety. Be sure to keep a clean camp, never bring food inside your tent, and put all cooking supplies and trash away as well. Lastly, and of most importance, never feed any wild animal. It's a sad fact that a fed bear is a dead bear.

47 Black Mountain Campground

Location: Off FR 472; north of the Blue Ridge Parkway, about 6 miles southwest of Busick
Season: Apr 14–Oct 31
Sites: 43
Maximum length: None
Facilities: Flush toilets, hot showers, water spigots dispersed, fire rings, picnic tables, lantern holders; pet friendly
Fee per night: $$
Management: Pisgah National Forest—Appalachian Ranger District; run by private concessioner
Contact: (828) 675-5616; www.fs.usda.gov/recarea/nfsnc/recreation/camping-cabins/recarea/?recid=48522&actid=29
Finding the campground: From the junction of FR 2074 and the Blue Ridge Parkway (BRP), drive north on FR 2074 for 2.4 miles to an intersection where a hard left leads into an open field, the left continues onto South Toe River Road (FR 472), and the right is Neel's Gap Road. Turn left at this intersection, and follow South Toe River Road for 0.6 mile to a right turn onto FR472A (Black Mountain Campground Road) and into the campground. *NOTE:* FR 2074 is located between Mileposts 349 and 350 on the BRP, just south of the Licklog Ridge Overlook.

From the junction of the BRP and NC 128 (unmarked NC 128 is at the Mt. Mitchell State Park sign), drive north on the BRP for 3.3 miles. Turn left onto FR 472, and follow the winding gravel road for 4.7 miles until you come to a large Pisgah National Forest sign for Black Mountain Campground. The campground is on the left.

From the junction of the BRP and NC 80, drive south on the BRP for 7.7 miles. Turn right onto FR 472, and follow directions above.

NOTE: FR 472 is located between Mileposts 351 and 352 on the Blue Ridge Parkway.
GPS coordinates: N35 45.089' / W82 13.250'
Maps: *DeLorme: North Carolina Atlas & Gazetteer:* Page 32 E2
About the campground: Black Mountain Campground is simply wonderful. The sites are well spaced out, and some of them are right alongside the South Toe River. One of the campground loops has a large open field where you could easily play a game of kickball, toss a Frisbee, or play some volleyball, whatever your fancy. There are hiking trails galore, whether you take a short stroll from your campsite to visit Setrock Creek Falls or, if you're looking for a challenge, hike the Mount Mitchell Trail. This strenuous 5.5-mile trail leads from the campground all the way to Mount Mitchell's summit.

At 6,684 feet Mount Mitchell is not only the tallest peak in North Carolina but also the tallest peak in the eastern United States. If you prefer to drive to the summit, a quick trip south on the Blue Ridge Parkway leads to the entrance to Mount Mitchell State Park.

48 Briar Bottom Group Camp

Location: Off FR 472, north of the Blue Ridge Parkway about 6 miles southwest of Busick. Briar Bottom Group Campground is located within the Black Bottom Campground.
Season: Apr 14–Oct 31

Sites: 6 group campsites, with a maximum of 50 people per site (reservations required)

Maximum length: n/a; tents only

Facilities: Flush toilets, fire ring, picnic shelter; hot showers available at nearby Black Mountain Campground; pet friendly

Fee per night: $$$

Management: Pisgah National Forest—Appalachian Ranger District; run by private concessioner

Contact: (828) 675-5616; www.fs.usda.gov/recarea/nfsnc/recreation/camping-cabins/recarea/?recid=48590&actid=33. For reservations call (877) 444-6777 or visit www.recreation.gov.

Finding the campground: From the junction of FR 2074 and the Blue Ridge Parkway (BRP), drive north on FR 2074 for 2.4 miles to an intersection where a hard left leads into an open field, the left continues onto South Toe River Road (FR 472), and the right is Neel's Gap Road. Go left at this intersection, and follow South Toe River Road for 0.6 mile to a right turn onto FR472A (Black Mountain Campground Road) and into the Black Mountain Campground. Take the first left once inside the campground. Follow the road up, ford the creek, and arrive at Briar Bottom Group Camp. *NOTE:* FR 2074 is located between Mileposts 349 and 350 on the BRP, just south of the Licklog Ridge Overlook.

From the junction of the BRP and NC 128 (unmarked NC 128 is at the Mt. MITCHELL STATE PARK sign), drive north on the BRP for 3.3 miles. Turn left onto FR 472, and follow the winding gravel road for 4.7 miles until you come to a large Pisgah National Forest sign for BLACK MOUNTAIN CAMP-GROUND. The campground is on the left.

From the junction of the BRP and NC 80, drive south on the BRP for 7.7 miles. Turn right onto FR 472, and follow directions above.

NOTE: FR 472 is located between Mileposts 351 and 352 on the Blue Ridge Parkway.

GPS coordinates: N35 44.931' / W82 13.556'

Maps: *DeLorme: North Carolina Atlas & Gazetteer:* Page 32 E2

About the campground: Briar Bottom Group Camp is located within the Black Mountain Campground. You have to cross a small creek to enter the campground, so you may want to warn those in your group to bring high-clearance vehicles. Each site has a fire ring and a large picnic shelter. A large open field in the middle of the campground is great for group activities and games. If you want to take the kids off into the forest, there are miles of hiking trails within easy reach of the campground. As a matter of fact, you can take a short 0.25-mile stroll to Setrock Creek Falls without ever leaving the property. Advance reservations are required.

49 South Toe River Dispersed Camping

Location: Off FR 472 and FR 2074, about 20 miles southwest of Little Switzerland

Season: Year-round

Sites: A handful of designated primitive campsites, available on a first-come, first-served basis

Maximum length: n/a; tents only

Facilities: Fire rings

Fee per night: None

Management: Pisgah National Forest—Appalachian Ranger District

Fields of wildflowers often grow along the roadside.

Contact: (828) 675-5616; www.fs.usda.gov/recarea/nfsnc/recreation/camping-cabins/recarea/?recid=49216&actid=34

Finding the campground: From the junction of FR 2074 and the Blue Ridge Parkway (BRP), drive north on FR 2074 for 2.4 miles to an intersection where a hard left leads into an open field, the left continues onto South Toe River Road (FR 472), and the right is Neel's Gap Road. There are handful of campsites along the roadside of FR 472 and FR 2074, from Neal's Creek to the Blue Ridge Parkway.

GPS coordinates: N35 44.592' / W82 12.763'

Maps: *DeLorme: North Carolina Atlas & Gazetteer:* Page 32 E2

About the campground: *Dispersed* is an understatement. There are only a handful of designated campsites in the area, but don't fret if all the primitive roadside sites are full when you arrive. Black Mountain Campground is right around the bend, off FR 472.

Even when the water level is up, you can't help but notice the character that oozes from the rocky riverbed of the South Toe River. This area is a great option for those wanting easy access to the Mountains-to-Sea Trail or the Blue Ridge Parkway. The 1,000-mile Mountains-to-Sea Trail literally makes its way from the mountains to the sea. It starts at Clingmans Dome in the Great Smoky Mountains and travels all the way to the Atlantic Ocean at Jockey Ridge in North Carolina's Outer

Banks. The modern-day trail was started in 1973 but is said to follow the original path taken by Native Americans hundreds of years ago.

50 Carolina Hemlocks Campground

Location: About 14 miles south of Burnsville and 5 miles north of Busick
Season: Apr 14–Oct 31
Sites: 37
Maximum length: 50 feet
Facilities: Flush toilets, hot showers, water, fire rings, picnic tables; pet friendly
Fee per night: $$
Management: Pisgah National Forest—Appalachian Ranger District; run by private concessioner
Contact: (828) 682-6146 or (828) 675-5509; www.fs.usda.gov/recarea/nfsnc/recreation/camping-cabins/recarea/?recid=48596&actid=29
Finding the campground: From the junction of NC 80 and the Blue Ridge Parkway near Busick, drive north on NC 80 for 5.3 miles to the campground on both your left and right.

From the junction of NC 80 and US 19 East in Micaville, drive south on NC 80 for approximately 8.6 miles to the campground on both your left and right.
GPS coordinates: N35 48.373' / W82 12.095'
Maps: *DeLorme: North Carolina Atlas & Gazetteer:* Page 32 D2
About the campground: Carolina Hemlocks has two separate sections—one on the west side and one on the east side of NC 80. Whichever you choose, you are in for a treat. The west side is wooded but not that private. A few of the campsites, however, sit high upon a ledge, overlooking the South Toe River. This, combined with a great wooded picnic area and a phenomenal stone-walled swimming hole, make the west side of the campground quite inviting.

While you don't have the river rushing by in the campground's eastern half, you do have lots more space and woods in between the campsites, giving you plenty of privacy and tranquility as you appreciate the lush land around you. Several trails are within easy reach and afford the opportunity to explore the Mount Mitchell Wildlife Management Area either on foot or on horseback. If you prefer a scenic drive, the Blue Ridge Parkway is just down the road.

51 Toe River Campground

Location: 225 Patience Park Rd., Burnsville; about 8 miles east of Burnsville and 11 miles west of Spruce Pine
Season: Apr–Oct
Sites: 93
Maximum length: None
Facilities: Flush toilets, hot showers, water, electric, fire rings, picnic tables, trash cans, camp store, ice and firewood for sale; pet friendly
Fee per night: $$$
Management: Yancey County Parks and Recreation

Contact: (828) 675-5104

Finding the campground: From the junction of NC 80 and the Blue Ridge Parkway, drive north on NC 80 for 9.8 miles. Turn right onto Blue Rock Road (SR 1152) at the sign for Toe River Campground, and travel 0.9 mile. Turn left onto Patience Park Road (SR 1201), and continue 0.2 mile to the campground's gated entrance. From the gate continue another 0.25 mile to the campground.

From the junction of NC 80 and US 19 East in Micaville, drive south on NC 80 for approximately 4.1 miles. Turn left onto Blue Rock Road (SR 1152), and follow directions above.

GPS coordinates: N35 52.405' / W82 11.999'

Maps: *DeLorme: North Carolina Atlas & Gazetteer:* Page 32 C2

About the campground: If you are staying in a tent, stop now; do not unpack your gear. Keep driving 4.5 miles farther south on NC 80 to Carolina Hemlocks Campground. Why? The Toe River Campground is an RV park. Not to say that tents aren't allowed. It just seems that tents were not in mind when the campground was designed. Not only is this more like an RV parking lot, but many of the RVs seem to be permanent fixtures, with decks and patios added on. I will say, the campground sits right beside the peaceful South Toe River. And there are plenty of activities available right on the premises, with a playground, volleyball court, basketball net, and picnic shelter.

52   Blue Ridge Parkway: Crabtree Meadows Campground

Location: On the Blue Ridge Parkway at Milepost 340, between NC 80 and NC 226; about 10 miles southwest of Little Switzerland

Season: Mid-May–Oct

Sites: 93

Maximum length: None

Facilities: Flush toilets, water spigots dispersed, fire rings, picnic tables, lantern holders, dump station, *no* showers; pet friendly

Fee per night: $$

Management: National Park Service—Blue Ridge Parkway

Contact: (828) 350-3821; www.nps.gov/blri/planyourvisit/camping-on-the-blue-ridge-parkway.htm

Finding the campground: The campground is located along the Blue Ridge Parkway at Milepost 340, between NC 80 and NC 226.

GPS coordinates: N35 48.851' / W82 08.753'

Maps: *DeLorme: North Carolina Atlas & Gazetteer:* Page 32 D3

About the campground: Crabtree Meadows is a great place to set up camp as you travel along the Blue Ridge Parkway. In general the campground has a few loops, each with an open grassy field in the middle. The campsites line the inner and outer edges of the loops, and the sites on the outer edge tend to offer more privacy than those inside the loop. If you prefer tent camping, you get a nice perk here. One of the loops is dedicated to tent camping only.

There's a picnic area just across the Parkway, and a great hiking trail leads from the campground to the base of picturesque Crabtree Falls. The crabapple tree (*Malus sylvestris*), or "wild crab tree," once flourished in this area. Orchards with their showy pink blooms and tart crabapples once sat just above the falls. Today very few crabapple trees can be found here, but don't be discouraged. What the trail lacks in the tree's pink blossoms, it more than makes up for with wild-flowers. This loop trail is home to more than forty species, making it an ideal place to hike during spring and summer.

53 Curtis Creek Campground

Location: About 7 miles north of Old Fort
Season: Apr 1–Oct 31
Sites: 14
Maximum length: 35 feet
Facilities: Vault toilets, water spigots dispersed, fire rings, picnic tables, lantern holders; pet friendly
Fee per night: $
Management: Pisgah National Forest—Grandfather Ranger District
Contact: (828) 675-5616; www.fs.usda.gov/recarea/nfsnc/recreation/camping-cabins/recarea/?recid=48956&actid=31
Finding the campground: From the junction of Curtis Creek Road and the Blue Ridge Parkway (BRP), drive south on Curtis Creek Road for 5.7 miles to the campground on your left. *NOTE:* Curtis Creek Road (unmarked) is directly across from FR 2074, between Mileposts 349 and 350 on the BRP, just south of the Licklog Ridge Overlook.

From the junction of Curtis Creek Road and US 70 near Old Fort, drive north on Curtis Creek Road for 5 miles to the campground on the right. *NOTE:* Curtis Creek Road (unmarked) is on the north side of US 70 and directly across from Green Lee Road. There is a small sign for Curtis Creek Campground. As you drive north from US 70, the pavement ends after 2.6 miles.
GPS coordinates: N35 41.390' / W82 11.808'
Maps: *DeLorme: North Carolina Atlas & Gazetteer:* Page 32 E2
About the campground: As you travel north on Curtis Creek Road from US 70, you notice that random campsites begin to appear on the side of the road. These sites are an isolated part of the campground, and although they are right on the side of the road, they are actually the nicest sites in the campground. They are extremely private, and you get the added bonus of waterfront property, as these sites sit right beside Curtis Creek.

As for the main body of the campground—well, *horrid* is one word that comes to mind. Picture a parking lot of campsites, sitting at an angle, all lined up in a row; one after the next, without a single tree to separate them. Yes, there are trees, but they are *surrounding* the sites, not in between them.

The campground is kept quite neat and clean. And my nostalgic side appreciates that this is part of the very first tract of land to become national forestland. Purchased under the Weeks Act back in 1911, it has remained in the caring hands of the USDA Forest Service ever since.

Marion to Morganton

	Total Sites	Hookup Sites	Max. RV Length	Hookups	Toilets	Showers	Drinking Water	Dump Station	Recreation	Fee	Reservations
54 Lake James State Park	20	0	n/a	n/a	F	Y	Y	N	H, S, F, B, P	$$	Y
55 South Mountains State Park	31	0	25'	N	V	N	Y	N	H, R, M, F, P	$$	Y
55 South Mountains State Park (Horse)	15	0	83'	N	F	Y	Y	N	H, R, M, F, P	$$-$$$	Y
55 South Mountains State Park (Group)	4	0	n/a	N	V	N	N	N	H, R, M, F, P	$$-$$$	Y

54 Lake James State Park

Location: About 5 miles northeast of Marion
Season: Mar 1–Nov 30
Sites: 20
Maximum length: n/a; tents only
Facilities: Flush toilets, hot showers, water spigots dispersed, fire rings, picnic tables, trash cans, firewood for sale; pet friendly
Fee per night: $$
Management: North Carolina Department of Natural Resources
Contact: (828) 584-7728 or (828) 584-7730; www.ncparks.gov/Visit/parks/laja/main.php. For reservations call (877) 722-6762 or visit www.reserveamerica.com
Finding the campground: From Marion follow US 70 to the junction of NC 126 and US 70 in Nebo. Drive northeast on NC 126 for approximately 2.6 miles to a left turn into Lake James State Park.

From Morganton travel west on I-40 to exit 94. After exiting the highway, travel north for 0.5 mile to a stop sign at US 70. Turn left onto US 70, and travel for approximately 5.6 miles. Turn right onto NC 126 in Nebo, and follow directions above.
GPS coordinates: N35 43.901' / W81 53.939'
Maps: *DeLorme: North Carolina Atlas & Gazetteer:* Page 33 E5
About the campground: Clean bathrooms, hot showers, flush toilets, and a 0.25-mile walk to paradise! Nestled away on its own pristine peninsula, the campground at Lake James State Park gets top marks from me. Actually, it ranks among my favorites. The sites are perfectly spaced out, and the crystal-clear lake water has quite an allure.

This is true waterfront camping. There are boat docks at the campground, so you can bring your boat, put in down the street at the Canal Bridge Boat Launch, and then leave your car overnight. Or if you prefer, bring a canoe or kayak and paddle out right from your own "backyard."

Lake James can be seen in the distance.

For a nominal ($) fee you can buy all the firewood you can burn. The state park requests and highly encourages that you take them up on this great deal. It helps protect the habitat by keeping out potential invasive species that you may inadvertently introduce by bringing in your own firewood. It's a small way that you can help protect this wonderful state park.

55 South Mountains State Park

Location: 3001 South Mountain Park Ave., Connelly Springs; about 20 miles south of Morganton
Season: Year-round; closed Christmas Day
Sites: 11 primitive sites, 15 equestrian sites with stalls available, 4 group camping areas (reservations required), 20 backpack sites

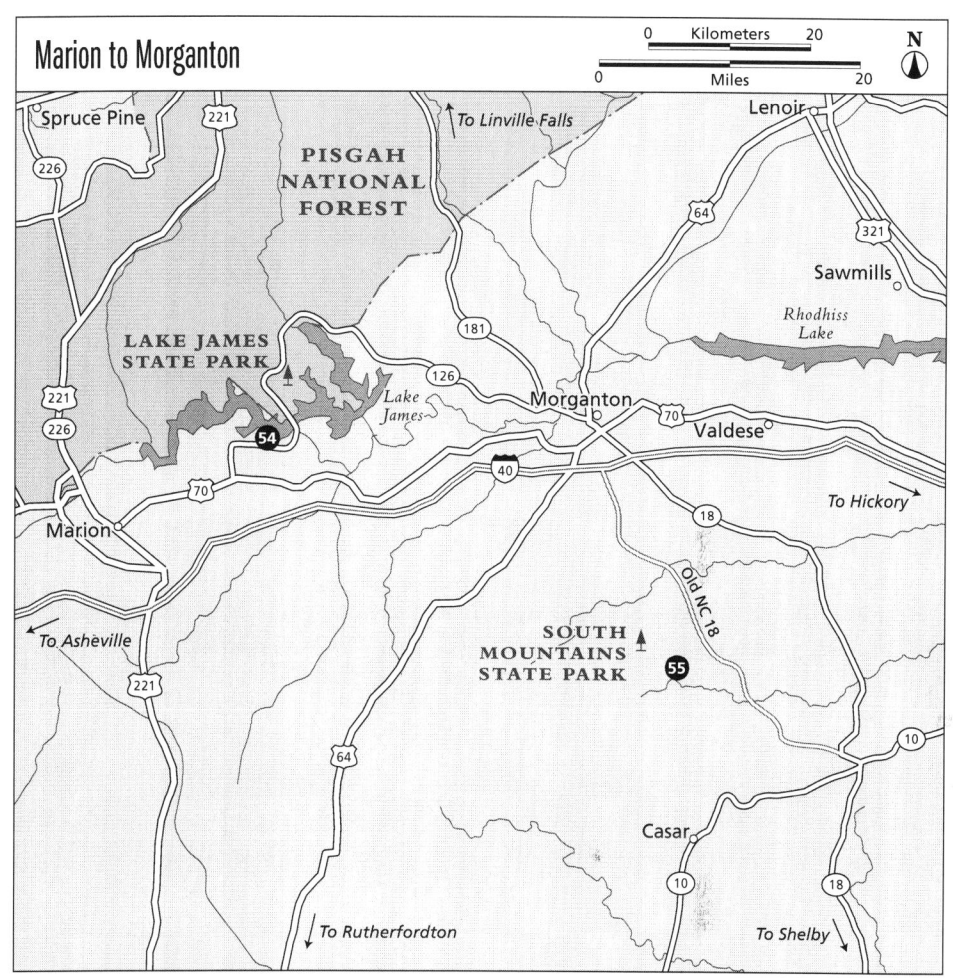

Marion to Morganton

Maximum length: Family camping: 25 feet; equestrian camping: 83 feet
Facilities: Primitive family camping—vault toilet, picnic tables, fire ring, drinking water; pet friendly. Equestrian camping—33-stall barn, flush toilets, hot showers, picnic tables, fire ring, drinking water; pet friendly
Fee per night: $$–$$$
Management: North Carolina Department of Natural Resources
Contact: (828) 433-4772 or (828) 433-4686; www.ncparks.gov/Visit/parks/somo/activities .php. For reservations call (877) 722-6762 or visit www.reserveamerica.com.
Finding the campground: From I-40 take exit 105 (NC 18), and drive south on NC 18 for 11 miles. Turn right onto Sugar Loaf Road (SR 1913) at the sign for SOUTH MOUNTAINS STATE PARK, and travel 4.2 miles to where it dead-ends at Old NC 18 (SR 1924). Turn left onto Old NC 18, and travel 2.6 miles. Turn right onto Wards Gap Road (SR 1901), and continue 1.3 miles to a fork. Bear right at the fork onto South Mountains Park Avenue, and follow it to the entrance to the park.

High Shoals Falls is one of the highlights of South Mountains State Park.

From the junction of NC 18 and NC 10, drive north on NC 18 for 0.6 mile. Turn left onto Old NC 18 (SR 1924), and travel 6 miles. Turn left onto Wards Gap Road (SR 1901), and follow directions above.

GPS coordinates: N35 36.136' / W81 37.752'

Maps: *DeLorme: North Carolina Atlas & Gazetteer:* Page 33 F7

About the campground: No matter what your pleasure, South Mountains State Park has a trail for you—more than 40 miles' worth designed for hiking, mountain biking, and horseback riding. Whether you take a hike up to High Shoals Falls or ride your horse to the top of Ben Knob, you are certain to enjoy the forested South Mountains that comprise this park. If you prefer an easy stroll, an interpretive nature trail runs alongside the Jacob Fork River. Or you can picnic near the water's edge or cast your lure into one of the many wild trout waters that flow through the park. Be sure to obtain a North Carolina state fishing license before casting your line.

The park offers backcountry camping, which entails packing in all your gear and hiking anywhere from 1.2 to more than 5 miles. There are also two developed campgrounds on the property. The family campground is small, primitive, and offers lots of privacy, but its designers did not have RVs in mind. The equestrian campground is much larger and can accommodate large RVs and horse trailers, but you must have a horse with you to camp here. For an additional fee you can also rent a stall and keep your horse protected from the elements inside the barn. You must show proof of a negative Coggins test to rent a horse stall. There is also group camping available near Shinny Creek; reservations are required.

Linville Falls to Blowing Rock and Lenoir

	Total Sites	Hookup Sites	Max. RV Length	Hookups	Toilets	Showers	Drinking Water	Dump Station	Recreation	Fee	Reservations
56 Linville Falls	70	0	None*	N	F	Y	Y	Y	H, F, P	$$	Y
57 Mortimer	19	0	50'	N	F	Y	Y	N	H, M, C, R, F, O, P	$$	N
58 Brown Mountain OHV (Dispersed)	*	0	n/a	N	N	N	N	N	H, M, C, O, P	No fee*	N*
59 Boone Fork	15	0	n/a	N	V	N	N	N	H, M, F, O, P	$	N
60 Julian Price	196	0	92'	N	F	Y	Y	Y	H, F, B*, L*, P	$$	Y

* See campground entry for specific information.

56 Blue Ridge Parkway: Linville Falls Campground

Location: On the east side of the Blue Ridge Parkway at Milepost 316, between US 221 and NC 181; about 2 miles north of the town of Linville Falls
Season: Mid-May–Oct
Sites: 70
Maximum length: A limited number of larger sites; most can accommodate RVs from 40 to 50 feet.
Facilities: Flush toilets, fire rings, picnic tables, lantern holders, water spigots dispersed, trash cans, dump station, firewood for sale, *no* showers; pet friendly
Fee per night: $$
Management: National Park Service—Blue Ridge Parkway
Contact: (828) 298-0398; www.nps.gov/blri/planyourvisit/camping-on-the-blue-ridge-parkway .htm. For reservations call (877) 444-6777 or visit www.recreation.gov.
Finding the campground: The campground is located on the east side of the Blue Ridge Parkway at Milepost 316, between US 221 and NC 181. Follow the Parkway toward the Linville Falls Visitor Center for 0.5 mile to the campground on the right.
GPS coordinates: N35 58.083' / W81 55.967'
Maps: *DeLorme: North Carolina Atlas & Gazetteer:* Page 33 B5
About the campground: The campground comprises two loops, keeping it small in comparison to some of the other campgrounds along the Blue Ridge Parkway. A wide-open grassy field sits in the middle of each loop, and as you would expect, the sites on the inside of the loop tend to have less privacy. The campsites are very well groomed, and scattered about is the occasional private campsite. The B Loop is a bit more wooded than the A Loop, and some sites are designated as tent-only campsites. These sites require a short 200-foot walk and are located right beside the Linville River. Dress warmly and pack accordingly—it's not uncommon for the area to get frost overnight, even in springtime. *Be prepared:* The self-pay station at the entrance to the campground requires exact change.

A short hike leads to Upper Linville Falls.

A short jaunt down the road, you will find the Linville Falls Visitor Center. From here you can take the small easy loop trail to Duggers Creek Falls, hike one of the trails to view the powerful and very popular Linville Falls, or spend an entire day exploring deeper into the Linville Gorge Wilderness.

57 Mortimer Campground

Location: On NC 90 in the town of Edgemont, about 24 miles northwest of Lenoir
Season: Apr 1–Nov 30
Sites: 19
Maximum length: 50 feet
Facilities: Flush toilets, hot showers, water spigots dispersed, fire rings, picnic tables, lantern holders; pet friendly
Fee per night: $$
Management: Pisgah National Forest—Grandfather Ranger District

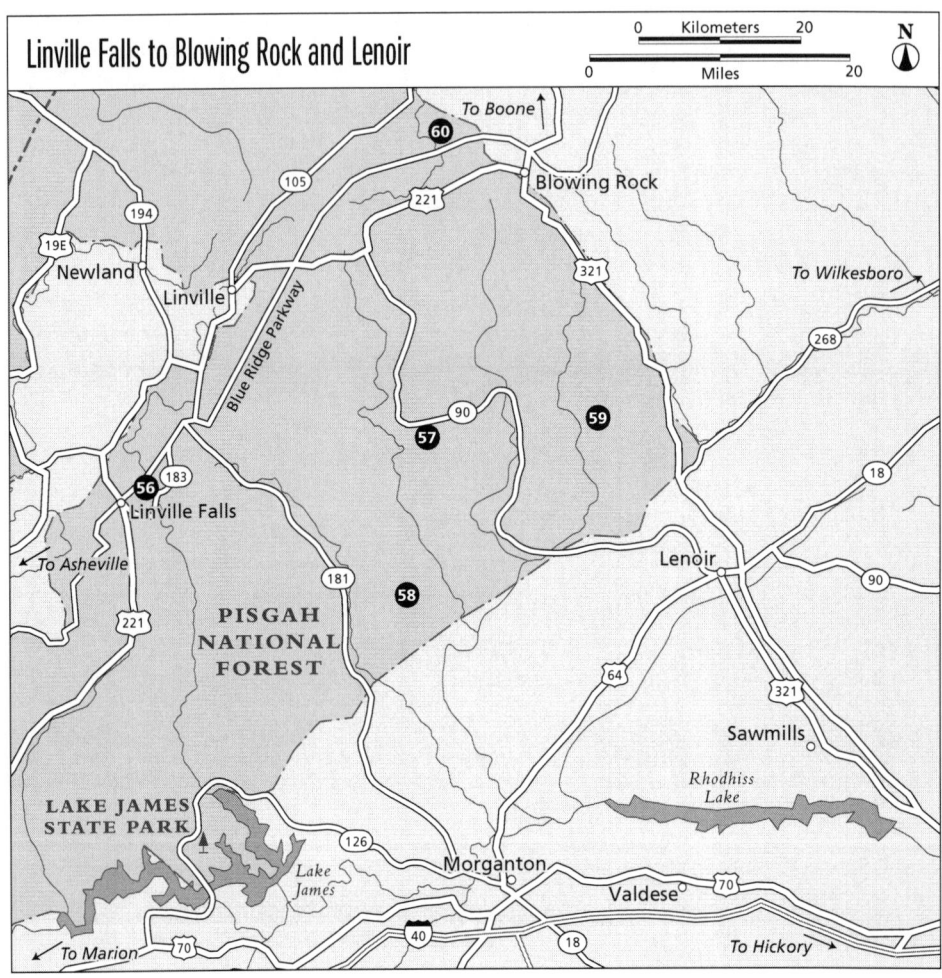

Linville Falls to Blowing Rock and Lenoir

Contact: (828) 675-5616; www.fs.usda.gov/recarea/nfsnc/recreation/camping-cabins/recarea/?recid=49006&actid=29

Finding the campground: From the junction of NC 90 and Brown Mountain Beach Road in Edgemont, drive north on NC 90 for less than 0.1 mile to the campground on your right.

From the junction of NC 90 and US 221 near Linville, drive south on NC 90 for approximately 14.7 miles to the campground on your left.

GPS coordinates: N35 59.475' / W81 45.685'

Maps: *DeLorme: North Carolina Atlas & Gazetteer:* Page 33 B6

About the campground: As remote as the Mortimer Campground seems, it fills up quickly on the weekends, primarily with locals. And just like night and day, if you camp here during the week, you are likely to have the place to yourself. There is a day-use picnic area just outside the campground entrance, and a quaint creek runs right through the property. Some of the sites are very private; a handful of them are tent only and sit on the other side of the creek. These tent-only sites are accessed by a footbridge over the creek. If you're in a tent, the short walk is worth the creekside camping. If you forget any provisions, from catsup to ice, Betsey's Store is within walking distance of the campground.

The area is surrounded by trails of every kind. Hike, mountain bike, horseback ride, or hop on your all-terrain vehicle (ATV). They are all welcome in this portion of the Pisgah National Forest.

If you prefer to simply sightsee, head up to the Blue Ridge Parkway for a scenic drive, or head over to NC 181 and stop at the Brown Mountain Overlook near dusk. On a clear night the mysterious "Brown Mountain Lights" can be seen wavering in the distance atop Brown Mountain. This strange phenomenon has mystified people for hundreds of years. Cherokee legend says the lights are the spirits of Indian maidens searching for their loved ones lost in battle. Others say the ghosts of Civil War veterans are doomed to carry candles across the mountain forever. Whether ghosts, spirits, foxfire, or a mirage, the lights have yet to be scientifically explained.

58 Brown Mountain OHV Camp

Location: About 16 miles north of Morganton and about 18 miles west of Lenoir
Season: Apr 1–Jan 1
Sites: Located throughout the area
Maximum length: n/a; tents only
Facilities: Vault toilet, fire rings, picnic table, lantern holder, off-highway vehicle (OHV) loading ramp; pet friendly
Fee per night: No fee for camping; OHV trail pass required for a nominal fee ($)
Management: Pisgah National Forest—Grandfather Ranger District
Contact: (828) 652-2144; www.fs.usda.gov/recarea/nfsnc/recreation/ohv/recarea/?recid=49004&actid=32
Finding the campground: From the junction of NC 181 and US 64 in Morganton, drive north on NC 181 for approximately 11.4 miles. Turn right onto Brown Mountain Beach Road, and travel approximately 3.6 miles. Turn left onto FR 299, and continue for approximately 1.5 miles to the parking area for the Brown Mountain OHV trail system.

From the junction of NC 181 and the Blue Ridge Parkway, drive south on NC 181 for approximately 15.1 miles. Turn left onto Brown Mountain Beach Road, and follow directions above.
GPS coordinates: N 35 53.680' / W81 45. 510'
Maps: *DeLorme: North Carolina Atlas & Gazetteer:* Page 33 C6
About the campground: There are not many places in the Pisgah National Forest where you are allowed to take motorized vehicles on the trail. So if you enjoy a good four-wheel drive, this 34-mile trail system is just for you. There are trails to accommodate all levels, from novice to expert. A handful of dispersed campsites sit along the side of FR 299 as you head to the trailhead. But remember, you came here to ride, not for peace and quiet. So embrace the rumble and roar of the OHV engine as it revs up in the background.

While the camping is free, a daily trail pass ($) is required to ride the trails. If you plan on frequenting the area, you can save yourself some money with a season pass ($$$). Passes can be purchased from several local vendors. Use the contact information above to get a list of vendors from the Grandfather District Ranger Station.

You may see the occasional mountain biker on the trail system, and the surfaced streets surrounding this area are popular with road cyclists. As you hit the trail, remember to always ride within your limits, and be aware that helmets and eye protection are mandatory gear.

59 Boone Fork Campground

Location: About 10 miles north of Lenoir
Season: Memorial Day–Labor Day
Sites: 14
Maximum length: 50 feet
Facilities: Vault toilets, water spigots dispersed, fire rings, picnic tables, lantern holders; pet friendly
Fee per night: $
Management: Pisgah National Forest—Grandfather Ranger District

Occasionally you come across a rundown waterwheel.

Contact: (828) 675-5616; www .fs.usda.gov/recarea/nfsnc/ recreation/camping-cabins/ recarea/?recid=49080&actid=29
Finding the campground: From the junction of NC 90 (Colletsville Road) and Valway Road in Lenoir, drive west on NC 90 for 4 miles. Turn right onto Mulberry Creek Road (SR 1368), across from the closed-down gas station in Olivette, and travel 4.5 miles. Turn right onto Boone Fork Road at the Boone Fork Campground sign, and continue 2 miles to the entrance to the campground. *NOTE:* When you're traveling from the east, NC 90 becomes a gravel road.
GPS coordinates: N36 00.621' / W81 37.288'
Maps: *DeLorme: North Carolina Atlas & Gazetteer:* Page 33 B8
About the campground: Well off the beaten path, this quaint, primitive campground doesn't see much traffic. With its picnic area and a fishing pond, this is a nice place to unwind, read a book, and simply lay low. There are a handful of mountain biking and hiking trails not too far away. Or if you prefer off-road vehicles, the Brown Mountain OHV trail system is near enough. Be sure to bring

single dollar bills with you, because the self-pay station at the entrance to the campground requires exact change.

60 Blue Ridge Parkway: Julian Price Memorial Park Campground

Location: On the Blue Ridge Parkway at Milepost 297, about 5 miles west of Blowing Rock
Season: Mid-May–Oct
Sites: 196
Maximum length: 92 feet
Facilities: Flush toilets, showers, water, electric, fire rings, picnic tables, lantern holders, trash cans, dump station, firewood for sale, boat rental; pet friendly
Fee per night: $$
Management: National Park Service—Blue Ridge Parkway
Contact: (828) 298-0398; www.nps.gov/blri/planyourvisit/camping-on-the-blue-ridge-parkway.htm. For reservations call (877) 444-6777 or visit www.recreation.gov.
Finding the campground: The campground is located along the Blue Ridge Parkway at Milepost 297, between US 221 and US 321.
GPS coordinates: N36 08.352' / W81 44.161'
Maps: *DeLorme: North Carolina Atlas & Gazetteer:* Page 13 F6–F7
About the campground: As the Blue Ridge Parkway's largest campground, this place is huge! They have a lovely lake, boat rentals, lots of hiking trails, an amphitheatre, and a large picnic area. There are loops for each camping category, whether you are in an RV, a travel trailer, or a tent. The RV loop sits right on Price Lake, giving you some lovely waterfront camping. The travel trailer loops are wooded and surprisingly well spaced. Unfortunately they dropped the ball with the tent loops. These sites seem to be crowded in, and while there are woods in the middle of the loops, there are no trees between the campsites. With the exception of a good spot here and there, you are pretty much open to the world.

If you have the chance to stay here during the week, you are in for a real treat. On the weekends you will be sharing it with the masses.

Wilkesboro

	Total Sites	Hookup Sites	Max. RV Length	Hookups	Toilets	Showers	Drinking Water	Dump Station	Recreation	Fee	Reservations
61 Fort Hamby	49	32	143'	E, W	F,V	Y	Y	Y	H, S, F, B, L, P, *	$$-$$$	Y
61 Fort Hamby (Group)	1	0	n/a	N	F	Y	N	N	H, S, F, B, L, P, *	$$$	Y
62 Bandit's Roost	100	85	148'	E, W	F	Y	Y	Y	H, S, F, B, L, O, P, *	$$-$$$	Y
62 Bandit's Roost (Group)	7	0	n/a	N	F	Y	Y	N	H, S, F, B, L, O, P, *	$$$	Y
63 Warrior Creek	72	53	145'	E, W	F	Y	Y	Y	H, M, S, F, B, L, P, *	$$-$$$	Y
63 Warrior Creek (Group)	2	0	n/a	N	F	Y	Y	N	H, M, S, F, B, L, P, *	$$$	Y

* See campground entry for specific information.

61   W. Kerr Scott Reservoir: Fort Hamby Campground

Location: On the north side of W. Kerr Scott Reservoir, about 8 miles west of Wilkesboro
Season: Apr 15–Oct 31
Sites: 49; also 1 group campsite that can accommodate up to 100 people
Maximum length: 143 feet
Facilities: Flush toilets, vault toilets, hot showers, water spigots dispersed, electric, fire rings, picnic tables, lantern holders, trash cans, dump station, firewood for sale; pet friendly
Fee per night: $$–$$$
Management: US Army Corps of Engineers
Contact: (336) 973-0104; www.saw.usace.army.mil/wkscott/index.htm. For reservations call (877) 444-6777 or visit www.recreation.gov.
Finding the campground: From the junction of US 421 and NC 16 North near Wilkesboro, drive north on US 421 for 3.1 miles. Turn left onto South Recreation Road at the Fт. Hᴀᴍʙʏ Pᴀʀᴋ sign, and continue 1.3 miles to the gate at the entrance to the Fort Hamby Campground.
GPS coordinates: N36 07.792' / W81 16.328'
Maps: *DeLorme: North Carolina Atlas & Gazetteer:* Page 14 F3
About the campground: Conveniently located on the north side of the reservoir and just a bit west of Wilkesboro, this is a great place to bring the family. Activities abound! Basketball, volleyball, horseshoe pits, and a playground are just a small taste of what Fort Hamby has to offer. With so much to do, the kids won't have time to get bored.

You can enjoy this campground by land or water. There's a swim beach and a boat launch, and the reservoir itself has over 55 miles of shoreline. The recreation possibilities are endless.

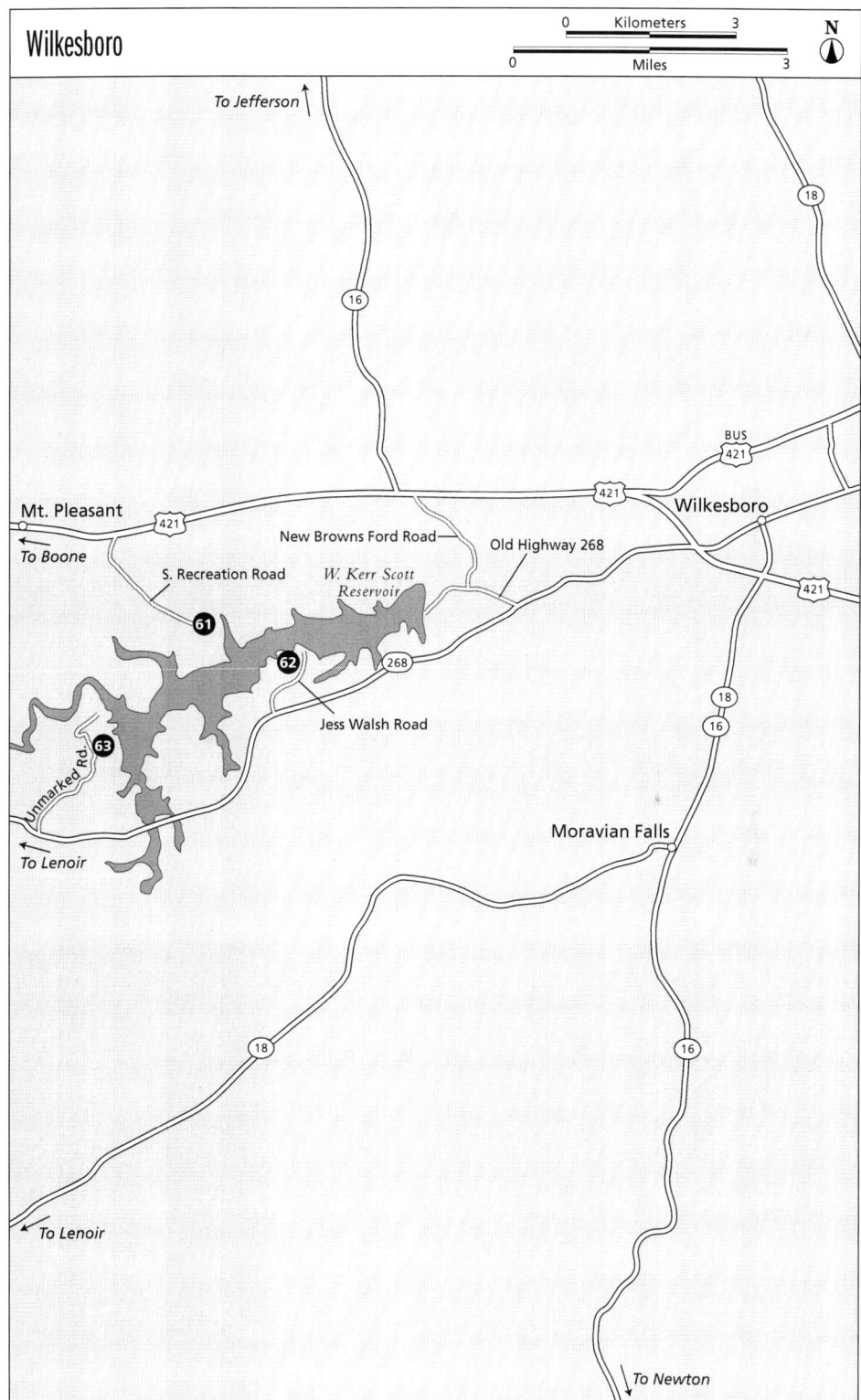

Wilkesboro

0   Kilometers   3
0   Miles   3

N

To Jefferson

18

16

BUS
421

Mt. Pleasant

421

421

Wilkesboro

US
421

New Browns Ford Road

Old Highway 268

To Boone

S. Recreation Road

W. Kerr Scott
Reservoir

61

62

268

421

18
16

Jess Walsh Road

63

Unmarked Rd.

Moravian Falls

To Lenoir

18

16

18

To Lenoir

To Newton

Many Canada Geese migrate to North Carolina in winter.

62 W. Kerr Scott Reservoir: Bandit's Roost Campground

Location: On the south side of W. Kerr Scott Reservoir, about 6 miles west of Wilkesboro

Season: Apr 1–Oct 31

Sites: 100; also 7 group campsites that can accommodate up to 50 people each

Maximum length: 148 feet

Facilities: Flush toilets, hot showers, water spigots dispersed, electric, fire rings, picnic tables, lantern holders, dump station, firewood for sale; pet friendly

Fee per night: $$–$$$

Management: US Army Corps of Engineers

Contact: (336) 921-3190; www.saw.usace.army.mil/wkscott/index.htm. For reservations call (877) 444-6777 or visit www.recreation.gov.

Finding the campground: From the junction of US 421 and NC 16 North near Wilkesboro, you will see that New Browns Ford Road (SR 1143) is on the south side of this intersection. Drive south on New Browns Ford Road (SR 1143) for 1.4 miles to where it dead-ends at a stop sign at the unmarked Old Highway 268 (SR 1176). Turn left and follow Old Highway 268 for 0.5 mile. Turn right onto NC 268, and travel west for 2.8 miles. Turn right onto Jess Walsh Road (SR 1141) immediately after the Goshen Fire Department, and continue 0.5 mile to the entrance to Bandit's Roost Campground.

From the junction of NC 268 and NC 321 near Lenoir, drive east on NC 268 for 22.8 miles. Turn left onto Jess Walsh Road (SR 1141) immediately before the Goshen Fire Department, and follow directions above.

GPS coordinates: N36 07.309' / W81 15.037'

Maps: *DeLorme: North Carolina Atlas & Gazetteer:* Page 14 F3

About the campground: Beautiful, simply beautiful. Many of the RV sites are right on the lake, and although they lack privacy, the waterfront view makes up for it. As for the sites in the middle of the loop, while they aren't on the lake, they are nicely shaded. There's a separate area for tent camping, and these sites are wooded and private! You simply take a quick jaunt down a few steps and, poof, you have your own happy wilderness home—a little piece of paradise.

If a great campsite isn't quite enough to entice you, there are hiking trails, basketball hoops, a boat launch, and a couple of swim beaches to keep you and the whole family entertained.

63   W. Kerr Scott Reservoir: Warrior Creek Campground

Location: On the south side of W. Kerr Scott Reservoir, about 8 miles west of Wilkesboro

Season: Apr 15–Oct 15

Sites: 72; also 2 group campsites that can accommodate up to 30 people in one and up to 50 people in the other

Maximum length: 143 feet

Facilities: Flush toilets, hot showers, water spigots dispersed, electric, fire rings, picnic tables, lantern holders, dump station, firewood for sale; pet friendly

Fee per night: $$–$$$

Management: US Army Corps of Engineers

Contact: (336) 921-2177; www.saw.usace.army.mil/wkscott/index.htm. For reservations call (877) 444-6777 or visit www.recreation.gov.

Finding the campground: From the junction of US 421 and NC 16 North near Wilkesboro, you will see that New Browns Ford Road (SR 1143) is on the south side of this intersection. Drive south on New Browns Ford Road (SR 1143) for 1.4 miles to where it dead-ends at a stop sign at the unmarked Old Highway 268 (SR 1176). Turn left and follow Old Highway 268 for 0.5 mile. Turn right onto NC 268, and continue west for 5.1 miles. Turn right onto an unmarked road at the sign for WARRIOR CREEK CAMPGROUND, and follow it to the entrance to the campground.

From the junction of NC 268 and NC 321 near Lenoir, drive east on NC 268 for 20.5 miles. Turn left onto an unmarked road at the sign for WARRIOR CREEK CAMPGROUND, and follow it to the entrance to the campground.

GPS coordinates: N36 06.623' / W81 17.450'

Maps: *DeLorme: North Carolina Atlas & Gazetteer:* Page 14 F3

About the campground: Much like its neighbor Bandit's Roost, Warrior Creek is perfectly located, off the beaten path on the south side of the W. Kerr Scott Reservoir. Although many of the RV sites are right on top of one another, the loops are small and intimate, so you have fewer neighbors to crowd you in. The tent sites sit on a nice inviting little cove on the lake.

While it has a playground, fishing piers, a boat launch, and a swim beach, Warrior Creek is best known for its world-class mountain biking. That's right. There's an 11-mile mountain bike trail system that has been nationally recognized by IMBA (International Mountain Bicycling Association). Fast, flowing, and fun—if you enjoy riding, don't miss the opportunity to ride here.

Jefferson to Sparta

	Total Sites	Hookup Sites	Max. RV Length	Hookups	Toilets	Showers	Drinking Water	Dump Station	Recreation	Fee	Reservations
64 New River State Park: US 221 Access	33	20*	67'	E, W	F	Y	Y	Y	H, F, B*, L*, P	$$-$$$	Y
64 New River State Park: US 221 Access (Group)	1	0	n/a	N	F	Y	Y	N	H, F, B*, L*, P	$$$	Y
64 New River State Park: Wagoner Access	10	0	n/a	N	F	Y	Y	N	H, F, B*, L*, P	$$-$$$	Y
64 New River State Park: Wagoner Access (Group)	1	0	n/a	N	F	Y	Y	N	H, F, B*, L*, P	$$$	Y
64 New River State Park: Alleghany Access	8	0	n/a	N	V	N	Y	N	F, B, L*	$$	N
65 Doughton Park	127	0	None*	N	F	Y	Y	Y	H, P	$$	Y
66 Stone Mountain State Park	88	40	95'	E	F	Y	Y	Y	H, R, F, P, *	$$-$$$	Y
66 Stone Mountain State Park (Group)	4	0	n/a	N	F	Y	Y	N	H, R, F, P, *	$$$	Y
67 Alleghany Fairgrounds	128	121	50'	E, W	F	Y*	Y	N	P	$$	Y

* See campground entry for specific information.

64 New River State Park

US 221 Access

Location: Off US 221, about 9 miles northeast of Jefferson and about 15.5 miles southwest of Sparta
Season: Year-round; closed Christmas Day
Sites: 33; also 1 group campsite (reservations required) that can accommodate up to 35 people
Maximum length: 67 feet
Facilities: Flush toilets, hot showers, electric, water and water spigots dispersed, fire rings, picnic tables, lantern holders, dump station; pet friendly
Fee per night: $$-$$$
Management: North Carolina Department of Natural Resources
Contact: (336) 982-2587; www.ncparks.gov/Visit/parks/neri/main.php. For reservations call (877) 722-6762 or visit www.reserveamerica.com.
Finding the campground: From the junction of US 221 North and NC 16 North near Jefferson, drive north on US 221 for 7.2 miles to the US 221 access area of New River State Park on your

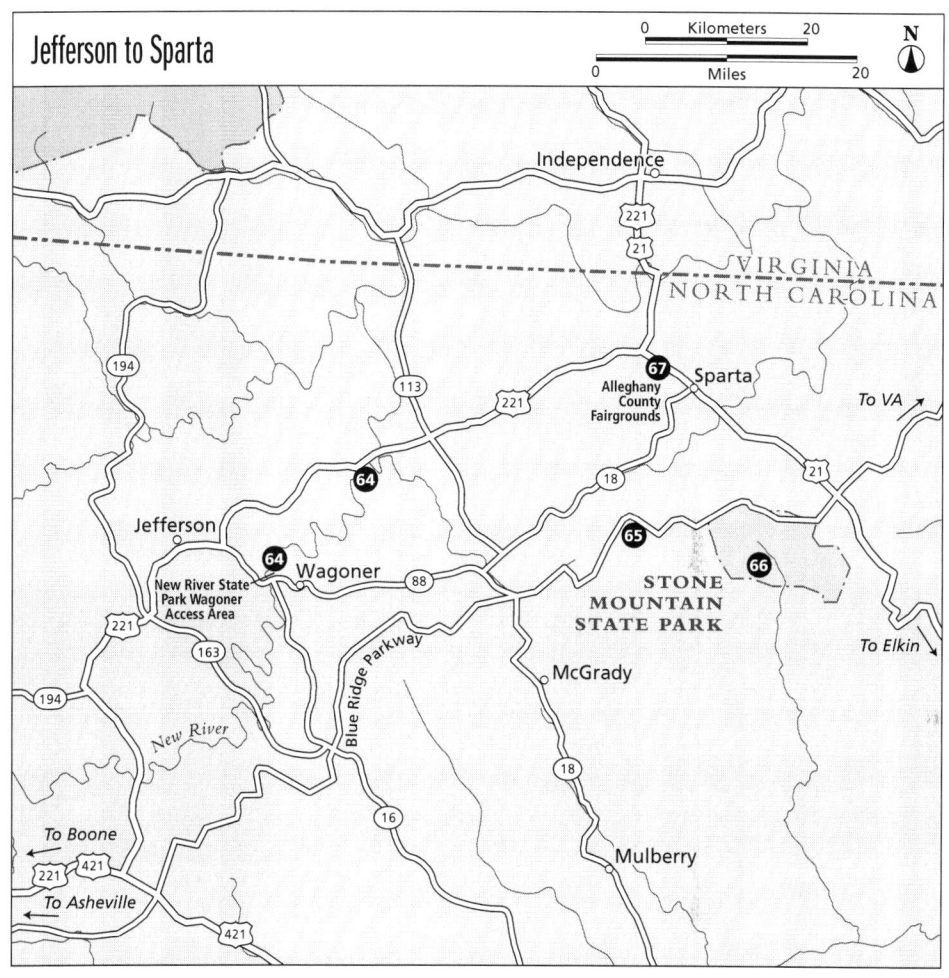

0   Kilometers   20

0   Miles   20

N

VIRGINIA
NORTH CAROLINA

Independence

Sparta

To VA

Alleghany
County
Fairgrounds

Jefferson

Wagoner

New River State
Park Wagoner
Access Area

STONE
MOUNTAIN
STATE PARK

To Elkin

Blue Ridge Parkway

McGrady

New River

To Boone

Mulberry

To Asheville

right. Drive up the hill 0.2 mile, and turn right to get to the drive up to the campground. To reach the hike-in campsites, head back to the main park road, and drive another 0.9 mile farther into the park to the primitive camping area.

From the junction of US 221 and NC 113, drive south on US 221 for 4.4 miles to the US 221 access area of New River State Park on your left. From the park entrance follow directions above.

GPS coordinates: N36 27.961' / W81 20.550'

Maps: DeLorme: North Carolina Atlas & Gazetteer: Page 14 B2

About the campground: The US 221 access area has two camping areas. One is for tent-camping only and can be accessed either by hiking less than 0.25 mile or by canoe. The park has kindly provided wheelbarrows to help you cart your stuff from the parking area. If you look at a map of the campground, it appears as though many of these sites are right next to the river. While they are next to the river, there's brush between the campsites and the river, so you can't really see the river from your tent.

The other camping area here is your traditional campground; you can drive right up to your site. These twenty sites all have electricity, and ten of them have a dedicated water hookup as well. Unfortunately, although these sites are well maintained, they are wide open, with no privacy whatsoever. If you're in an RV, this is less of an issue, but if you're in a tent, I recommend heading to the primitive camping here—or going down the road to the Wagoner access area.

Wagoner Access

Location: Off NC 88; about 5.5 miles east of Jefferson and about 21 miles southwest of Sparta
Season: Year-round; closed Christmas Day
Sites: 10; also 1 group campsite (reservations required) that can accommodate up to 35 people
Maximum length: n/a; tents only
Facilities: Flush toilets, hot showers, water spigots dispersed, fire rings, picnic tables, lantern holders; pet friendly
Fee per night: $$–$$$
Contact: (336) 982-2587; www.ncparks.gov/Visit/parks/neri/main.php. For reservations call (877) 722-6762 or visit www.reserveamerica.com.
Finding the campground: From the junction of NC 88 and NC 16, drive east on NC 88 for 1.4 miles. Turn left onto Wagoner Access Road (SR 1590) at the sign for New River State Park. From the entrance to the park, drive 0.3 mile down the hill and around the bend. When you get to the bottom of the hill, the campground is on your right.

From the junction of NC 88 and NC 18, drive west on NC 88 for 8.6 miles. Turn right onto Wagoner Access Road (SR 1590) at the sign for New River State Park, and follow directions above.
GPS coordinates: N36 24.943' / W81 23.196'
Maps: DeLorme: North Carolina Atlas & Gazetteer: Page 14 C2
About the campground: Christmas tree farms abound along the route to the Wagoner access area, and when you arrive you're in for a pleasant surprise. A 250-foot walk with your gear leads you past a small butterfly garden and to this wonderful primitive campground. The large sites are spaced out just right, giving you plenty of privacy, and a few of them sit right alongside the river. There are a few short hiking trails, but I also recommend bringing a canoe to really explore the park's namesake.

Alleghany County Access

Location: Along the New River, just south of the Virginia state line; about 18 miles northeast of Jefferson
Season: Year-round; closed Christmas Day
Sites: 8; also 1 canoe-to group campsite that can accommodate up to 35 people
Maximum length: n/a; tents only
Facilities: Vault toilets, drinking water; pet friendly
Fee per night: $$
Contact: (336) 982-2587; www.ncparks.gov/Visit/parks/neri/main.php.
Finding the campground: Accessible by canoe only
Maps: DeLorme: North Carolina Atlas & Gazetteer: Page 14 A2
About the campground: The Alleghany County access campground is canoe-to camping only. There are many launch sites along the New River, depending on how far you want to paddle. For maps of the river and additional information, contact the state park directly at the number above.

65 Blue Ridge Parkway: Doughton Park Campground

Location: On the Blue Ridge Parkway at Milepost 240, between NC 18 and US 21; about 33 miles north of Wilkesboro and 17 miles south of Sparta
Season: Mid-May–Oct
Sites: 127
Maximum length: 90 feet
Facilities: Flush toilets, fire rings, picnic tables, lantern holders, trash cans, dump station, firewood for sale, *no* showers; pet friendly
Fee per night: $$
Management: National Park Service—Blue Ridge Parkway
Contact: (828) 298-0398; www.nps.gov/blri/planyourvisit/camping-on-the-blue-ridge-parkway.htm. For reservations call (877) 444-6777 or visit www.recreation.gov.
Finding the campground: The campground is located on the Blue Ridge Parkway at Milepost 240, between NC 18 and US 21.

Dogwood trees are one of the many blooming trees that can be found along the Blue Ridge Parkway.

GPS coordinates: RV campground: N36 25.674' / W81 09.361'; tent campground: N36 25.730' / W81 09.261'

Maps: *DeLorme: North Carolina Atlas & Gazetteer:* Page 14 C4

About the campground: Doughton Park has several loops, depending on what you're camping in. The RV loop is small and quite peaceful. There's a loop for pop-ups and tents where each campsite has its own well-manicured grassy area to pitch your tent or park your pop-up. While this loop is wooded, there's not a lot of privacy. If you're in a tent and want more privacy, there is a tent-only area that requires a short 100-foot walk to you campsite.

The campground is great for families, with a large community campfire, an amphitheater, and large open grassy fields that are great for tossing a Frisbee or kicking a ball around. As always, the Blue Ridge Parkway is a perfect place to take a scenic drive, and this area of the Parkway is well known for its wildlife viewing.

66 Stone Mountain State Park

Location: 3042 Frank Pkwy., Roaring Gap; about 6 miles southwest of Roaring Gap

Season: Year-round; closed Christmas Day

Sites: 88; also 4 group campsites (reservations required) that can accommodate up to 25 people each

Maximum length: 95 feet

Facilities: Flush toilets, hot showers, water spigots dispersed, electric, fire rings, picnic tables, dump stations, firewood for sale; pet friendly

Fee per night: $$–$$$

Management: North Carolina Department of Natural Resources

Contact: (336) 957-8185; www.ncparks.gov/Visit/parks/stmo/main.php. For reservations call (877) 722-6762 or visit www.reserveamerica.com.

Finding the campground: Take exit 83 (US 21) off I-77, and follow US 21 north for approximately 10.7 miles. Turn left onto Traphill Road at the sign for Stone Mountain State Park, and travel for 4.3 miles. Turn right onto John P. Frank Parkway, and continue 2.3 miles to the gated entrance to South Mountains State Park.

From the junction of US 21 and the Blue Ridge Parkway, travel south on US 21 for 4.4 miles. Turn right onto Oklahoma Road (SR 1100), and travel 3 miles to where it ends at John P. Frank Parkway. Turn right onto John P. Frank Parkway; the gated entrance to Stone Mountain State Park is directly in front of you.

GPS coordinates: N36 22.780' / W81 01.546'

Maps: *DeLorme: North Carolina Atlas & Gazetteer:* Page 14 C4–15 C5

About the campground: A visit to Stone Mountain State Park will leave you in awe. There are wonderful waterfalls, meadows filled with wildflowers, wooded hiking and bridle trails, and of course the shining star itself: Stone Mountain. This 600-foot-tall granite dome has a 4-mile circumference and is said to be over 360 million years old. Rock climbers and rappellers alike travel from afar to climb or descend the face of this National Natural Landmark.

As for the camping, well, it's not the reason you would visit this park. Although the sites are well groomed, they are not very wooded or private. But just keep in mind all the wonderful other things this state park has to offer, and you won't be disappointed. There are six primitive

A doe and her fawn graze at Stone Mountain State Park.

backcountry campsites also available. Getting to these sites requires hiking anywhere from 1.5 to 3 miles, but they offer the privacy that the campground does not. Advance reservations are required for the group campsites.

67 Alleghany County Fairgrounds

Location: Off US 21, about 1.5 miles north of Sparta and 4 miles south of the Virginia state line
Season: Year-round
Sites: 28; also a field that can accommodate up to 100 campers using shared electric and water stations (reservations required)
Maximum length: 50 feet
Facilities: Flush toilets, hot showers, electric, water, dump station, *no* fires; pet friendly
Fee per night: $$
Management: Alleghany County Department of Recreation
Contact: (336) 372-2942

Finding the campground: From the junction of US 21 and NC 18 in Sparta, drive north on US 21 for 1.5 miles to the entrance to the Alleghany County Fairgrounds on your left.

From the junction of US 21 and US 221 North in Twin Oaks, drive south on US 21 for 1.3 miles to the entrance to the Alleghany County Fairgrounds on your right.

GPS coordinates: N36 30.979' / W81 08.652'

Maps: *DeLorme: North Carolina Atlas & Gazetteer:* Page 14 B4

About the campground: Alleghany Fairgrounds is not a traditional campground. Although camping is open to the public, the facility was designed for larger events, such as the Alleghany County Fiddler's Convention. There are twenty-one campsites lined up in a row, each with its own dedicated electric and water hookups. There's a wooded hilltop that can accommodate up to seven tent campsites, but the sites are not marked out. There are no picnic tables or fire rings.

The other one hundred "campsites" are located in a large open field and are also not marked out. As you approach the field, you will see that the county has provided six power/water stations. Each of these stations has multiple hookups and can supply water and electric to several RVs.

While the price is right, the camping is not very private, and the sites are fairly close to US 21, so you may hear traffic passing by at night. Keep this in mind before you plan your visit, or perhaps save this one until there's a convention in town. There are no campfires allowed. The shower facilities are kept locked, so if you will need the on-site showers, be sure to let the park staff know when you make your reservations. Reservations are required and can be made using the contact number provided above.

Gastonia to Charlotte

	Total Sites	Hookup Sites	Max. RV Length	Hookups	Toilets	Showers	Drinking Water	Dump Station	Recreation	Fee	Reservations
68 McDowell Nature Preserve	62	13	38'	W, E	F	Y	Y	Y	H, S, F, P	$$–$$$	Y
69 Copperhead Island (Group)	6	0	n/a	n/a	F	N	Y	N	S, F, B, L, P	$$$	Y

68 McDowell Nature Preserve Campground

Location: 15222 York Rd., Charlotte; about 6 miles southwest of Charlotte
Season: Year-round
Sites: 56; also 2 small group campsites that can accommodate up to 20 people each and 4 large group sites that can accommodate more than 20 people
Maximum length: 38 feet
Facilities: Flush toilets, hot showers, water spigots dispersed, electric, fire rings, charcoal grills, picnic tables, trash cans, ice and firewood for sale; pet friendly
Fee per night: $$–$$$
Management: Mecklenburg County Parks and Recreation
Contact: (704) 583-1284; www.parkandrec.com. Call for reservations between 9 a.m. and 5 p.m., 7 days a week.
Finding the campground: From the junction of NC 49 and the North Carolina–South Carolina state line, drive east on NC 49 for 1 mile to the signed entrance to McDowell Nature Preserve on your left. After entering the nature preserve, continue 0.1 mile to the campground on your left.

From the junction of NC 49 and NC 160 (Steel Creek Road), drive west on NC 49 for 2.1 miles to McDowell Nature Preserve on your right. Enter the nature preserve, and follow directions above.
GPS coordinates: N35 05.795' / W81 01.425'
Maps: *DeLorme: North Carolina Atlas & Gazetteer:* Page 57 F5
About the campground: Sitting right on the banks of Lake Wylie, the McDowell Nature Preserve is a great place to get back to nature, without ever leaving the city. Although the campground is not directly on Lake Wylie, the nature preserve is. So you have all the amenities of lakeside camping. There are several fishing piers and picnic areas for enjoying the lake, as well as miles of hiking trails for exploring the interior of the preserve. You can take the kids to the nature center or join in on one of the many interactive programs offered here.

The campsites are wooded but seem a bit crowded and on top of one another. There's a separate area for tent campers, which is a bit more secluded.

For a different kind of camping experience, try the "rent-a-tent" feature. These ten sites include a 9 X 12-foot tent and two cots. The tents are already set up and waiting for you, making this an easy option for a quick weekend getaway.

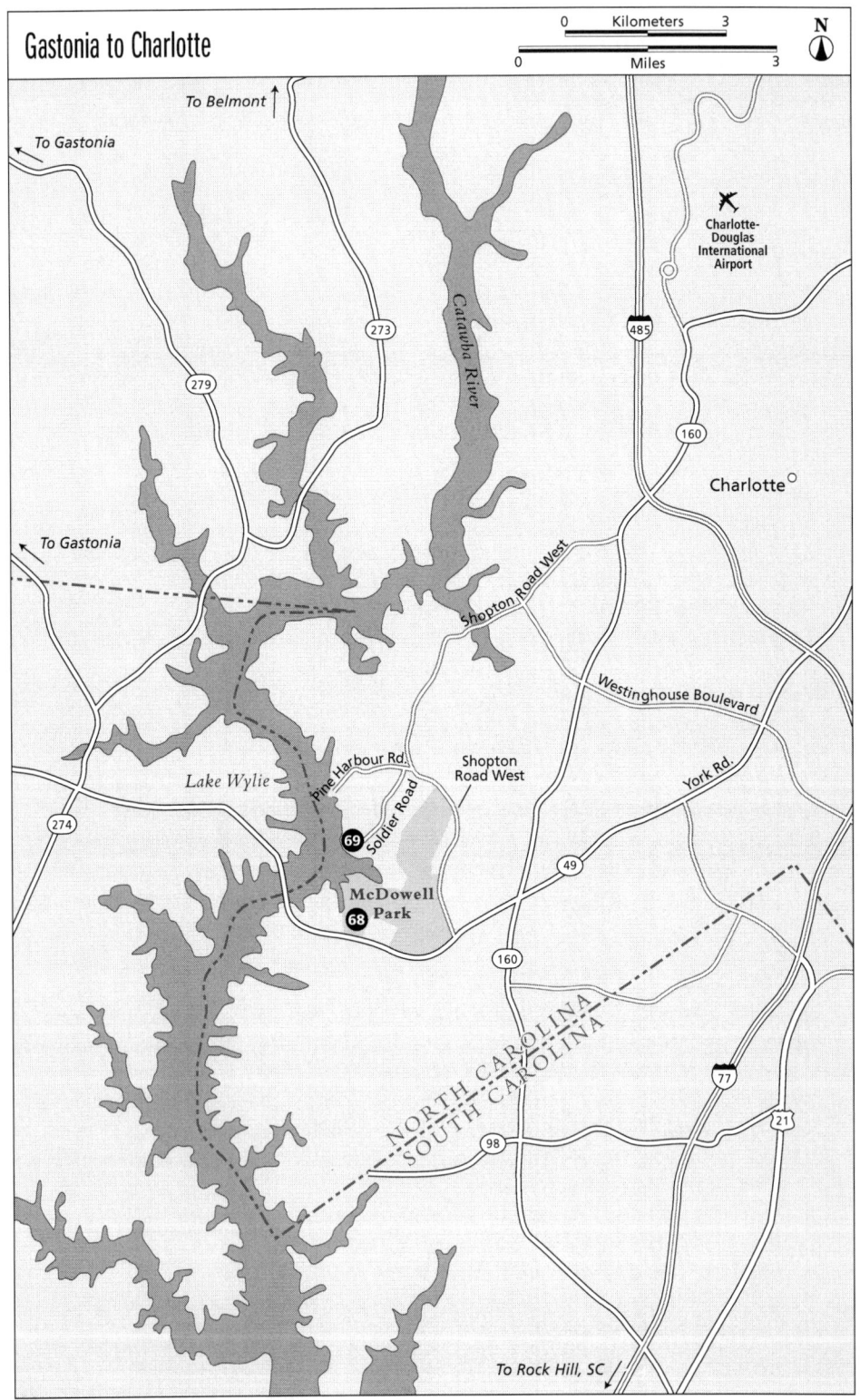

Gastonia to Charlotte

To Belmont
To Gastonia
Catawba River
273
279
Charlotte-Douglas International Airport
485
160
Charlotte
To Gastonia
Shopton Road West
Westinghouse Boulevard
Pine Harbour Rd.
Shopton Road West
York Rd.
Lake Wylie
Soldier Road
274
69
McDowell Park
68
49
160
NORTH CAROLINA
SOUTH CAROLINA
77
21
98
To Rock Hill, SC

0   Kilometers   3
0   Miles   3
N

69 Copperhead Island Group Camp

Location: 15200 Soldier Rd., Charlotte; about 6 miles southwest of Charlotte
Season: Year-round
Sites: 6 sites (reservations required, and you must rent the entire island)
Maximum length: n/a; tents only
Facilities: Flush toilets, water spigots dispersed, fire rings, picnic tables; pet friendly
Fee per night: $$$
Management: Mecklenburg County Parks and Recreation
Contact: (704) 583-1284; www.parkandrec.com. Call for reservations between 9a.m. and 5 p.m., 7 days a week.
Finding the campground: From the junction of NC 49 and the North Carolina–South Carolina state line, drive east on NC 49 for 2.1 miles. Turn left onto Shopton Road West, and travel 2.2 miles. Turn left onto Pine Harbor Road, and drive less than 0.1 mile to Soldier Road. Turn left onto Soldier Road, and continue for 1 mile to the entrance to Copperhead Island on your left. As soon as you enter the park, immediately turn right, which leads to the group camping area.

From the junction of NC 49 and NC 160 (Steel Creek Road), drive west on NC 49 for 1 mile. Turn right onto Shopton Road West, and follow directions above.
GPS coordinates: N35 06.560' / W81 01.501'
Maps: *DeLorme: North Carolina Atlas & Gazetteer:* Page 57 F5
About the campground: *NOTE:* Unlike most other group camps listed in this guide, you do not have to be part of a nonprofit organization to camp here.

Copperhead Island is a great place for a large group of friends to just get away and get outside and play! If you're the one planning the trip, rather than dealing with the logistics of getting several campsites together, you can simply rent the entire island. And you must do exactly that if you camp here. Talk about privacy!

The fee includes a picnic shelter that can accommodate up to eighty people, six lakefront campsites, a volleyball court, horseshoe pits, and four boat ramps. So bring your boat, canoe, or kayak; grab your fishing pole (and applicable licenses); and enjoy this camping experience by land and water. No matter what the occasion—family reunion, holiday bash, special birthday, or you just want to get away—you are certain to enjoy camping at Copperhead!

Statesville

	Total Sites	Hookup Sites	Max. RV Length	Hookups	Toilets	Showers	Drinking Water	Dump Station	Recreation	Fee	Reservations
70 Lake Norman State Park	33	0	71'	N	F	Y	Y	Y	H, M, S, F, B, L, P	$$	Y
70 Lake Norman State Park (Group)	5	0	n/a	N	F	N	Y	N	H, M, S, F, B, L, P	$$-$$$	Y

70 Lake Norman State Park

Location: 159 Inland Sea Lane, Troutman; about 10 miles south of Statesville and about 6 miles
north of Mooresville
Season: Mar 15–Nov 30; group camping open Apr–Nov
Sites: 33; also has 5 group camping areas (reservations required) that can accommodate up to
25 people each
Maximum length: 71 feet
Facilities: Flush toilets, hot showers, water spigots dispersed, fire rings, picnic tables, lantern hold-
ers, dump station, firewood for sale; pet friendly

Lake Norman is surrounded by horse country.

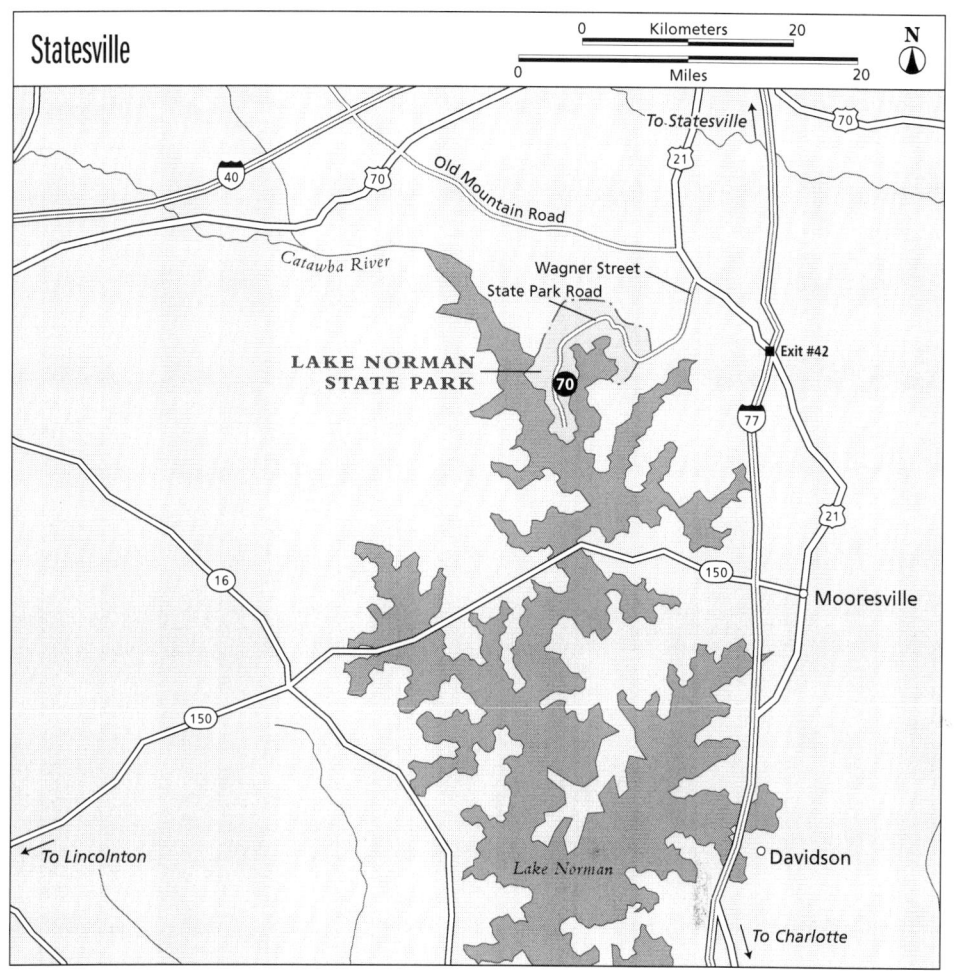

Fee per night: $$

Management: North Carolina Department of Natural Resources

Contact: (704) 528-6350; www.ncparks.gov/Visit/parks/lano/main.php. For reservations call (877) 722-6762 or visit www.reserveamerica.com.

Finding the campground: From Mooresville travel north on I-77 to exit 42 (US 21/NC 115). Drive north on US 21 for 2.8 miles, and turn left onto Wagner Street at the sign for LAKE NORMAN STATE PARK. Follow Wagner Street for 1.5 miles, and turn right onto State Park Road (SR 1321) at another sign for LAKE NORMAN STATE PARK. Continue on State Park Road for 2.1 miles to where the road dead-ends at the park entrance.

From Statesville travel south on I-77 to exit 42 (US 21/NC 115). Drive north on US 21, and follow directions above.

GPS coordinates: N35 38.779' / W80 56.585'

Maps: *DeLorme: North Carolina Atlas & Gazetteer:* Page 35 F6

About the campground: The campground at Lake Norman State Park is a popular weekend getaway spot for many locals. It sits at the northern end of Lake Norman and is conveniently located less than an hour from both Charlotte and Statesville. The park has a great mountain bike trail system and miles of hiking trails that skirt the edge of the lake. The campsites are very wooded and very private—so much so that you can barely see the lake even though it's just a stone's throw away.

Since the park is practically surrounded by water, it has a swim beach, fishing piers, a boat ramp, and boat rentals to help you make the most of your visit. The group camping area is hike-in only, and reservations are required.

Salisbury to Lexington

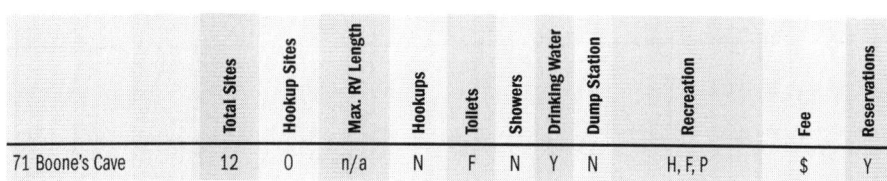

	Total Sites	Hookup Sites	Max. RV Length	Hookups	Toilets	Showers	Drinking Water	Dump Station	Recreation	Fee	Reservations
71 Boone's Cave	12	0	n/a	N	F	N	Y	N	H, F, P	$	Y

71 Boone's Cave Park Campground

Location: 3552 Boone's Cave Rd., Lexington; about 10 miles west of Lexington and 9 miles north of Salisbury

Season: Year-round, Friday and Saturday nights only

Sites: 8; also 4 primitive campsites that require a 0.25-mile hike to reach (advance reservations required)

Maximum length: n/a; tents only

Facilities: Flush toilets, tent pads, community fire rings; pet friendly

Fee per night: $

Management: Davidson County Parks and Recreation

Contact: (336) 752-2322

Finding the campground: From the junction of NC 150 and US 64 near Reeds Crossroads, drive south on NC 150 for 7.3 miles. Turn right onto Boone's Cave Road at the sign for Boone's Cave Park, and travel 3.4 miles to the park on the left. Enter the park, and continue 0.4 mile to the parking area.

Take exit 83 (NC 150) off I-85, and travel north on NC 150 for 5 miles. Turn left onto Boone's Cave Road, and follow directions above.

GPS coordinates: N35 47.771' / W80 27.765'

Maps: *DeLorme: North Carolina Atlas & Gazetteer:* Page 36 D2

About the campground: For a small county park, Boone's Cave has quite a bit to offer any nature enthusiast. The park, and the cave for which it was named, rest alongside the banks of the Yadkin River. Fishing is permitted, but you must obtain a North Carolina state fishing license before you break out the bait. Five miles of hiking trails run through the park, and the Cottonwood Trail leads to the largest cottonwood tree on record within the state of North Carolina. With a 16-foot diameter, it's quite a sight to see. You may also want to bring your binoculars along—the park is home to tons of migratory birds and more than eighty species of butterflies.

The campground is primitive, with a few community fire rings and a separate area with several picnic tables. Both groups and individuals are welcome to camp here. You can access the campsites by car, but once you set up, there is a designated parking area just outside the campground loop for your vehicle. Reservations are required and must be made at least two weeks in advance.

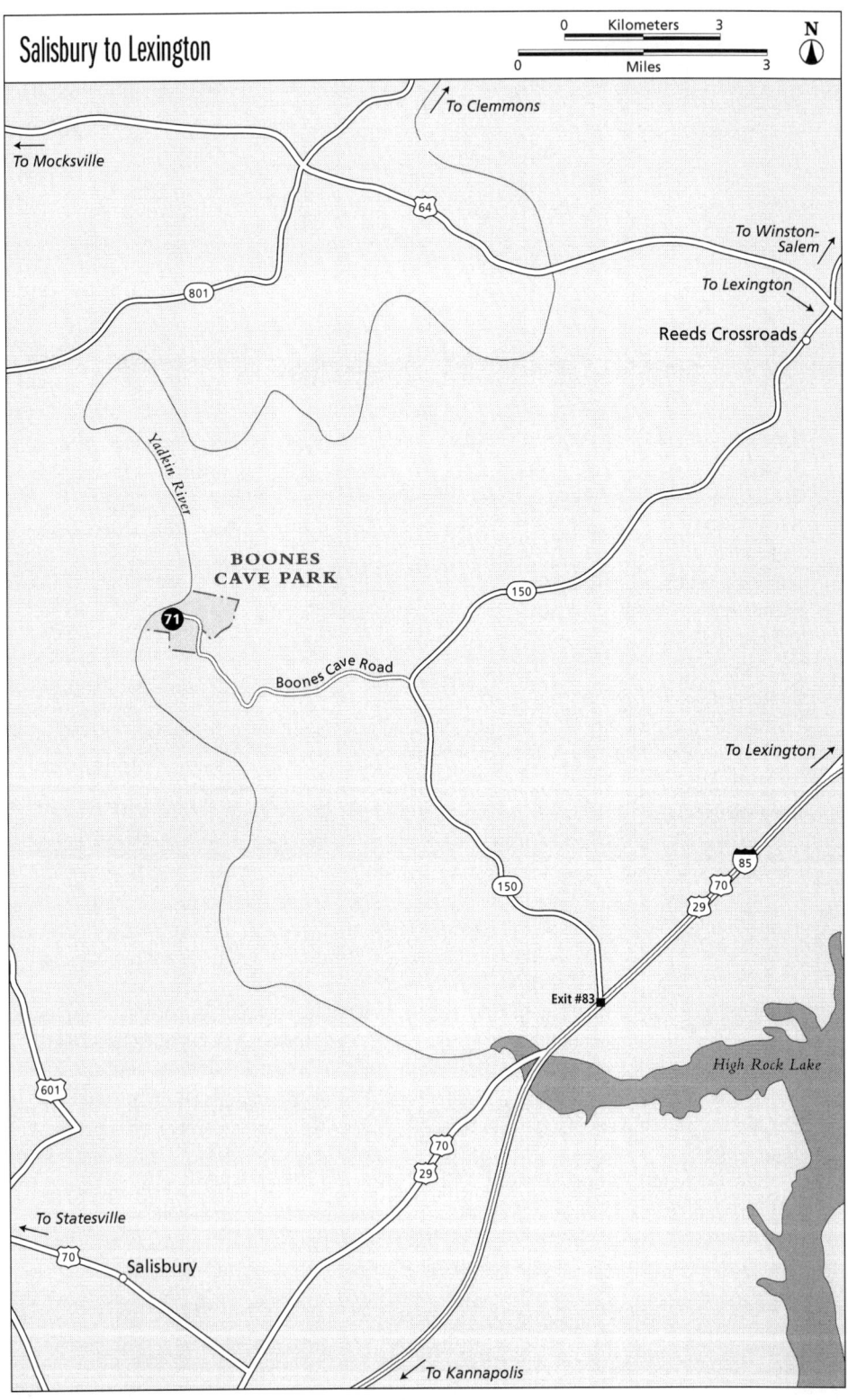

0 Kilometers 3

0 Miles 3

N

To Clemmons

To Mocksville

64

801

To Winston-Salem

To Lexington

Reeds Crossroads

Yadkin River

BOONES CAVE PARK

71

150

Boones Cave Road

To Lexington

150

85

70

29

Exit #83

High Rock Lake

601

70

29

To Statesville

70

Salisbury

To Kannapolis

Winston-Salem

	Total Sites	Hookup Sites	Max. RV Length	Hookups	Toilets	Showers	Drinking Water	Dump Station	Recreation	Fee	Reservations
72 Tanglewood Park	44	44	None	W, E	F	Y	Y	Y	H, M, R, S, F, B, P, *	$$$	Y
73 Pilot Mountain State Park	49	0	35'	N	F	Y	Y	N	H, C, R, P, *	$$	Y
73 Pilot Mountain State Park: Yadkin River (Group)	2	0	n/a	N	V	N	N	N	H, R, B*, P	$$	Y
73 Pilot Mountain State Park (Canoe)	2	0	n/a	N	N	N	N	N	B*, L*	$$	Y
74 Hanging Rock State Park	73	0	60'	N	F	Y	Y	N	H, S, R, F, B*, L*, P, *	$$-$$$	Y
74 Hanging Rock State Park (Group)	5	0	n/a	N	V	N	Y	N	H, S, R, F, B*, L*, P, *	$$-$$$	Y

* See campground entry for specific information.

72 Tanglewood Park Campground

Location: 4201 Manor House Circle, Clemmons
Season: Year-round
Sites: 44; no tents allowed
Maximum length: None
Facilities: Flush toilets, hot showers, water, electric, dump station, picnic tables, wireless Internet connection, *no* campfires allowed; pet friendly
Fee per night: $$$
Management: Forsyth County Parks and Recreation
Contact: (336) 778-6300; www.forsyth.cc/Parks/Default.aspx?StoryID=17574
Finding the campground: From I-40 in Clemmons, take exit 182 (Harper Road) and travel south for 0.1 mile to US 158 (Clemmons Road). Turn right onto US 158, and travel west 0.3 mile. Turn left into Tanglewood Park, and go 0.1 mile. Turn left, and continue to follow the park road around for less than 1 mile, past the open fields to the campground.

From the junction of NC 801 and US 158 (Clemmons Road), drive east on US 158 for 1.7 miles. Turn right into Tanglewood Park at the large stone sign. After entering the park, follow directions above.
GPS coordinates: N36 00.844' / W80 24.344'
Maps: *DeLorme: North Carolina Atlas & Gazetteer:* Page 36 A3–B3

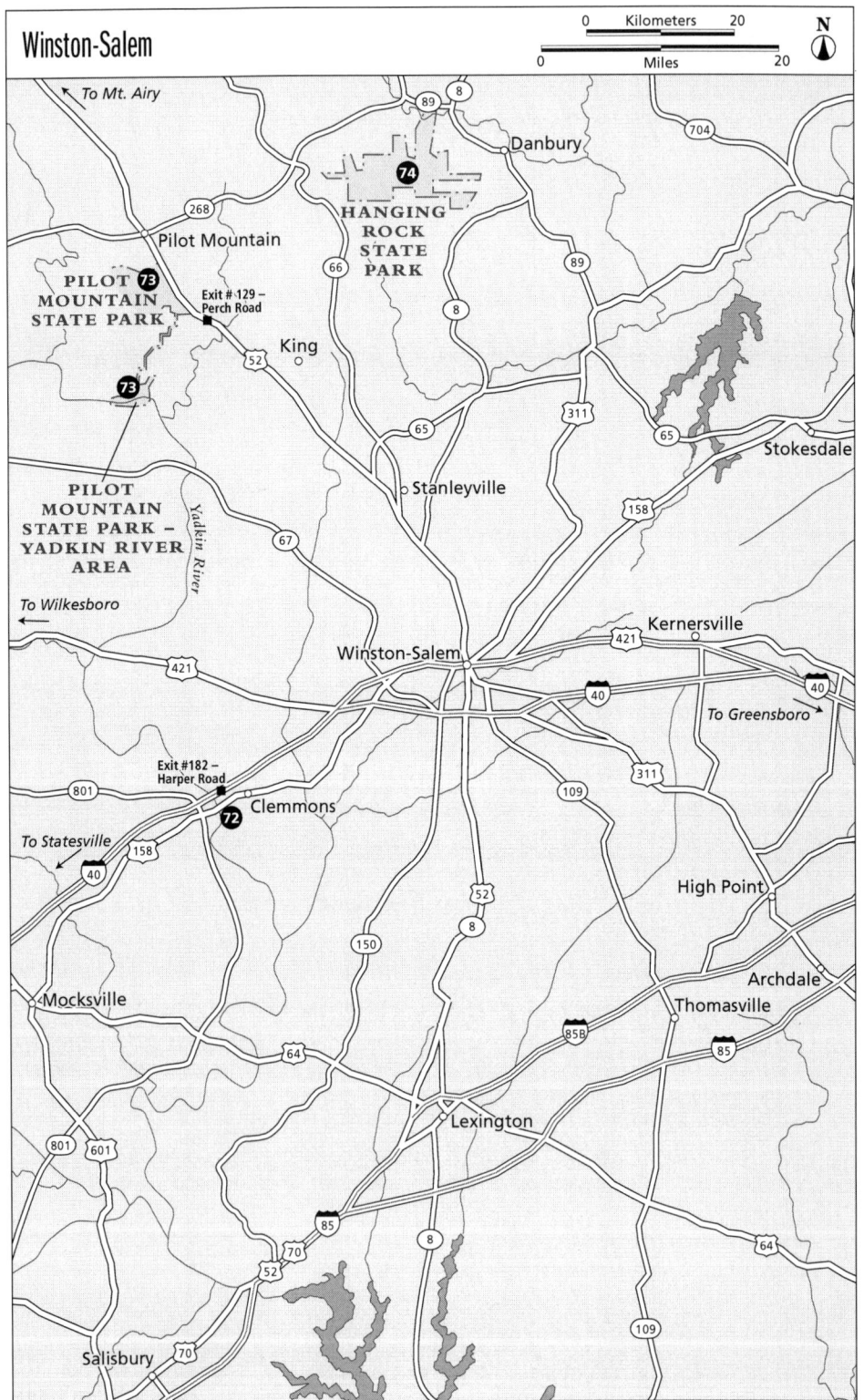

Winston-Salem

0 Kilometers 20
0 Miles 20

N

To Mt. Airy

704
8
89
Danbury

74

HANGING ROCK STATE PARK

268
Pilot Mountain

PILOT 73 MOUNTAIN STATE PARK

Exit # 129 – Perch Road

66
89
8

52
King

311
65

65
Stokesdale

73

PILOT MOUNTAIN STATE PARK – YADKIN RIVER AREA

Yadkin River

67
Stanleyville
158

To Wilkesboro

421
Winston-Salem
421
Kernersville
40
40
To Greensboro

801
Exit #182 – Harper Road
311
109

72 Clemmons

To Statesville
158
40
52
8
High Point

150

64
Mocksville
85B
Thomasville
85
Archdale

801 601
Lexington

85
52 70 8
64

109

Salisbury 70

About the campground: There are no tents allowed here—period. So if you're not in an RV or a pop-up, read no further. Instead head down the road to either Lake Norman State Park or Dan Nicholas Park to pitch your tent.

Tanglewood Park is quite lovely. With mountain bike trails, walking paths, gardens, tennis courts, an aquatic center, and a golf course, you are sure to be entertained. No matter what your pleasure, Tanglewood Park has it. There's even a horse stable where they offer riding lessons. Or you can take a guided trail ride along the Yadkin River.

Now that you've heard how wonderful the park is, here's the bad news: The campground is more like a giant parking lot, literally. The campsites are lined up, row upon row, with absolutely no privacy. No open fires are allowed either, so leave the marshmallows at home. There's a give and take here. In exchange for all the wonderful activities you get, you sacrifice sitting by a campfire in a peaceful wooded setting. If you know these things going in, you won't be disappointed.

Sunflowers can grow up to 9 feet tall.

73 Pilot Mountain State Park

Location: 1792 Pilot Knob Park Rd., Pinnacle; about 16 miles north of Winston-Salem and 14 miles south of Mt. Airy
Season: Mar 15–Nov 30
Sites: 49; canoe camping also available
Maximum length: 35 feet
Facilities: Flush toilets, hot showers, water spigots dispersed, fire rings, picnic tables, trash cans; pet friendly
Fee per night: $$
Management: North Carolina Department of Natural Resources
Contact: (336) 325-2355; www.ncparks.gov/Visit/parks/pimo/main.php. For reservations call (877) 722-6762 or visit www.reserveamerica.com.
Finding the campground: From US 52 in Winston-Salem, drive north on US 52 to the Pilot Mountain State Park exit. There is no exit number, but there is a PILOT MOUNTAIN STATE PARK sign. Turn left after exiting the highway, and travel west for 0.3 mile to the entrance of the park. Follow the park road as it climbs for 0.5 mile to a right turn toward the family camping area. Continue 0.4 mile to the campground.
GPS coordinates: N36 20.847' / W80 28.273'
Maps: *DeLorme: North Carolina Atlas & Gazetteer:* Page 16 D2

About the campground: Pilot Mountain State Park is quite diverse. The park is split into two separate sections—the mountains and the river—each with its own unique qualities. The mountain section, which houses the family campground, is home to Pilot Mountain itself. This 1,400-foot pinnacle stands high above the surrounding countryside. Rock climbers have a heyday in this section of the park along several routes, but a permit must be obtained prior to climbing.

This portion of the park is also popular with cyclists. The road leading to the top of Pilot Mountain climbs at grades from 10 to 16 percent. That's quite a challenge on two wheels—both uphill and screaming downhill. There are hiking and bridle trails as well.

The campsites are very wooded and well spaced, giving you privacy at almost every site in the campground. Canoe camping is also available along the Yadkin River; contact the park for more information.

Pilot Mountain: Yadkin River Group Camp

Location: About 20 miles northwest of Winston-Salem and about 21 miles southeast of Mt. Airy
Season: Year-round
Sites: 2, each accommodating up to 25 people (advance reservations required)
Maximum length: n/a; tents only
Facilities: Vault toilets, fire rings, charcoal grills, picnic tables, trash cans; pet friendly
Fee per night: $
Finding the campground: Take exit 129 (Pinnacle) off US 52, and travel west on Perch Road for 3.3 miles to a fork. Bear right at the fork onto Hauser Road (SR 2072) at the sign for YADKIN ISLAND PARK. Continue on Hauser Road as you enter Surry County. At 2.1 miles Hauser Road bends left and Caudle Road (SR 2070) goes straight ahead. Go left here, following Hauser Road for another 0.8 mile. Turn left into the park at the sign for the YADKIN RIVER SECTION OF PILOT MOUNTAIN STATE PARK. Follow the park road for 0.4 mile as it fords three small creeks. The group camping area is on the right, immediately after the picnic area.
GPS coordinates: N36 15.857' / W80 29.262'
Maps: *DeLorme: North Carolina Atlas & Gazetteer:* Page 16 E2
About the campground: The group camp can be found in the Yadkin River section of Pilot Mountain State Park. To access the camping here, you must ford a few creeks with your car, so you may want to be driving a high-clearance vehicle if there's been a lot of rain prior to your visit.

This section of the park is not huge, but there is a picnic area, and you can access the river. Several hiking and bridle trails also can be accessed here, including the Yadkin River Trail, a 130-mile hiking trail that closely follows the Yadkin and Pee Dee Rivers. Advance reservations are required.

74 Hanging Rock State Park

Location: 1790 Hanging Rock Park Rd., Danbury; 2 miles west of the town of Danbury
Season: Year-round; closed Christmas Day; bathhouse closed Dec 1-Mar 15 (vault toilet available during off-season)
Sites: 73; also 5 group campsites (reservations required) that can accommodate up to 16 people each; 10 cabins available for rent (no pets allowed in cabins)
Maximum length: 60 feet

Lower Cascades at Hanging Rock State Park is a favorite with the locals.

Facilities: Flush toilets (vault toilet during winter months), hot showers (closed during winter months), water, electric, fire rings, picnic tables, trash cans, firewood for sale; pet friendly
Fee per night: $$–$$$
Management: North Carolina Department of Natural Resources
Contact: (336) 593-8480; www.ncparks.gov/Visit/parks/haro/main.php. For reservations call (877) 722-6762 or visit www.reserveamerica.com.
Finding the campground: From the northernmost junction of NC 8 and NC 89 near Danbury, drive south on NC 8 for 1.4 miles. Turn right onto Hanging Rock Park Road, and travel 3.2 miles. Turn left and continue toward the visitor center.

From the southernmost junction of NC 8 and NC 89 near Danbury, drive north on NC 8 for 5.1 miles. Turn left onto Hanging Rock Park Road, and follow directions above.
GPS coordinates: N36 23.700' / W80 15.981'
Maps: *DeLorme: North Carolina Atlas & Gazetteer:* Page 16 C4
About the campground: Waterfalls, a lake, rock cliffs, amazing views, and several unique natural features all greet you at Hanging Rock State Park. With so much to explore, this is a hiker's dream, but the activities are certainly not limited to that. Climbers frequent the park for a number of cliff walls that can be found here. There's a small lake with a swim area and a fishing pier, and you can rent a canoe or rowboat on the weekends. No private boats are allowed on the lake, but there is a canoe/kayak or tube launch at the north end of the park, where you can access the Dan River with your own craft.

The campground is nicely wooded, but the sites are kind of close together. You can camp here year-round, but be forewarned: Showers and flush toilets are not available in winter. Reservations are required for the group camping and cabin rentals.

The Piedmont

As the mountains fade, the foothills of the Piedmont begin. Here you'll find rolling hills and vast farmland sprawling out across the center of the state. Explore the forested pine-lands of the Uwharrie National Forest, or camp along the shores of Badin, Falls, Jordan, or Kerr Lake. With ospreys circling overhead, bald eagles roosting, and stunning sunsets, this is as good as it gets in lakeside camping! Ample opportunities for swimming, fishing, and boating abound. The region also offers miles of hiking, mountain bike, bridle, and off-road-vehicle trails. From Charlotte to Raleigh, Greensboro to Fayetteville, camping in the Piedmont can be easily accessed from every corner of the region.

Lakeside camping is a highlight of the Piedmont.

Piedmont Overview

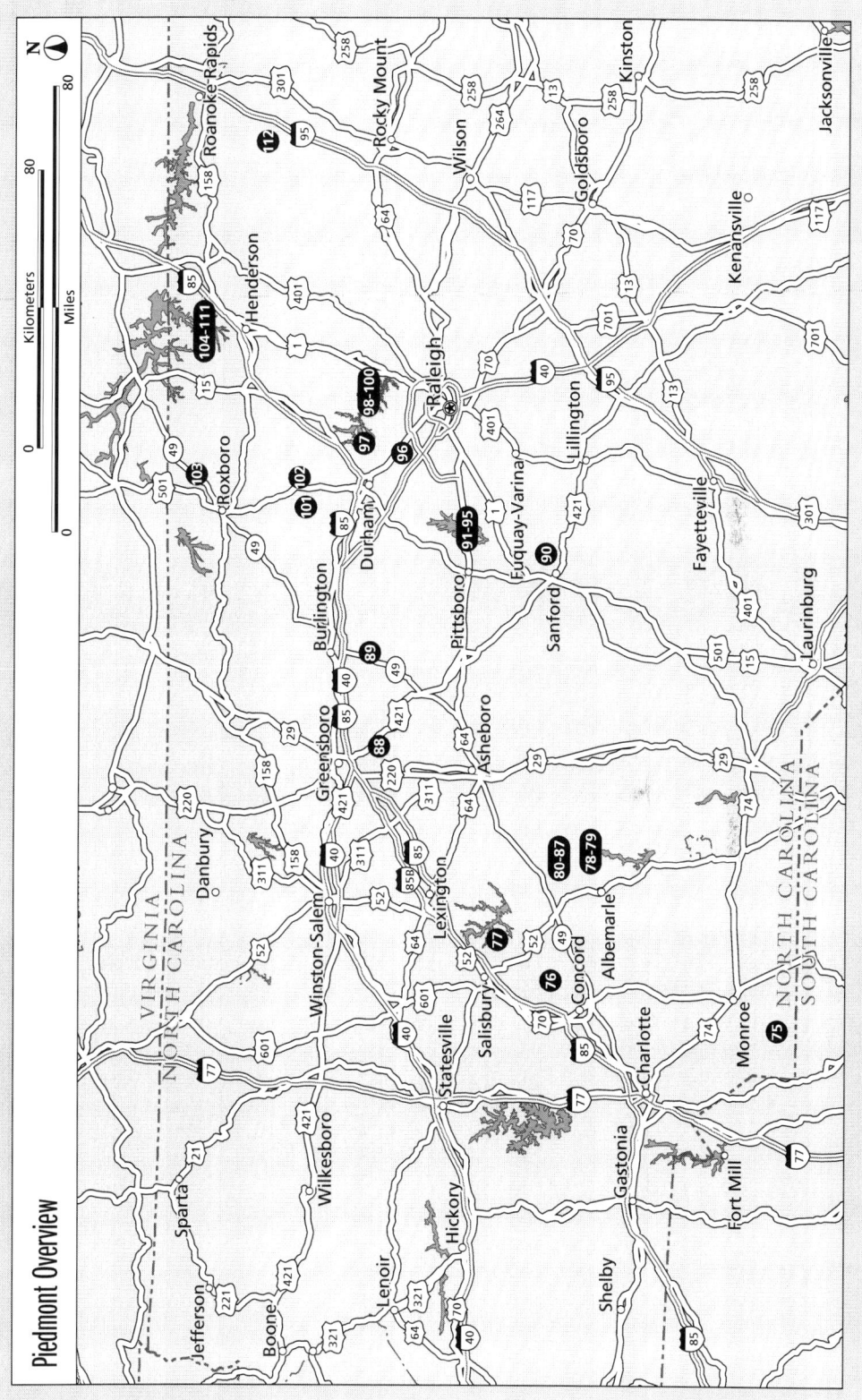

Monroe

	Total Sites	Hookup Sites	Max. RV Length	Hookups	Toilets	Showers	Drinking Water	Dump Station	Recreation	Fee	Reservations
75 Cane Creek Park	118	108	50'	W, E, S*	F	Y	Y	Y	S, F, B, L, P	$$–$$$	Y

* See campground entry for specific information.

75 Cane Creek Park Campground

Location: 5213 Harkey Rd., Waxhaw; about 12.5 miles northeast of Lancaster and about 17.5 miles southwest of Monroe
Season: Year-round
Sites: 118; also group camping areas available that can accommodate up to 20 or 30 people; 6 rustic cabins also available for rent
Maximum length: 50 feet
Facilities: Flush toilets, hot showers, water spigots dispersed, fire rings, picnic tables, lantern holders, dump station, camp store; pet friendly
Fee per night: $$–$$$
Management: Union County Parks and Recreation
Contact: (704) 843-3919; www.unioncountync.us/Departments/ParksRecreation.aspx
Finding the campground: From the junction of NC 200 and NC 522 near Monroe, drive south on NC 200 for 5.4 miles. Turn left onto Providence Road South, and continue 2.8 miles. Turn left onto Cane Creek Road (SR 1212), and travel 1.5 miles to where the road ends at the entrance to the campground.

From the junction of NC 200 and US 521 Bypass in Lancaster, drive north on NC 200 for approximately 10.1 miles. Turn right onto Providence Road South, and follow directions above.
GPS coordinates: N34 50.050' / W80 40.719'
Maps: *DeLorme: North Carolina Atlas & Gazetteer:* Page 70 C4
About the campground: The campground at Cane Creek Park is much like your typical RV park. The sites are all lined up in a row, one after the other, without much in the category of privacy. A separate "wilderness" camping area is set aside for tent campers only. These sites are walk-in sites, and a short walk of less than 0.1 mile leads you through the longleaf pines to your campsite. Each tent campsite has a picnic table and a fire ring, but there's not a lot of underbrush, so there's not a ton of privacy here either. Plus the wilderness area is right next to the boat ramp, so on weekends you are inundated with all the boat traffic as well.

Cane Creek Park is loaded with activities. The park is split into two sections: the campground and the day-use area. The campground has a boat ramp, a swim beach, a volleyball net, an open field to toss a ball in, and a camp store. The day-use area is located about 5 miles from the campground, but you have full access to the area when you stay at the campground. The day-use

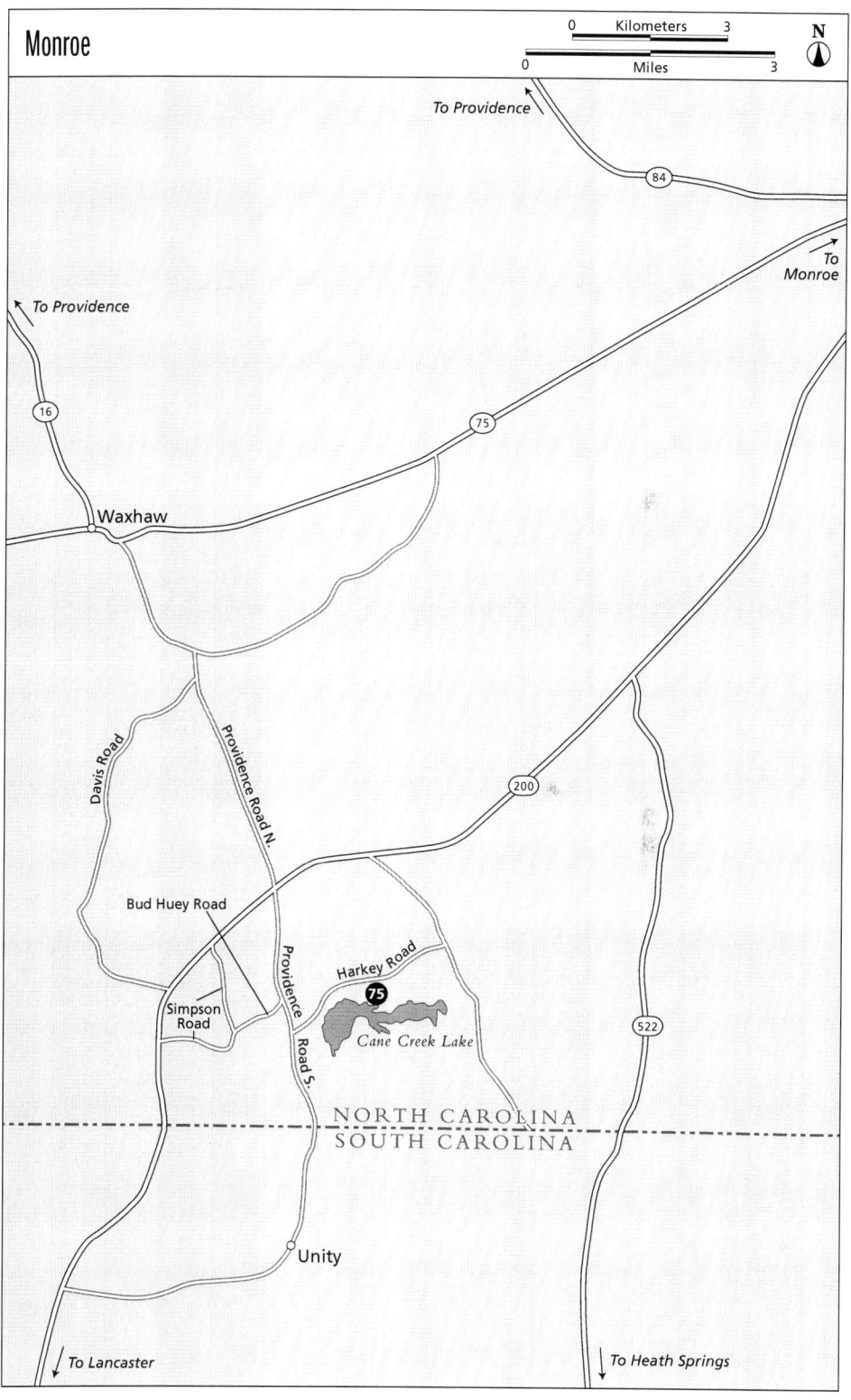

area has an abundance of things to do: softball/baseball field, soccer field, volleyball nets, horse-shoe pits, shuffleboard, a small climbing wall in one of several playgrounds, a minigolf course, picnic areas, a swim beach, fishing piers, a boat ramp, and a boat rental station where they rent paddleboats, canoes, and rowboats.

Separate fees may be charged for certain activities; contact the park for specifics. All the activities available within the day-use area help offset the lack of privacy within the campground.

	Total Sites	Hookup Sites	Max. RV Length	Hookups	Toilets	Showers	Drinking Water	Dump Station	Recreation	Fee	Reservations
76 Camp T. N. Spencer Park	16*	0	n/a	N	F	Y	Y	N	H, S, F, P	$$-$$$	Y
77 Dan Nicholas Park	70	67	45'	E, W	F	Y	Y	Y	H, F, B*, P, *	$$-$$$	Y

* See campground entry for specific information

76 Camp T. N. Spencer Park

Location: 3155 Foxford Rd., Concord; about 5 miles northeast of Concord and 20 miles northwest of Albemarle
Season: Year-round
Sites: 7 tent sites; 9 group campsites for organized nonprofit groups only; cabin rentals also available
Maximum length: n/a; tents only
Facilities: Flush toilets, hot showers, fire rings, picnic tables, trash cans; *no* pets overnight
Fee per night: $$-$$$
Management: Cabarrus County Parks and Recreation
Contact: (704) 795-4492; www.cabarruscounty.us/government/departments/active-living-parks/parks/camp-spencer/Pages/default.aspx. For reservations call (704) 920-3351.
Finding the campground: From the junction of NC 73 and NC 3 in Concord, drive east on NC 73 for 1.1 miles. Turn left onto Gold Hill Road and travel 4.5 miles. Turn left onto Rimer Road at the sign for T. N. SPENCER PARK. Follow Rimer Road for 0.3 mile, and veer to the left onto Fox Ford Drive (SR 2468) to enter the park.

From the junction of NC 73 and NC 49 in Mt. Pleasant, drive west on NC 73 for 1.4 miles. Turn right onto Saint John's Church Road (SR 2414), and continue 2.9 miles. Turn right onto Gold Hill Road, and follow it for 0.9 mile. Turn left onto Rimer Road, and follow directions above.
GPS coordinates: N35 27.701' / W80 29.500'
Maps: *DeLorme: North Carolina Atlas & Gazetteer:* Page 58 B2
About the campground: This wonderful small community park gives you a lot of bang for your buck! The campsites are tent only, and some of them sit right on the edge of a lovely little fishing pond. The camping here gets pretty hot in summer, but the park has a swimming pool, so if you do camp here in summer, at least you have a way to cool down.

Because it offers so many activities, Camp T. N. Spencer is very popular with the locals. There's a playground, a volleyball net, horseshoe pits, a fishing pond, and picnic areas. They even loan out fishing rods, and on occasion, the park will lead guided nature hikes along the hiking trails. If you prefer to hit the trails on your own, you can try your hand at navigating the geocaching course.

If the weather's bad, or you just don't feel like roughing it, you can rent one of the adorable cabins that rest alongside the shore of the pond.

77 Dan Nicholas Park Campground

Location: 6800 Bringle Ferry Rd., Salisbury; about 5 miles east of Salisbury
Season: Year-round
Sites: 70
Maximum length: 45 feet
Facilities: Flush toilets, hot showers, water, electric, fire rings, picnic tables, dump station, camp store, ice and firewood for sale; pet friendly
Fee per night: $$-$$$
Management: Rowan County Parks and Recreation
Contact: (704) 216-7808; www.dannicholas.net
Finding the campground: From the junction of US 52 and I-85 in Salisbury (exit 76), drive south on US 52 for 0.4 mile. Turn left onto Newsome Road at the sign for Dan Nicholas Park, and

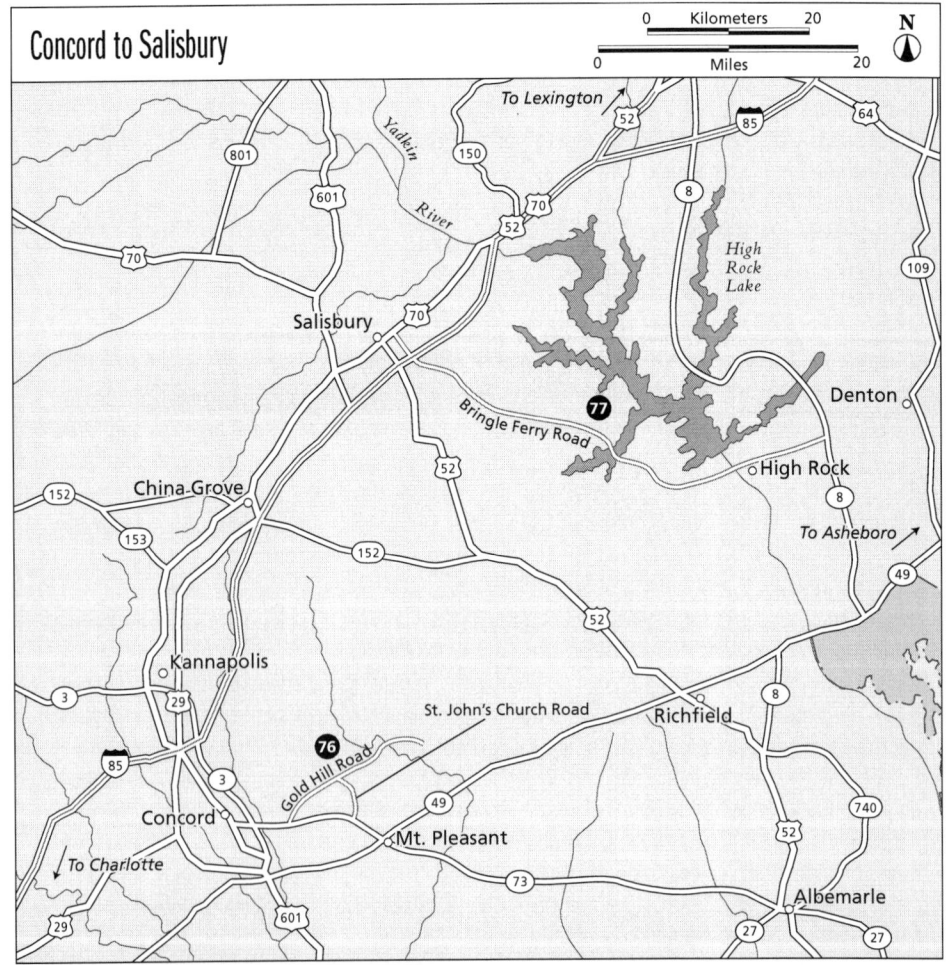

Concord to Salisbury

travel for 0.9 mile. Turn right onto Bringle Ferry Road, and travel for 5.7 miles to a left turn into Dan Nicholas Park. After entering the park, continue straight ahead for 0.4 mile and then go left toward the campground. Head down the hill, and follow the road for another 0.4 mile to the campground entrance.

From the junction of Bringle Ferry Road and NC 8 near Denton, drive west on Bringle Ferry Road for 3.3 miles to a right turn into Dan Nicholas Park. After entering the park, follow directions above.

GPS coordinates: N35 38.099' / W80 21.014'

Maps: *DeLorme: North Carolina Atlas & Gazetteer: Page 36 F3*

About the campground: Where do I even begin? I suppose I should begin by telling you to visit the website above. Dan Nicholas Park has more activities than any other campground, or park, in this book. Things you wouldn't even fathom, like a carousel, a petting zoo, and train rides, can be found at Dan Nicholas. Of course the park has the typical playgrounds and picnic areas, but there's an endless list of other things to do and see here as well—from gem mining to horseshoes, or try your hand at putt-putt golf. Whatever your pleasure, you are likely to find it here, and the whole family is sure to be entertained. They even have live wildlife exhibits with a real live black bear, bobcat, and bald eagle.

The campground sits on the northern end of Lake Murtis and has an interesting layout. There are loops within loops, and some of the sites back up to the lake, with a bit of forest in between the sites and the lake. The campground is wooded but not super private. But with all the amazing things to do at Dan Nicholas Park, it's worth a visit.

A red-tailed hawk shows off its impressive wingspan.

Albemarle

	Total Sites	Hookup Sites	Max. RV Length	Hookups	Toilets	Showers	Drinking Water	Dump Station	Recreation	Fee	Reservations
78 Morrow Mountain State Park	106	22	55'	E	F	Y	Y	Y	H, R, S, F, B, P	$$–$$$	Y
78 Morrow Mountain (Group)	6	0	n/a	N	F	Y	Y	N	H, R, S, F, B, P	$$$	Y
79 Yates Place	7	0	n/a	N	V	N	N	N	H, M, R, S, F, B, L, O, P	No fee	N
80 West Morris	14	0	50'	N	V	N	N	N	H, M, R, S, F, B, L, O, P	$	N
80 West Morris (Group)	2	0	n/a	N	V	N	N	N	H, M, R, S, F, B, L, O, P	$$$	Y
81 Uwharrie Hunt Camp	8	0	n/a	N	V	N	Y	N	H, M, R, S, F, B, L, O, P	$	N
82 Badin Lake (Horse)	*	0	n/a	N	V	N	N	N	H, M, R, S, F, B, L, O, P	No fee	N
83 Canebrake (Horse)	28	28	85'	E	F	Y	Y	Y	H, M, R, S, F, B, L, O, P	$$–$$$	Y
84 Overflow (Horse)	*	0	n/a	N	N*	N	N	N	H, M, R, S, F, B, L, O, P	No fee	N
85 Badin Lake	34	0	40'	N	F	Y	Y	Y*	H, M, R, S, F, B, L, O, P	$$–$$$	Y
85 Badin Lake (Group)	3	0	n/a	N	F	Y	Y	Y*	H, M, R, S, F, B, L, O, P	$$$	Y
86 Arrowhead	50	33	45'	E	F	Y	Y	Y	H, M, R, S, F, B, L, O, P	$$–$$$	Y
87 Art Lilley (OHV)	*	0	n/a	N	V	N	N	N	H, M, R*, S, F, B, L, O, P	No fee*	N

* See campground entry for specific information.

78 Morrow Mountain State Park

Location: 49104 Morrow Mountain Rd., Albemarle; about 7 miles east of Albemarle and about 21 miles west of Troy
Season: Year-round; closed Christmas Day
Sites: 106; 6 group campsites (reservations required) available and can accommodate up to 35 people each; also 6 cabins available for rent
Maximum length: 55 feet

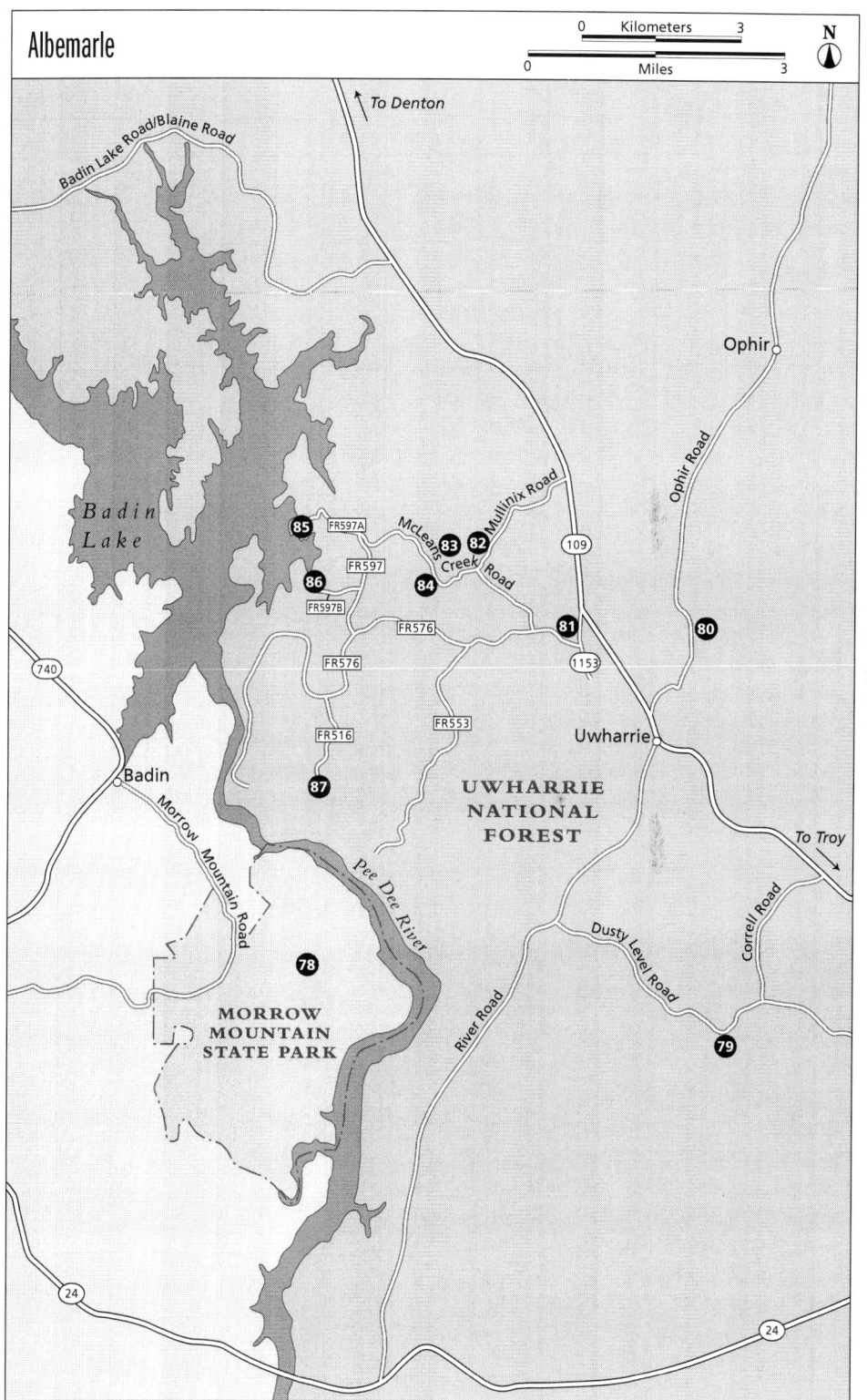

Facilities: Flush toilets, hot showers, water spigots dispersed, electric, fire rings, picnic tables, lantern holders, dump station; pet friendly
Fee per night: $$–$$$
Management: North Carolina Department of Natural Resources
Contact: (704) 982-4402; www.ncparks.gov/Visit/parks/momo/activities.php. For reservations call (877) 722-6762 or visit www.reserveamerica.com.
Finding the campground: From the junction of NC 740 and NC 24 in Albemarle, drive north on NC 740 for approximately 1.8 miles. Turn right onto Morrow Mountain Road at the sign for MORROW MOUNTAIN STATE PARK, and travel 1.7 miles to a stop sign at Valley Road. Continue straight across and continue on Morrow Mountain Road for another 1.4 miles to the park entrance.

From the junction of NC 24/27 and NC 73 South near Albemarle, drive west on NC 24/NC 27/NC 73 for 3.7 miles. Turn right onto Valley Road, and continue 3.2 miles. Turn right onto Morrow Mountain Road (SR 1798), and travel 1.4 miles to the park entrance.
GPS coordinates: N35 22.346' / W80 04.390'
Maps: *DeLorme: North Carolina Atlas & Gazetteer: Page 59 C6*
About the campground: Rich in geological and cultural history, Morrow Mountain houses the largest prehistoric quarry in the state of North Carolina. The park's museum exhibits a large variety of tool styles that were used throughout the ages when Native Americans inhabited the area. Along with the quarry and museum, the park has a picnic area and a swimming pool that is very popular with the locals.

The property borders Lake Tillery and the Pee Dee and Yadkin Rivers. You can rent a canoe or rowboat from the riverside concession stand or bring your own boat and use the park's launch site. Bridle trails loop around the outskirts of the park, and hiking trails traverse throughout, some leading to a handful of backpack campsites.

Morrow Mountain is the closest thing to a mountain in the Piedmont region, and the family campground is set among rolling hills. The sites are wooded, but there's not a lot of underbrush, so it's hit or miss as to whether you have privacy. The group camp is isolated and sits well off the beaten path atop a knoll. Reservations are required for the group camp.

79 Yates Place Campground

Location: About 6.5 miles west of Troy and about 21.5 miles south of Denton
Season: Year-round
Sites: 7
Maximum length: n/a; tents only
Facilities: Vault toilets, fire rings, picnic tables, lantern holders; pet friendly
Fee per night: None
Management: Uwharrie National Forest—Uwharrie Ranger District
Contact: (910) 576-6391; www.fs.usda.gov/recarea/nfsnc/recreation/camping-cabins/recarea/?recid=48948&actid=29
Finding the campground: From the junction of NC 109 and NC 24/27 in Troy, drive north on NC 109 for 4.8 miles. Turn left onto Correll Road (SR 1147) at the sign for YATES PLACE CAMP, and travel 1.8 miles. Turn right onto Dusty Level Road (SR 1146) at the YATES PLACE sign. Follow Dusty Level Road for 0.6 mile to Yates Place on your left.

A fawn grazes peacefully in the Uwharrie National Forest.

From the junction of NC 109 and NC 49 near Denton, drive south on NC 109 for approximately 14.2 miles. Turn right onto Correll Road (SR 1147), and follow directions above.
GPS coordinates: N35 21.900' / W79 59.329'
Maps: *DeLorme: North Carolina Atlas & Gazetteer:* Page 59 C7
About the campground: If you're looking to explore the Uwharrie National Forest but want a low-cost alternative, Yates Place has seven primitive campsites where you can camp for free. You get the typical picnic table, lantern holder, and fire ring, but there's no running water on site. For the price, it's not a bad option.

The campground is surrounded by wooded, rolling hill terrain. There's easy access to the Uwharrie Trail; stretching 20 miles, it's the only National Recreation Trail in the Uwharrie National Forest. If you prefer your recreation on two wheels, the trailhead for the Wood Run Mountain Bike Trail is just a few miles away.

80 West Morris Campground

Location: About 8 miles northwest of Troy and about 18 miles south of Denton
Season: Year-round
Sites: 14; also 2 group camping areas available that can accommodate up to 50 people
Maximum length: 50 feet
Facilities: Vault toilets, water spigots dispersed, fire rings, picnic tables, lantern holders; pet friendly

Fee per night: $

Management: Uwharrie National Forest—Uwharrie Ranger District

Contact: (910) 576-6391; www.fs.usda.gov/recarea/nfsnc/recreation/camping-cabins/recarea/?recid=48944&actid=29

Finding the campground: From the junction of NC 109 and NC 24/27 in Troy, drive north on NC 109 for 7.8 miles. Turn right onto the unmarked Ophir Road at the sign for WEST MORRIS MOUNTAIN AND BIRKHEAD WILDERNESS, and travel 1 mile. Turn right onto FR 549 at the sign for WEST MORRIS MOUNTAIN, and continue 0.2 miles to a fork. The Uwharrie Trailhead is on the left and the campground is on your right.

From the junction of NC 109 and NC 49 near Denton, drive south on NC 109 for approximately 11.2 miles. Turn left onto the unmarked Ophir Road (SR 1134) at the sign for WEST MORRIS MOUNTAIN, and follow directions above.

GPS coordinates: N35 25.647' / W79 59.636'

Maps: *DeLorme: North Carolina Atlas & Gazetteer:* Page 59 B7

About the campground: If you can live without flush toilets and hot showers, I highly recommend West Morris. Surrounded by a pine and hardwood mixed forest, each site here is very wooded and very private. With the Uwharrie Trailhead right around the bend, you can literally hike right from your tent and explore the foothills of the Uwharrie.

Although the sites offer seclusion, this campground fills up quickly during hunting season. Keep this in mind, since all the sites at West Morris are on a first-come, first-served basis.

81 Uwharrie Hunt Camp

Location: About 8 miles northwest of Troy and about 18 miles south of Denton

Season: Year-round

Sites: 8

Maximum length: n/a; tents only

Facilities: Vault toilets, water spigots dispersed, fire rings, picnic tables, lantern holders, tent pads; pet friendly

Fee per night: $

Management: Uwharrie National Forest—Uwharrie Ranger District

Contact: (910) 576-6391; www.fs.usda.gov/recarea/nfsnc/recreation/wateractivities/recarea/?recid=48946&actid=78

Finding the campground: From the junction of NC 109 and NC 24/27 in Troy, drive north on NC 109 for 9.3 miles. Turn left onto SR 1153 at the sign for BADIN LAKE RECREATION AREA, and travel 0.4 mile to the campground on your right.

From the junction of NC 109 and NC 49 near Denton, drive south on NC 109 for approximately 9.7 miles. Turn right onto SR 1153 at the sign for BADIN LAKE RECREATION AREA, and follow directions above.

GPS coordinates: N35 25.746' / W80 01.180'

Maps: *DeLorme: North Carolina Atlas & Gazetteer:* Page 59 B6

About the campground: In this tent-only, primitive campground, perfectly manicured campsites sit on a hillside, with a drainage/dry creekbed running through the middle. Even though the sites are very close to one another, the fact that they are built on a hillside rather than on level ground adds to the appeal. The downside: The campground is right off SR 1153, so all the traffic entering the forest from this route, or heading to the small community of Uwharrie, will be passing by. The upside: You are within easy reach of miles and miles of trails. No matter what you are searching for—hiking, mountain biking, bridle, or OHV trail—you can easily access it from the Uwharrie Hunt Camp.

82 Badin Lake Horse Camp

Location: About 11.5 miles northwest of Troy and about 15 miles south of Denton
Season: Year-round
Sites: Open field; no set number of designated campsites
Maximum length: None
Facilities: A few randomly placed primitive fire rings, horse tie-offs; pet friendly
Fee per night: None
Management: Uwharrie National Forest—Uwharrie Ranger District
Contact: (910) 576-6391; www.fs.usda.gov/recarea/nfsnc/recreation/horseriding-camping/recarea/?recid=48952&actid=30
Finding the campground: From the junction of NC 109 and NC 24/27 in Troy, drive north on NC 109 for 10.6 miles. Turn left onto Mullinix Road (SR 1154) at the sign for Badin Lake Recreation Area, and continue 1.4 miles to the Badin Lake Horse Camp on your right.

From the junction of NC 109 and NC 49 near Denton, drive south on NC 109 for approximately 8.4 miles. Turn right onto Mullinix Road (SR 1154) at the sign for Badin Lake Recreation Area, and follow directions above.
GPS coordinates: N35 26.560' / W80 02.412'
Maps: *DeLorme: North Carolina Atlas & Gazetteer:* Page 59 B6
About the campground: Badin Lake Horse Camp is the polar opposite of Canebrake Horse Camp. In essence, this horse "camp" is simply an open field, and the field is not on level ground. There are posts galore, lined up on one end of the field, for you to tie your horse up to. This is the one plus, because tying your horses up to trees can damage the trees. There are a few primitive fire rings randomly placed here and there, no bathroom, not even a vault toilet. As a matter of fact, if you didn't know this was a horse camp, you would pass right by without a thought.

The upside of Badin Horse Camp is that there is a small trail leading from the campground to a horse watering hole along West Branch Creek. Another plus is that it is free. So if you are looking for a horse camp within easy access of the miles and miles of bridle trails within Uwharrie National Forest and are on a strict budget, this may be the place for you. If you are looking for a campground with a bathroom and other amenities, head down the road to the Canebrake Horse Camp.

83 Canebrake Horse Camp

Location: About 11.5 miles northwest of Troy and about 15 miles south of Denton
Season: Year-round
Sites: 28
Maximum length: 85 feet
Facilities: Flush toilets, hot showers, water spigots dispersed, electric, fire rings, picnic tables, lantern holders, dump station, horse washing station, manure management system; pet friendly
Fee per night: $$-$$$
Management: Uwharrie National Forest—Uwharrie Ranger District
Contact: (910) 576-6391; www.fs.usda.gov/recarea/nfsnc/recreation/camping-cabins/recarea/?recid=48950&actid=29. For reservations call (877) 444-6777 or visit www.recreation.gov.
Finding the campground: From the junction of NC 109 and NC 24/27 in Troy, drive north on NC 109 for 10.6 miles. Turn left onto Mullinix Road (SR 1154) at the sign for Badin Lake Recreation Area, and travel 1.5 miles to where it ends at a T at FR 544 (McLeans Creek Road). Turn right onto FR 544, and continue 0.3 mile to the campground on your right.

From the junction of NC 109 and NC 49 near Denton, drive south on NC 109 for approximately 8.4 miles. Turn right onto Mullinix Road (SR 1154) at the sign for Badin Lake Recreation Area, and follow directions above.
GPS coordinates: N35 26.376' / W80 02.747'
Maps: *DeLorme: North Carolina Atlas & Gazetteer: Page 59 B6*
About the campground: Wow! What a nice facility for those looking for a place to camp with their horses. The Uwharrie National Forest has gone above and beyond and has really set the bar with the Canebrake Horse Camp. The campground has all the amenities of a family campground but has added horse tie-offs, so you don't have to tie your horse to the trees, which can damage them.

There are garden hoses at the horse-washing station, and the forest service is diligently working with local horse clubs on a manure management system. They have provided rakes, shovels, and wheelbarrows to help remove the excess waste from the campground. The manure is then put back into use as fertilizer throughout the forest. Once you set up camp at Canebrake, there is no need to trailer your horse any further. You can saddle up from your campsite and access miles of bridle trails without ever leaving the campground.

84 Overflow Horse Camp

Location: About 11.5 miles northwest of Troy and about 15 miles south of Denton
Season: Year-round; opens as needed when the Canebrake Horse Camp is full
Sites: Open field; no set number of designated campsites
Maximum length: None
Facilities: Horse tie-offs; pet friendly
Fee per night: None
Management: Uwharrie National Forest—Uwharrie Ranger District

Campers use one of the many "hitching posts" provided at Canebrake Horse Camp.

Contact: (910) 576-6391; www.fs.usda.gov/recarea/nfsnc/recreation/horseriding-camping/recarea/?recid=49596&actid=30

Finding the campground: From the junction of NC 109 and NC 24/27 in Troy, drive north on NC 109 for 10.6 miles. Turn left onto Mullinix Road (SR 1154) at the sign for Badin Lake Recreation Area, and travel 1.5 miles to a where it ends at a T at FR 544 (McLeans Creek Road). Go right onto FR 544 and travel 0.5 mile to the campground on your left.

From the junction of NC 109 and NC 49 near Denton, drive south on NC 109 for approximately 8.4 miles. Turn right onto Mullinix Road (SR 1154) at the sign for Badin Lake Recreation Area, and follow directions above.

GPS coordinates: N35 26.369' / W80 02.941'

Maps: *DeLorme: North Carolina Atlas & Gazetteer:* Page 59 B6

About the campground: The Overflow Horse Camp is just that. This is an "overflow" campground and is only opened up when the Canebrake Horse Camp is full. Much like Badin Lake Horse Camp, there are no facilities, simply an open field with some posts to tie your horses off to. You can use the bathroom facilities at Canebrake, but it's about a 0.25-mile walk to get there. Miles of bridle trails are available within the surrounding Uwharrie National Forest, and several trailheads can be easily reached from the Overflow Horse Camp.

85 Badin Lake Campground

Location: About 13.5 miles northwest of Troy and about 17 miles south of Denton

Season: Year-round

Sites: 34; also a separate group camping area with 3 campsites that can accommodate up to 50 people each

Maximum length: 40 feet

Facilities: Flush toilets, hot showers, water spigots dispersed, fire rings, picnic tables, lantern holders; pet friendly

Fee per night: $$–$$$

Management: Uwharrie National Forest—Uwharrie Ranger District

Contact: (910) 576-6391; www.fs.usda.gov/recarea/nfsnc/recreation/camping-cabins/recarea/?recid=48940&actid=29. For reservations call (877) 444-6777 or visit www.recreation.gov.

Finding the campground: From the junction of NC 109 and NC 24/27 in Troy, drive north on NC 109 for 10.6 miles. Turn left onto Mullinix Road (SR 1154) at the sign for Badin Lake Recreation Area, and travel 1.5 miles to a where it ends at a T at FR 544 (McLeans Creek Road). Turn right onto FR 544 and continue 1.6 miles to where the road ends at FR 597 (Badin Lake Road). Turn right onto FR 597 and follow it for 0.2 mile to a fork. Bear left at the fork onto FR 597A, and travel 0.5 mile to another fork. The right leads less than 0.1 mile to the group campground on the right. Instead bear left at the fork and continue on FR 597A for 0.3 mile to the Badin Lake Family Campground.

From the junction of NC 109 and NC 49 near Denton, drive south on NC 109 for approximately 8.4 miles. Turn right onto Mullinix Road (SR 1154) at the sign for Badin Lake Recreation Area, and follow directions above.

GPS coordinates: Family campground: N35 26.918' / W80 04.723'; group camp: N35 27.052' / W80 04.330'

Boaters enjoy stunning sunsets on Badin Lake.

Maps: *DeLorme: North Carolina Atlas & Gazetteer:* Page 59 B6

About the campground: This little hidden gem sits at the northeastern corner of the Uwharrie National Forest and along the banks of Badin Lake. This is a great location for those wanting to enjoy the lake by boat. Many of the campsites are right along the edge of the lake, so you can literally pull your boat right up to your campsite, wake up in the morning, hop in the boat, and head out to play, fish, swim, and explore. The Cove Boat Ramp is just down the road a bit, off FR 597B near the Arrowhead Campground. Be forewarned: Although Arrowhead is much closer to the boat ramp, it does not have any waterfront campsites.

It's a mixed bag at Badin Lake Campground. Some of the sites are right on top of one another; others area tucked away, offering lots of privacy. The King's Mountain Point day-use area is less than 1 mile away and has a picnic area, a swim beach, fishing piers, and an open field atop Kings "Mountain" where you can toss a Frisbee or football or get a game of kickball together. Miles of hiking, mountain bike, bridle, and OHV trails run throughout the Uwharrie National Forest. You can easily access them all from the Badin Lake Family Campground and the Badin Lake Group Camp.

The group camp is at a separate location, just a few tenths of a mile from the family campground. Unlike most of the national forest group camps, you do not have to be affiliated with a nonprofit organization to camp here. Everyone is welcome. At first glance this group camp looks like any other, with a wide-open field in the middle and a bathhouse at one end. When you arrive at any one of the three campsites, however, you're in for a great surprise. Each of the group sites is almost like having your own private campground. The tent pads are tucked away in the woods, so you still have some privacy from the rest of the group, and each site has a water spigot, a large community fire ring, picnic tables, and charcoal grills. Both the family campground and the group camp are among my favorites in the Piedmont region.

86 Arrowhead Campground

Location: About 13.5 miles northwest of Troy and about 17 miles south of Denton
Season: Year-round
Sites: 50
Maximum length: 45 feet
Facilities: Flush toilets, hot showers, water spigots dispersed, electricity, fire rings, charcoal grills, picnic tables, lantern holders, dump station; pet friendly
Fee per night: $$–$$$
Management: Uwharrie National Forest–Uwharrie Ranger District
Contact: (910) 576-6391; www.fs.usda.gov/recarea/nfsnc/recreation/camping-cabins/recarea/?recid=48938&actid=29. For reservations call (877) 444-6777 or visit www.recreation.gov.
Finding the campground: From the junction of NC 109 and NC 24/27 in Troy, drive north on NC 109 for 10.6 miles. Turn left onto Mullinix Road (SR 1154) at the sign for Badin Lake Recreation Area, and travel 1.5 miles to a where it ends at a T at FR 544 (McLeans Creek Road). Turn right onto FR 544, and travel 1.6 miles to where the road ends at FR 597 (Badin Lake Road). Turn left onto FR 597 and follow it for 0.5 mile. Turn right onto FR 597B at the Arrowhead CG sign, and continue 0.3 mile to the entrance to Arrowhead Campground.

From the junction of NC 109 and NC 49 near Denton, drive south on NC 109 for approximately 8.4 miles. Turn right onto Mullinix Road (SR 1154) at the sign for Badin Lake Recreation Area, and follow directions above.

GPS coordinates: N35 26.293' / W80 04.195'

Maps: *DeLorme: North Carolina Atlas & Gazetteer:* Page 59 B6

About the campground: Its location, less than 1 mile from the Cove Boat Ramp, makes Arrowhead a great place to appreciate Badin Lake from the water, whether you want to swim, fish, water-ski, or just tool around in your boat. Unfortunately, although it appears to be right on the water, Arrowhead has no waterfront campsites. If you are looking for a place where you can pull your boat right up to the campsite, head up the road to the Badin Lake Family Campground.

What Arrowhead does have is electricity. So if you're in an RV, this may be a great option for you. With paved campsites rather than gravel and many pull-through sites, it affords easy RV access. That's not to say Arrowhead isn't suitable for tent campers. Actually the campground is nicely wooded, and many of the sites offer quite a bit of privacy. Bring your boat, kayak, mountain bike, or OHV, and enjoy the many miles of trails that run nearby. Stop in the ranger station to grab a trail map and see what this wonderful forest has to offer.

87 Art Lilley Off-Highway Vehicle (OHV) Camp

Location: About 13 miles northwest of Troy and about 21 miles south of Denton

Season: Apr 1–Dec 15

Sites: No set number of designated campsites

Maximum length: n/a; tents only

Facilities: Vault toilet, a handful of primitive fire rings; pet friendly

Fee per night: No fee for camping; daily fee ($) to ride on the OHV trails

Management: Uwharrie National Forest—Uwharrie Ranger District

Contact: (910) 576-6391; www.fs.usda.gov/recarea/nfsnc/recreation/ohv/recarea/?recid=49884&actid=32

Finding the campground: From the junction of NC 109 and NC 24/27 in Troy, drive north on NC 109 for 9.3 miles. Turn left onto SR 1153 at the sign for Badin Lake Recreation Area, and travel 0.4 mile. Turn right onto FR 576 (Moccasin Creek Road), and continue 2.9 miles. Turn left onto FR 516, and travel 1.1 miles to a fork. The left leads to the Falls Dam Trailhead parking area. Bear right at the fork and continue 0.1 mile to the Art Lilley Memorial Campground.

From the junction of NC 109 and NC 49 near Denton, drive south on NC 109 for approximately 9.7 miles. Turn right onto SR 1153 at the sign for Badin Lake Recreation Area, and follow directions above.

GPS coordinates: N35 24.247' / W80 04.417'

Maps: *DeLorme: North Carolina Atlas & Gazetteer:* Page 59 C6

About the campground: Depending on which map you use, it may look as though FR 516 ends well before the campground. Actually a very well-maintained, smooth gravel road leads all the way to the Art Lilley Campground. While there are a few ruts here and there, the road is suitable for cars with or without four-wheel drive.

Once you arrive at the "campground," you will see that it's really just a very large gravel parking area with a loading ramp for OHVs and a vault toilet at one end. The parking lot is surrounded by forest, with open, flat areas to pitch a tent and the occasional primitive stone fire ring. There are no set campsites, and the area is subject to first-come, first-served camping. A second OHV-loading ramp is located right next door at the Falls Dam Trailhead and is great for busy weekends.

An OHV is required to head any deeper into the forest from here, as the trails narrow and criss-cross throughout the forest. Use caution as you barrel through the forest. It's common to come across a hiker, mountain biker, or someone on horseback, as these multiuse trails intersect the OHV trails regularly.

There's no fee to camp at Art Lilley, but you must obtain an OHV pass prior to heading off-road on any motorized vehicle. Passes can be obtained at the ranger station or at self-pay stations at some but not all of the trailheads. There is a nominal fee to obtain a pass (good for one day); seasonal passes are also available.

Greensboro to Burlington

	Total Sites	Hookup Sites	Max. RV Length	Hookups	Toilets	Showers	Drinking Water	Dump Station	Recreation	Fee	Reservations
88 Hagen-Stone Park	89	70	45'	E, W	F	Y	Y	Y	H, M, S, F, B*, L*, P	$$-$$$	N*
89 Cedarock Park	*	0	n/a	N	F	N	N	N	H, M, R, F, B*, L*, P*, *	$-$$	Y

* See campground entry for specific information.

88 Hagen-Stone Park Campground

Location: About 6 miles south of Greensboro and about 13 miles northwest of Liberty
Season: Year-round
Sites: 86; also 3 group tent camping sites (reservations required) that can accommodate up to 30 people each
Maximum length: 45 feet
Facilities: Flush toilets, hot showers, electric and water (RV sites only), water spigots dispersed, picnic tables, fire rings, lantern holders (tent sites only), dump station; pet friendly
Fee per night: $$-$$$
Management: City of Greensboro Parks and Recreation
Contact: (336) 674-0472; www.greensboro-nc.gov/index.aspx?page=1193
Finding the campground: From the junction of US 421 and NC 62 near Climax, drive north on US 421 for 4.2 miles. Turn left onto Hagen-Stone Park Road (SR 3411) at the sign for HAGEN-STONE PARK, and continue 2.2 miles to the park entrance on your right.

From I-85 near Greensboro, take exit 126 and drive south on US 421 for approximately 3.2 miles. Turn right onto Hagen-Stone Park Road (SR 3411) at the sign for HAGEN-STONE PARK, and continue 2.2 miles to the park entrance on your right.
GPS coordinates: N35 56.995' / W79 44.178'
Maps: *DeLorme: North Carolina Atlas & Gazetteer:* Page 38 B1
About the campground: Hagen-Stone is another giant town park with lots of activities for locals and visitors alike. The campground is divided into loops like most, and there is a separate area designated for tent campers only. The RV loop is a bit disappointing. There's an open field, and the sites are lined up one after the next, much like a parking lot. They do have water and electric, so RV campers won't need to run their generators, but privacy is heavily lacking in this loop. A second RV loop offers a bit more tree cover and a tad more privacy, but not much. The tent campsites are slightly more wooded and well spaced, but a heavily used hiking trail passes right by some of the sites, so choose your spot wisely.

The park itself is wonderful. It has several playgrounds, areas for volleyball and softball, horseshoe pits, an orienteering course, and a swimming pool that's open seasonally. There are hiking

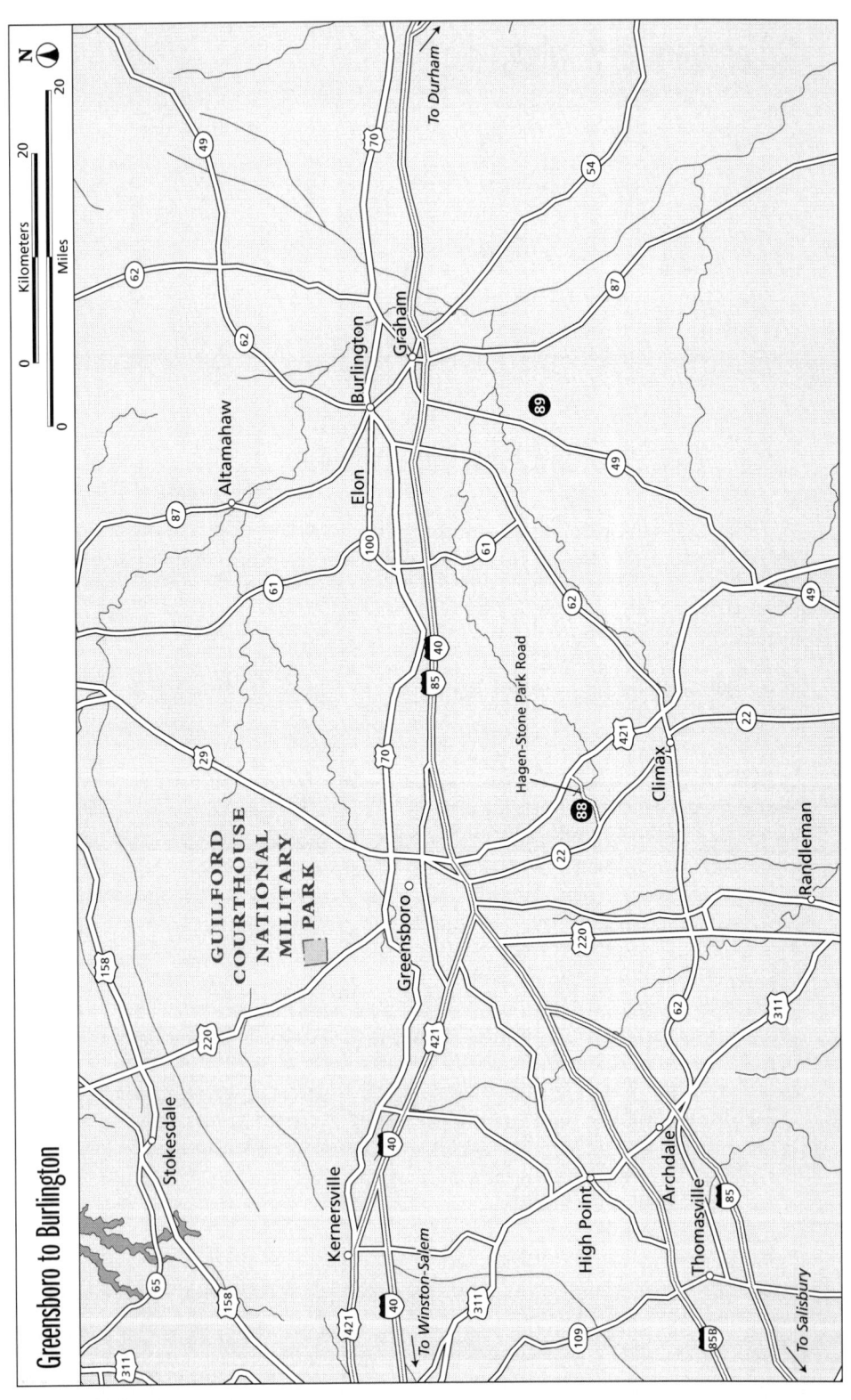

Greensboro to Burlington

An old farmhouse sits on the outskirts of Hagen-Stone Park.

and biking trails and four lakes where you can fish or launch a canoe or kayak and tool about. The group camping areas have a large open field surrounded by woods. There are picnic tables and a large community fire ring. The group camping is tent only, and reservations are required.

89 Cedarock Park Campground

Location: 4242 R. Dean Coleman Rd., Burlington; about 6 miles south of Burlington and about 12 miles northeast of Liberty
Season: Year-round
Sites: Large open field with no set campsites; hike-in only
Maximum length: n/a; tents only
Facilities: Flush toilets about 0.25 mile from the campsites, community fire rings, *no* potable water; pet friendly
Fee per night: $-$$
Management: Alamance County Department of Recreation and Parks

Contact: (336) 570-6759; www.alamance-nc.com/d/recreation-and-parks/parks-and-centers/cedarock-park.html

Finding the campground: From I-40 in Burlington, take exit 145 and travel south on NC 49 (Maple Avenue) for 5.9 miles. Turn left onto Friendship Patterson Mill Road (SR 1130) at the sign for CEDAROCK PARK, and continue 0.2 mile. Turn left onto R. Dean Coleman Road, and travel 0.5 mile to where the road dead-ends at the park entrance.

From the junction of NC 49 and US 421 in Liberty, drive north on NC 49 for approximately 14 miles. Turn right onto Friendship Patterson Mill Road (SR 1130), and follow directions above.

GPS coordinates: N35 59.191' / W79 27.002'

Maps: *DeLorme: North Carolina Atlas & Gazetteer:* Page 38 B4

About the campground: Of all the amenities Cedarock Park has to offer, camping is not the highlight. The "campground" is really a large open grassy field with a bench and a fire ring here and there. There are no designated sites, so it's basically first come, first served as far as where you pitch your tent. A short hike of less than 0.25 mile leads to the camping area, The park does have flush toilets, but you have to hike back out to the main area to use them.

What Cedarock Park has done right is just about everything else in the park. There is a historic farm you can tour; hiking, mountain bike, and bridle trails grace the park; and there's a lake with a canoe and kayak launch. If you don't have your own boat, you can rent a canoe from the park. This very busy park also offers basketball, volleyball, and a full Frisbee/disc golf course. Whether you sit with the kids at the playground or meet with friends for a picnic, this park is fantastic. But the campground itself is lackluster.

Sanford to Fayetteville

	Total Sites	Hookup Sites	Max. RV Length	Hookups	Toilets	Showers	Drinking Water	Dump Station	Recreation	Fee	Reservations
90 San Lee Park	16	3	40'	E, W	F	Y	Y	Y	H, M, F, B*, P	$$	N

* See campground entry for specific information.

90   San Lee Park Campground

Location: About 2 miles west of Sanford
Season: RV sites open year-round; tent campsites open Apr–Oct
Sites: 16
Maximum length: 40 feet
Facilities: Flush toilets, hot showers, water spigots dispersed, fire rings, fire wood, charcoal grills, picnic tables, lantern holders, trash cans, dump station; pet friendly
Fee per night: $$

A red-shouldered hawk keeps a keen eye out.

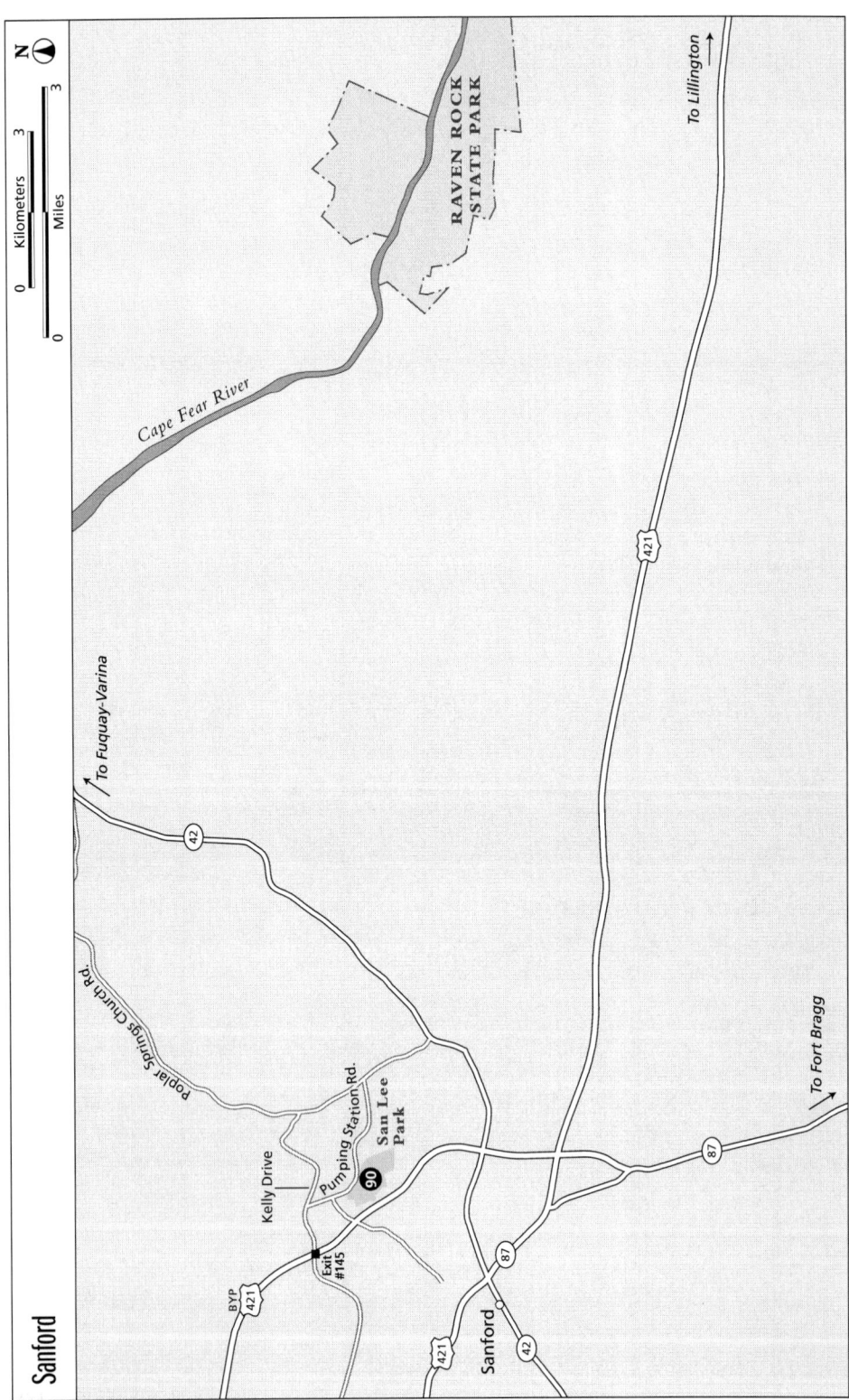

Sanford

Management: Lee County Department of Parks and Recreation

Contact: (919) 776-6221; www.leecountync.gov/Departments/SanLeePark.aspx

Finding the campground: From the junction of NC 42/US 421 Bypass and NC 42 Connector in Sanford, drive north on US 421 Bypass for 1.7 miles. Take exit 145 (Kelly Drive), and follow Kelly Drive northeast for 0.3 mile. Turn right onto Pumping Station Road (SR 1510), and continue 0.2 mile to the park entrance on the right.

GPS coordinates: N35 29.083' / W79 07.599'

Maps: *DeLorme: North Carolina Atlas & Gazetteer:* Page 61 B7

About the campground: What a treat you will find at San Lee Park—with the park itself more than the campgrounds. This small community park has two separate camping areas, one for RVs and one for tents only. Scattered amid the campsites are stacks of firewood lined up and free for the burning. Both campgrounds sit atop a knoll on the outskirts of the park and are fairly well shaded. Although the campsites are not the most secluded, what they lack in privacy the park itself more than makes up for. There's a playground, picnic shelters, 4 miles of hiking trails, and an 11-mile mountain bike trail system that offers some of the best riding in the region. Creeks run throughout the park, and there are two ponds where you can fish or even rent a canoe or paddleboat from the park and paddle or peddle your way around.

All of this, and I still haven't gotten to the highlight that really makes San Lee stand out: a nature center with a full-time outdoor education specialist on staff. There are exhibits, nature programs, and an aviary within which you can see several species of birds of prey up close and personal. Hazel the barred owl may cluck for you, or you might hear the call of the red-tailed hawks as you venture past their pen. Both white and Canada geese walk freely about the property, and the spillway from the upper pond creates a small waterfall. A small outdoor chapel next to the upper pond is worth a visit—so is this fabulous county park.

Raleigh-Durham

	Total Sites	Hookup Sites	Max. RV Length	Hookups	Toilets	Showers	Drinking Water	Dump Station	Recreation	Fee	Reservations
91 Jordan Lake: Vista Point	55	50	40'	E, W	F	Y	Y	N	H, S*, F, B, L, P*	$$$	Y
92 Jordan Lake: Parker's Creek	250	120	116'*	E, W	F	Y	Y	Y	H, S, F, B, L, P	$$$	N
92 Jordan Lake: Parker's Creek (Group)	6	0	n/a	N	F	Y	Y	Y	H, S, F, B, L, P	$$$	Y
93 Jordan Lake: New Hope Overlook	24	0	n/a	N	V	N	Y	N	H, F, B, L	$$	N
94 Jordan Lake: Poplar Point	579	363	136'*	E, W	F	Y	Y	Y	H, S, F, B, L	$$$	Y*
95 Jordan Lake: Crosswinds	182	134	146'*	E, W	F	Y	Y	Y	H, S, F, B, L	$$$	Y
96 William B. Umstead State Park	28	0	30'	N	F	Y	Y	N	H, M, R, S*, F, B, P	$$$	Y
96 William B. Umstead State Park (Group)	2	0	n/a	N	F	Y	Y	N	H, M, R, S*, F, B, P	$$$	Y
97 Falls Lake: Rollingview	115	80	115'	E, W	F	Y	Y	Y	H, S, F, B, L, P	$$-$$$	Y
97 Falls Lake: Rollingview (Group)	4	0	n/a	N	F	Y	Y	Y	H, S, F, B, L, P	$$$	Y
98 Falls Lake: Shinleaf	47	0	n/a	N	F	Y	N	N	H, L*	$$	Y
98 Falls Lake: Shinleaf (Group)	9	0	n/a	N	F	Y	N	N	H, L*	$$$	Y
99 Falls Lake: Holly Point	153	89	120'	E, W	F	Y	Y	Y	H, S, B, L	$$-$$$	Y
100 Falls Lake: B. W. Wells (Group)	11	0	n/a	N	F	Y	Y	N	H, B, L	$$$	Y
101 Little River Park (Group)	1	0	n/a	N	F	N	Y	N	H, M, P	$$$	Y*
102 Spruce Pine Lodge (Group)	7	0	n/a	N	V	N	N	N	H, F, B, L, P	$$$	Y*

* See campground entry for specific information.

Jordan Lake State Recreation Area: Sites 91-95

Jordan Lake encompasses almost 14,000 acres of water and approximately 200 miles of shoreline. Named for B. Everett Jordan, a former North Carolina senator, much of this massive lake is now owned and operated by the North Carolina Department of Natural Resources. Jordan Lake Recreation Area is divided into a dozen smaller recreation areas. Five of these dozen areas have some sort of camping to offer. From primitive tent to group RV camping, the state park system has done a fabulous job at providing the public with a variety of camping opportunities along the shores of Lake Jordan. Every campground on the lake has its own boat ramp, several swim

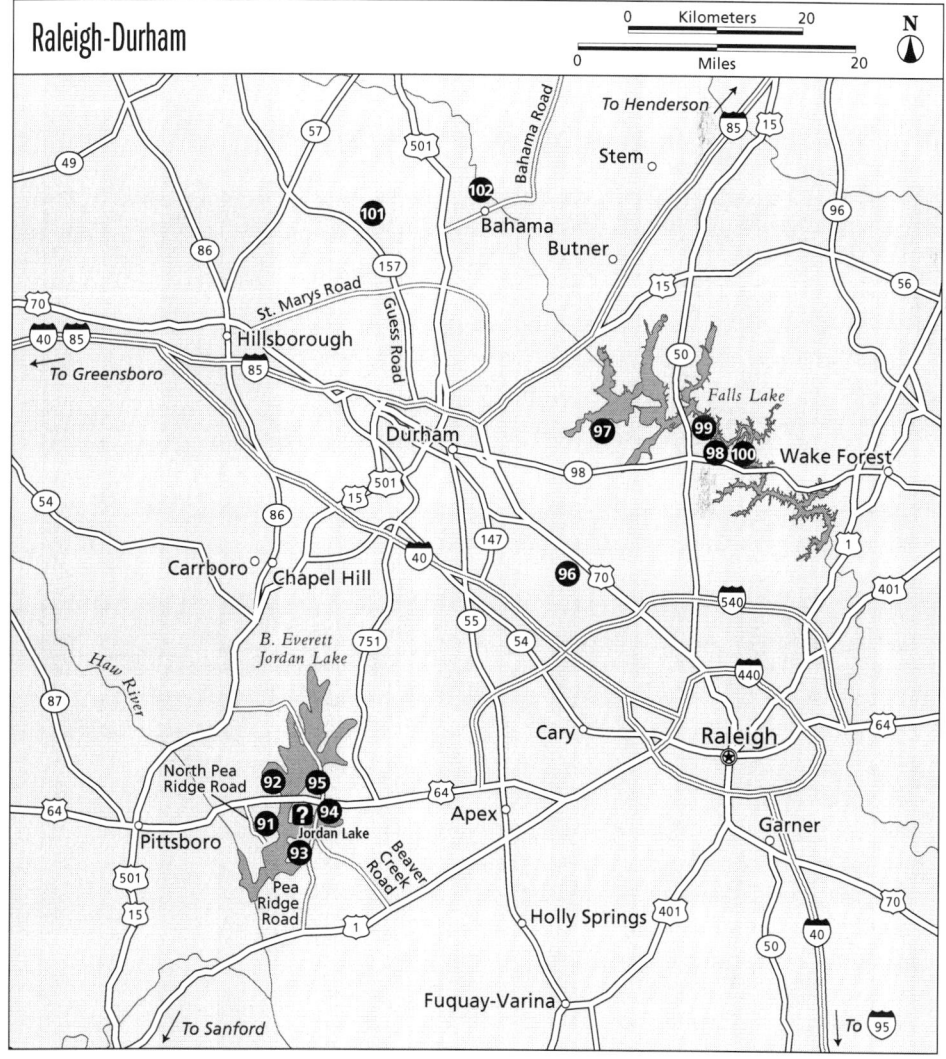

beaches grace the area, and hiking trails passing through each campground give you the opportunity to appreciate the lake by water or by land. The sunsets are stunning whether you camp on the east or west side. Ospreys circle overhead; bald eagles roost here as well.

To preserve the area, the state park system keeps only one campground open year-round. The rest are open typically from April through October. Each year a different campground is chosen to be the lucky winter winner. Be sure to call ahead if you plan on camping in the winter months so that you know which campground will be open. During the summer Lake Jordan sees heavy usage; reservations are recommended to ensure you get a spot. For more information visit their website at www.ncparks.gov/Visit/parks/jord/main.php. Maps are available online or at the visitor center, located on the south side of US 64, just east of the lake.

GPS coordinates for the visitor center: N35 43.957' / W79 01.014'

91 Jordan Lake State Recreation Area: Vista Point Group Camp

Location: On the southwest side of Jordan Lake
Season: Year-round
Sites: 50 RV sites for group camping only; 5 tent group sites also available that can accommodate up to 30 people each (reservations required)
Maximum length: 40 feet
Facilities: *RV sites:* Flush toilets, hot showers, water spigots, electric, dump station; pet friendly. *Primitive group camp area:* fire rings, water spigots dispersed, *no* electric
Fee per night: $$$
Management: North Carolina Department of Natural Resources
Contact: (919) 362-0586; www.ncparks.gov/Visit/parks/jord/main.php. For reservations (required) call (877) 722-6762.
Finding the campground: From the junction of US 64 Business and US 501/US 15 in downtown Pittsboro, drive east on US 64 for 5.5 miles. Turn right onto North Pea Ridge Road (SR 1700), and travel 2.4 miles to where the road ends at the Vista Point Recreation Area.

From the junction of US 64 and NC 751 near Wilsonville, drive west on US 64 for 7.5 miles. Turn left onto North Pea Ridge Road (SR 1700), and follow directions above.
GPS coordinates: N35 42.548' / W79 03.526'
Maps: *DeLorme: North Carolina Atlas & Gazetteer:* Page 39 E7
About the campground: Vista Point is on the western bank of Jordan Lake. There are two camping areas within this part of the recreation area, and both are designed for group camping only. Although these group camps are just a short walk apart, they are polar opposites. The tents-only group camp has five campsites. The sites here are quite wooded and spacious, and there's plenty of privacy. Each site has a community fire ring, a charcoal grill, and a few picnic tables. There's a playground in the middle of the loop, and Jordan Lake is in view from almost every site. The only downfall to the tent group camp at Vista Point is that you have to share the bathhouse with the RV group camp.

The full moon rises through the longleaf pines.

The upside of the RV group camp is that it's the only public campground in the state designed specifically for RVs. Every site has electric and water, but that's it. The sites are lined up in the grass, much like a parking lot, one right on top of the next all in a row. Because this is designed for groups of RVs to come together, there is one large picnic shelter, which can be rented for an additional fee. The shelter has picnic tables, and a single fireplace sits in the middle of the shelter and vents through the roof. It's a really neat idea, especially great when the weather is bad. It gives you the opportunity to still sit by a fire with your friends rather than having to hibernate inside your RV. It's also the only fire ring/fireplace in the group camp area. So if you want to appreciate a campfire while you camp in your RV at Vista Point, you're kind of forced to rent the shelter.

Jordan Lake is obviously the highlight of this and every campground within the recreation area. Vista Point has a boat ramp for motorized boats and also has a sailboat launch area. There's a sandy beach here, but no swimming is allowed. The nearest swimming area would be either Seaforth or Parker's Creek. You can try your hand at fishing, but be sure you have your state fishing license before casting your line. If you enjoy hiking, two loop trails wind through the Vista Point area. Reservations are required at both the RV and tent campsites.

92 Jordan Lake State Recreation Area: Parker's Creek Campground

Location: On the northwest side of Jordan Lake
Season: Each year Jordan Lake State Recreation Area keeps one campground open year-round, while the others are typically open Apr–Oct. Which campground they keep open changes annually, so if you plan on camping in the winter months, please check with the park office ahead of time to see which campground is open.
Sites: 250; also 6 group camping sites (reservations required) that can accommodate up to 30 people each
Maximum length: 116 feet
Facilities: Flush toilets, hot showers, electric, water, water spigots dispersed, fire rings, picnic tables, lantern holders, dump station; pet friendly
Fee per night: $$$
Management: North Carolina Department of Natural Resources
Contact: (919) 362-0586; www.ncparks.gov/Visit/parks/jord/main.php. For reservations call (877) 722-6762.
Finding the campground: From the junction of US 64 Business and US 501/US 15 in downtown Pittsboro, drive east on US 64 for 8 miles. Turn left onto Parkers Creek Recreation Road, and drive north approximately 0.3 mile to the campground entrance on your right.

From the junction of US 64 and NC 751 near Wilsonville, drive west on US 64 for 5.1 miles. Turn right onto Parkers Creek Recreation Road, and follow directions above.
GPS coordinates: N35 44.491' / W79 02.329'
Maps: *DeLorme: North Carolina Atlas & Gazetteer:* Page 39 E7
About the campground: Ospreys call out to one another on a regular basis as they circle overhead at Parker's Creek. Unfortunately, along with the ospreys you can also hear the traffic passing by on US 64. Four main loops compose this campground. Loop 1 has some wonderful private

campsites within view of Jordan Lake, but this loop is closer to the highway, so the sound of the traffic is a bit more apparent here than it is in Loop 2. I'm not saying the sound is overwhelming, simply that it's there and you do notice it. The deeper you go into the park, the farther you are from US 64, and the less apparent the sound of the traffic becomes. The last loop is dedicated to group camping, and the sites are for tent camping only. Each of the six group campsites can accommodate up to thirty people, and reservations are required.

Although Parker's Creek sits on the west side of Jordan Lake, Mother Nature puts on quite a show at sunset. The colors of the sky over the lake are absolutely stunning, so you may want to bring a camera along. A hiking trail connects the loops and traverses the Parker's Creek area. There's a boat ramp that is dedicated to campers only and a large swim beach that's open to the public. Fishing is permitted as long as you have your North Carolina state fishing license.

93 Jordan Lake State Recreation Area: New Hope Overlook Campground

Location: On the southeast side of Jordan Lake
Season: Each year Jordan Lake State Recreation Area keeps one campground open year-round, while the others are typically open Apr–Oct. Which campground they keep open changes annually, so if you plan on camping in the winter months, please check with the park office ahead of time to see which campground is open.
Sites: 24
Maximum length: n/a; tents only
Facilities: Vault toilets, water spigots dispersed, fire rings, picnic tables; pet friendly
Fee per night: $$
Management: North Carolina Department of Natural Resources
Contact: (919) 362-0586; www.ncparks.gov/Visit/parks/jord/main.php.
Finding the campground: From the junction of US 64 Business and US 501/US 15 in downtown Pittsboro, drive east on US 64 for 10.2 miles. Turn right onto Beaver Creek Road (SR 1008), and travel 3.1 miles. Turn right onto Pea Ridge Road (SR 1972) and continue 2.2 miles. Turn right onto W. H. Jones Road, and travel 0.4 mile to where the road ends at the entrance to the New Hope Overlook Recreation Area.

From the junction of US 64 and NC 751 near Wilsonville, drive west on US 64 for 2.8 miles. Turn left onto Beaver Creek Road (SR 1008), and follow directions above.

From US 1 near Moncure, drive north on Pea Ridge Road (SR 1972) for 2.8 miles. Turn left onto W. H. Jones Road, and travel 0.4 mile to where the road ends at the entrance to the New Hope Overlook Recreation Area.
GPS coordinates: N35 40.719' / W79 02.834'
Maps: *DeLorme: North Carolina Atlas & Gazetteer:* Page 39 E7
About the campground: The camping at New Hope Overlook is tent only and requires a short hike. A less than 0.25-mile walk leads you to the primitive camping in Area A on the east side of the park. Head in the other direction, and you soon come to Area B on the west side of the park. Area A puts you closer to the lakes edge, but you are still sheltered from the elements, with just enough trees between you and the water. Area B is unique for this area, because the sites run along the top of a small spur.

Unlike Parker's Creek, the only traffic you can hear at New Hope Overlook is the motor of the occasional boat as it passes by. Six boat ramps grace this portion of the recreation area, and since they are open to the public, they do see a bit of traffic. New Hope has just over 8 miles of hiking trails, so you may want to bring a daypack along as well. You can fish anywhere in the park, but make sure you have your state fishing license in hand prior to launching your lure. The nearest swim beach is just up the road at Ebenezer.

94   Jordan Lake State Recreation Area: Poplar Point Campground

Location: On the southeast side of Jordan Lake

Season: Each year Jordan Lake State Recreation Area keeps one campground open year-round, while the others are typically open Apr–Oct. Which campground they keep open changes annually, so if you plan on camping in the winter months, please check with the park office ahead of time to see which campground is open.

Sites: 579

Maximum length: 136 feet

Facilities: Flush toilets, hot showers, electric, water, water spigots dispersed, fire rings, picnic tables, lantern holders, dump station; pet friendly

Fee per night: $$$

Management: North Carolina Department of Natural Resources

Contact: (919) 362-0586; www.ncparks.gov/Visit/parks/jord/main.php. For reservations call (877) 722-6762.

Finding the campground: From the junction of US 64 Business and US 501/US 15 in downtown Pittsboro, drive east on US 64 for 10.2 miles. Turn right onto Beaver Creek Road (SR 1008), and continue 0.5 mile to the campground entrance on the right.

From the junction of US 64 and NC 751 near Wilsonville, drive west on US 64 for 2.8 miles. Turn left onto Beaver Creek Road (SR 1008), and follow directions above.

GPS coordinates: N35 43.742' / W79 00.253'

Maps: *DeLorme: North Carolina Atlas & Gazetteer:* Page 39 E8

About the campground: With nearly 600 campsites, Poplar Point is by far the largest campground in the Jordan Lake Recreation Area. You would think that squeezing this many campsites into one area would make them crowded, but that isn't the case. Several loops make up the campground, and the layout is quite nice. It's almost as though every loop is on a peninsula of its own, jutting out into the lake. The campsites are fairly well spaced, but much like Parker's Creek, the closer you are to US 64, the more you notice the sound of the traffic passing by.

There's a boat ramp and a swim beach that are only available for campers to use. Fishing is allowed anywhere on Jordan Lake, but you must obtain a North Carolina state fishing license prior to casting your line. A hiking trail leads from loop to loop, taking you from one end of the park to the other.

95 Jordan Lake State Recreation Area: Crosswinds Campground

Location: On the northeast side of Jordan Lake
Season: Each year Jordan Lake State Recreation Area keeps one campground open year-round, while the others are typically open Apr–Oct. Which campground they keep open changes annually, so if you plan on camping in the winter months, please check with the park office ahead of time to see which campground is open.
Sites: 182
Maximum length: 146 feet
Facilities: Flush toilets, hot showers, electric, water, water spigots dispersed, fire rings, picnic tables, lantern holders, dump station; pet friendly
Fee per night: $$$
Management: North Carolina Department of Natural Resources
Contact: (919) 362-0586; www.ncparks.gov/Visit/parks/jord/main.php. For reservations call (877) 722-6762 or visit www.reserveamerica.com.
Finding the campground: From the junction of US 64 Business and US 501/US 15 in downtown Pittsboro, drive east on US 64 for 10.2 miles. Turn left onto Farrington Road (SR 1008), and travel 0.3 mile to the campground entrance on the right.

From the junction of US 64 and NC 751 near Wilsonville, drive west on US 64 for 2.8 miles. Turn right onto Farrington Road (SR 1008), and travel 0.3 mile to the campground entrance on the right.
GPS coordinates: N35 44.533' / W79 00.108'
Maps: *DeLorme: North Carolina Atlas & Gazetteer:* Page 39 E8
About the campground: Crosswinds is on the smaller side compared with the other RV campgrounds in the Jordan Lake Recreation Area. But unlike the others, this one sits in a cove in a large finger of Jordan Lake rather than on a peninsula. As you explore the campground, you see that the layout is much the same as the rest. Each loop has a handful or two of waterfront campsites; the rest are set inland.

The sites are fairly well spaced and wooded, and a hiking trail leads from one end of the campground to the other. The boat ramp and swim beach are dedicated to campers only. Keeping the facilities "in house" like this cuts back on the traffic passing through, and makes for a much more pleasant camping experience. If you plan on fishing, whether from the lakeshore or from your boat, be sure to obtain a North Carolina state fishing license before you even bait your line.

96 William B. Umstead State Park

Location: 8801 Glenwood Ave., Raleigh; 11 miles west of Raleigh
Season: Mar 15–Dec 15; group camp with cabins open Apr–Oct; primitive group camp areas open year-round; closed Christmas Day
Sites: 28; 2 group camping areas with cabins can accommodate up to 120 people each; 2 primitive group camping areas can accommodate up to 25 people each (reservations required for group camping)
Maximum length: 30 feet

Facilities: Flush toilets, hot showers, water spigots dispersed, fire rings, picnic tables, lantern holders; pet friendly
Fee per night: $$$
Management: North Carolina Department of Natural Resources
Contact: (919) 571-4170; www.ncparks.gov/Visit/parks/wium/main.php. For reservations (required for all group camping) call (877) 722-6762 or visit www.reserveamerica.com.
Finding the campground: Take exit 7 (US 70) off I-440 in Raleigh. Drive north on US 70 for approximately 5.8 miles to the entrance to the park entrance on the left.

Take exit 4 (US 70) off I-540 in Raleigh. Drive south on US 70 for 1.4 miles to the park entrance on the right.
GPS coordinates: N35 53.406' / W78 45.048'
Maps: *DeLorme: North Carolina Atlas & Gazetteer: Page 40 C2*
About the campground: With easy access to both Raleigh and Durham, William B. Umstead Park is a diamond in the rough. This surprisingly

Daffodils bloom in spring throughout the Piedmont.

nice patch of forest encompasses more than 5,500 acres and is made up of wooded rolling hills. You can stroll through the forest on one of the many hiking trails or hop on your horse or mountain bike and hit the trail a bit harder. There are three man-made lakes for fishing. Or if you prefer, you can rent a canoe or bring your own and enjoy a nice easy paddle. Several creeks wind through the park, and swimming is allowed at Sycamore Lake, but only for registered group campers.

The campground at Umstead Park offers shady wooded sites and makes a nice retreat from the busy city around it. But don't be surprised if you hear an occasional siren in the distance. There are two types of group camping also available: primitive group camping, which is for tent camping only, and group camping, which has cabins to bunk in. Whichever you choose, you must be affiliated with a nonprofit organization to use these facilities. Advance reservations are required for all group camping.

Falls Lake State Recreation Area: Sites 97–100

Falls Lake Recreation Area lies just outside Durham and minutes north of Raleigh. With such easy access from the state's capital, you are likely to notice the many weekend warriors that frequent Falls Lake, especially during the warmer months of spring and summer. The recreation area is divided into seven separate smaller areas, each offering its own variety of outdoor opportunities. If you prefer to stay on dry land, hop on your mountain bike and tour the rolling hills at Beaverdam. Or put one foot in front of the other on any of the many hiking trails located throughout the area.

The Falls Lake Trail skirts the southern edge of the lake for nearly 30 miles and is part of one of the state's most famous hiking trails: the Mountains-to-Sea Trail (MST). The MST begins in Tennessee at Clingmans Dome and traverses the entire state of North Carolina, ending alongside the Atlantic Ocean at Jockey's Ridge on the Outer Banks.

While the biking and hiking at Falls Lake are worth a visit, the lake itself is why most people leave the hustle and bustle of the city and make their way here. The recreation area offers ample opportunity for you to get out and explore this 12,000-acre lake firsthand. You can bring your own boat and put in at one of many boat ramps throughout the park or head to the Rollingview Marina and rent one for the day. Several swim beaches are open to the public, while others are reserved for campers only. Fishing is allowed just about anywhere in the recreation area as long as you have a North Carolina state fishing license. You can obtain your license ahead of time at www.ncwildlife.org. If you enjoy birding, bring your binoculars; a large variety of bird species can be seen by water or by land. For more information, visit Fall Lake's website at www.ncparks.gov/Visit/parks/fala/main.php. Maps are available online or at the visitor center, located off NC 50 north of NC 98 and south of the lake.

GPS coordinates for the visitor center: N36 01.053' / W78 41.139'

97 Falls Lake State Recreation Area: Rollingview Campground

Location: On the south side of Falls Lake, west of NC 50 and north of NC 98
Season: Portion of the campground open year-round; entire campground open Mar 15–Oct 31; closed Christmas Day
Sites: 115; 4 group campsites (reservations required) also available that can accommodate up to 30 people each
Maximum length: 115 feet
Facilities: Flush toilets, hot showers, electric, water spigots, fire rings, picnic tables, lantern holders, dump station; pet friendly
Fee per night: $$–$$$
Management: North Carolina Department of Natural Resources
Contact: (919) 676-1027; www.ncparks.gov/Visit/parks/fala/main.php. For reservations call (877) 722-6762 or visit www.reserveamerica.com.
Finding the campground: From the north take I-85 South to exit 191; drive east toward Creedmoor to NC 50. Turn right on NC 50, and drive south for 9.8 miles to NC 98. (*NOTE:* You will pass the park's visitor center on your left at 8.3 miles.) Turn right, and drive west on NC 98. for 5.5 miles. Turn right onto Baptist Road (SR 1807), and continue 4.3 miles to where it dead-ends at Rollingview.

From the junction of NC 98 and US 70 in Durham, drive east on NC 98 for approximately 4.7 miles. Turn left onto Baptist Road (SR 1807), and follow directions above.

From the junction of NC 98 and NC 50 near Raleigh, drive west on NC 98 for 5.5 miles. Turn right onto Baptist Road (SR 1807), and follow directions above.

GPS coordinates: N36 00.517' / W78 43.701'
Maps: *DeLorme: North Carolina Atlas & Gazetteer:* Page 40 B2
About the campground: Smack dab in the middle of Falls Lake you will find the Rollingview Campground. Although Rollingview sits on a peninsula and is practically surrounded by water, the layout of the campground only provides a few "waterfront" sites. I use the quotation marks because although you can see the lake from these sites, none actually butt up to the shoreline. They are, however, quite well spaced and offer lots of wooded privacy. The group camping area sits at the northern end of the peninsula and is isolated from the family campground. These sites are just a short walk from the lake, and two of the four group sites are wheelchair accessible.

Rollingview has lots of activities to keep you and the family on the go. There are picnic areas and playgrounds. Hiking trails run throughout the area, and the nearby Falls Lake Trail is also part of the famous Mountains-to-Sea Trail—a 1,000-mile-long trail that literally makes its way from the Great Smoky Mountains to the Atlantic Ocean. To enjoy the lake firsthand, a swim beach, a few fishing piers, and a boat ramp are conveniently located on the property.

98 Falls Lake State Recreation Area: Shinleaf Campground

Location: On the south side of Falls Lake, east of NC 50 and north of NC 98
Season: Mar 15–Oct 31; closed Christmas Day
Sites: 47 hike-in sites; 9 group campsites (reservations required) also available that can accommodate up to 35 people each
Maximum length: n/a; tents only
Facilities: Flush and vault toilets, hot showers, water spigots at bathhouse, fire rings, picnic tables, lantern holders, charcoal grills (at group campsites only); pet friendly
Fee per night: $$
Management: North Carolina Department of Natural Resources
Contact: (919) 676-1027; www.ncparks.gov/Visit/parks/fala/main.php. For reservations call (877) 722-6762 or visit www.reserveamerica.com.
Finding the campground: From the junction of NC 98 and NC 50 near Raleigh, drive east on NC 98 for 1.4 miles. Turn left onto New Light Road (SR 1907), and continue 0.6 mile to a right turn into the parking lot for the Shinleaf Area.

From the junction of NC 98 and US 1 in Wake Forest, drive west on NC 98 for approximately 6.9 miles. Turn right onto New Light Road (SR 1907), and follow directions above.
GPS coordinates: N35 59.640' / W78 39.450'
Maps: *DeLorme: North Carolina Atlas & Gazetteer:* Page 40 B3
About the campground: Shinleaf provides the only backpack camping in the Falls Lake Recreation Area. Depending on which campsite you choose, you can hike as little as a few hundred feet or as far as nearly 0.5 mile to get to your site. You must pack in all your supplies, including water. There is a wash sink at the trailhead, and there are water spigots at the main bathhouse, but there are no water spigots within the camping area. A wide gravel "road" leads to the campsites, so you could bring a wheelbarrow to cart your belongings if you were so inclined. But that kind of defeats the purpose of backpack camping.

Stunning sunsets greet you at Falls Lake.

The hiking trail continues beyond the campground all the way out to a horseshoe at the tip of the peninsula. Shinleaf also has a canoe/kayak launch, so if you prefer to see this part of Falls Lake by water, leave the wheelbarrow, and bring your canoe and paddle along instead. The group campsites are far more accessible, and you can drive right up to them. Reservations are required for the group camping.

99 Falls Lake State Recreation Area: Holly Point Campground

Location: On the east side of Falls Lake, north of NC 98
Season: Mar 15–Oct 31; closed Christmas Day
Sites: 153
Maximum length: 120 feet
Facilities: Flush toilets, hot showers, electric, water spigots, fire rings, picnic tables, lantern holders, dump station; pet friendly
Fee per night: $$–$$$
Management: North Carolina Department of Natural Resources
Contact: (919) 676-1027; www.ncparks.gov/Visit/parks/fala/main.php. For reservations call (877) 722-6762 or visit www.reserveamerica.com.

Finding the campground: From the junction of NC 98 and NC 50 near Raleigh, drive east on NC 98 for 1.4 miles. Turn left onto New Light Road (SR 1907), and travel 2 miles to the campground entrance on your right.

From the junction of NC 98 and US 1 in Wake Forest, drive west on NC 98 for approximately 6.9 miles. Turn right onto New Light Road (SR 1907), and follow directions above.

GPS coordinates: N36 00.571' / W78 39.395'

Maps: *DeLorme: North Carolina Atlas & Gazetteer:* Page 40 B3

About the campground: Holly Point Campground is located along a narrow twist on the east side of Falls Lake. This is the largest campground in the recreation area, but most of the sites sit inland rather than on the edge of the lake. There's a boat ramp and two swim beaches that are dedicated for campers only. A hiking trail makes its way from one end of Holly Point to the other, and the typical playground and picnic areas sit within view of the lake, at the south end of the campground.

100 Falls Lake State Recreation Area: B. W. Wells Group Camp

Location: 1630 Bent Rd. in Wake Forest; approximately 11 miles north of Raleigh, about 16 miles east of Durham, and about 7.5 miles northwest of Wake Forest

Season: Sept 1–June 1; closed Christmas Day

Sites: 11 group campsites (reservations required) that can accommodate up to 35 people each

Maximum length: n/a; tents only

Facilities: Flush toilets, hot showers, water spigots, fire rings, charcoal grills, picnic tables, lantern holders; pet friendly

Fee per night: $$$

Management: North Carolina Department of Natural Resources

Contact: (919) 676-1027; www.ncparks.gov/Visit/parks/fala/main.php. For reservations call (877) 722-6762 or visit www.reserveamerica.com.

Finding the campground: From the junction of NC 98 and NC 50 near Raleigh, drive east on NC 98 for 4.2 miles. Turn left onto Stony Hill Road (SR 1917), and travel 1 mile. Turn left onto Bud Morris Road (SR 1918) at the BW WELLS sign; go 0.25 mile. Turn left onto Bent Road (SR 1919), and continue 0.8 mile to the entrance to the group campground.

From the junction of NC 98 and US 1 in Wake Forest, drive west on NC 98 for approximately 4.1 miles. Turn right onto Stony Hill Road (SR 1917), and follow directions above.

GPS coordinates: N35 59.734' / W78 37.507'

Maps: *DeLorme: North Carolina Atlas & Gazetteer:* Page 40 B3

About the campground: The eleven group campsites at B. W. Wells are nestled in a forest of pine trees with the occasional hardwood mixed in. Some of these well-wooded sites require a short hike in; others are just off the side of the road. A quick jaunt up some steps, and you've arrived at your home sweet home in the forest. A community fire ring accompanies each site, creating a great atmosphere for telling ghost stories or for you and your group to simply sit back and enjoy the flicker of the flames. Two loop trails meander through the forest, and a steep boat ramp is available for campers only. Reservations are required.

Benches surround a community fire ring at B. W. Wells Group Camp.

101 Little River Regional Park & Natural Area Group Camp

Location: 301 Little River Park Way, Rougemont; about 10 miles north of Durham and about 17 miles south of Roxboro
Season: Feb–Nov
Sites: Large group camping area (reservations required) for up to 30 people; nonprofit organizations only
Maximum length: n/a; tents only
Facilities: Flush toilets, water spigots, *no* showers; pet friendly
Fee per night: $$$
Management: Orange County Parks and Recreation
Contact: (919) 732-5505; www.co.orange.nc.us/deapr/parks/little_river_regional_park.asp
Finding the campground: From the junction of NC 157 and NC 57 in Caldwell, drive south on NC 157 for 3.7 miles. Turn left onto Little River Park Way at the entrance to the park.
    From I-85 in Durham, take exit 175 to NC 157 (Guess Road). Travel north for approximately 10.6 miles to a right onto Little River Park Way at the entrance to the park.
GPS coordinates: N36 09.724' / W78 58.498'
Maps: *DeLorme: North Carolina Atlas & Gazetteer:* Page 19 F8

About the campground: Deep within horse country, you will pass horse pasture after horse pasture on your way to Little River Park. This small county park offers group camping only, and you must be affiliated with a nonprofit organization to use the camping facility. The group camp area is for tent camping only and is really just a small open field, hidden away behind the bathhouse. There are flush toilets and a water spigot, but there are no fire pits or picnic tables in the camping area.

The park itself has a large picnic shelter and charcoal grills, which you will have access to when you camp here. There's a lovely flower garden, a playground, and another large open field big enough to get a game of kickball or Wiffle ball going. If you feel like exploring, the park has a paved walking path, hiking trails, and biking trails. Advance reservations are required.

102 Spruce Pine Lodge and Group Camp

Location: 2235 Bahama Rd., Bahama; about 5 miles north of Durham
Season: Year-round
Sites: 7 sites for group camping only; nonprofit organizations only
Maximum length: n/a; tents only
Facilities: Vault toilets, a single water spigot of nonpotable water, fire rings, charcoal grills, picnic tables, trash cans; pet friendly
Fee per night: $$$
Management: City of Durham Parks and Recreation
Contact: (919) 560-4358; http://durhamnc.gov/ich/op/prd/Pages/Special-Facilities.aspx
Finding the campground: From US 501 in Rougemont, drive south on US 501 for approximately 2.2 miles. Turn left onto Quail Roost Road (SR 1615), and travel 2.4 miles. Turn left onto Bahama Road (SR 1616), and continue 0.85 mile. Turn left at the sign for Spruce Pine Lodge, and follow the road to the lodge on your right. The road continues past the lodge to where it dead-ends at the group campground.

Take exit 176 off I-85 in Durham, and drive north on US 501 (North Roxboro Street) for 9.2 miles. Turn right onto Bahama Road (SR 1616), and travel 2.75 miles. Turn left at the sign for Spruce Pine Lodge, and follow the road to the lodge on your right. The road continues past the lodge to where it dead-ends at the group campground.

GPS coordinates: N36 10.563' / W78 52.019'
Maps: *DeLorme: North Carolina Atlas & Gazetteer:* Page 20 F1
About the campground: Spruce Pine Group Camp is a well-kept secret near the city of Durham. If you have a nonprofit organization, this is a great place to take your group, get outdoors, and introduce them to camping. There's a large community fire ring, plus individual fire rings at each site. A vault toilet and a single water spigot are shared by all. The campground has seven individual campsites surrounded by forest, yet it's just minutes from civilization.

You can hike the Waterfall Nature Trail, which leads you steeply down, up, and down again to a small but lovely waterfall. The historical Spruce Pine Lodge is also on the property and is available to rent for special occasions. The lodge sits atop a hill overlooking Lake Michie. You can fish from the banks of the lake, or bring a canoe or kayak and float about the cool waters of the Piedmont.

Roxboro

	Total Sites	Hookup Sites	Max. RV Length	Hookups	Toilets	Showers	Drinking Water	Dump Station	Recreation	Fee	Reservations
103 Mayo Park	30	14	None	E, W	F	Y	Y	Y	H, F, B, L, P, *	$$–$$$	Y

* See campground entry for specific information.

103 Mayo Park Campground

Location: 1013 Neal's Store Rd., Roxboro; about 9 miles northeast of Roxboro
Season: Year-round
Sites: 30; cabin rentals also available
Maximum length: None
Facilities: Flush toilets, hot showers, water spigots dispersed, electric, fire rings, picnic tables, lantern holders, dump station; pet friendly
Fee per night: $$–$$$
Management: Person County Parks and Recreation
Contact: (336) 597-7806 or (336) 597-1755; www.personcounty.net/index.aspx?page=277
Finding the campground: From the junction of NC 49 and US 501 in Roxboro, drive north on NC 49 for approximately 8.8 miles. Turn left onto Neal's Store Road (SR 1515), and travel 0.6 mile to Mayo Park on your left.

From the junction of NC 49 and NC 96 S in Virgilina, Virginia, drive south on NC 49 for 6.7 miles. Turn right onto Neal's Store Road (SR 1515), and follow directions above.
GPS coordinates: N36 28.899' / W78 52.067'
Maps: *DeLorme: North Carolina Atlas & Gazetteer:* Page 20 B1
About the campground: Gravel roads "pave" the way through this surprisingly pleasant county park. With wooded, rolling hill terrain and lakeside campsites, this is a real treat. A hiking trail passes just below the campsites, which are lined up right next to one another, so they lack privacy. But the fabulous view of the lake below balances it out. The bathrooms were not the cleanest when I visited, so you may want to bring "shower shoes" with you. If you don't feel like roughing it, rental cabins sit high above, overlooking the Mayo Reservoir.

Despite the lack of privacy in the campground, the park itself packs a punch. They have playgrounds, picnic shelters, an amphitheater, horseshoe pits, and an open field for tossing a Frisbee or a ball. There's nearly 6 miles of hiking trails, and the park also offers canoe and kayak rentals. There's a large boat ramp just down the road, so if you have a motorized boat, you can put in and really explore the Mayo Creek and Reservoir to the fullest.

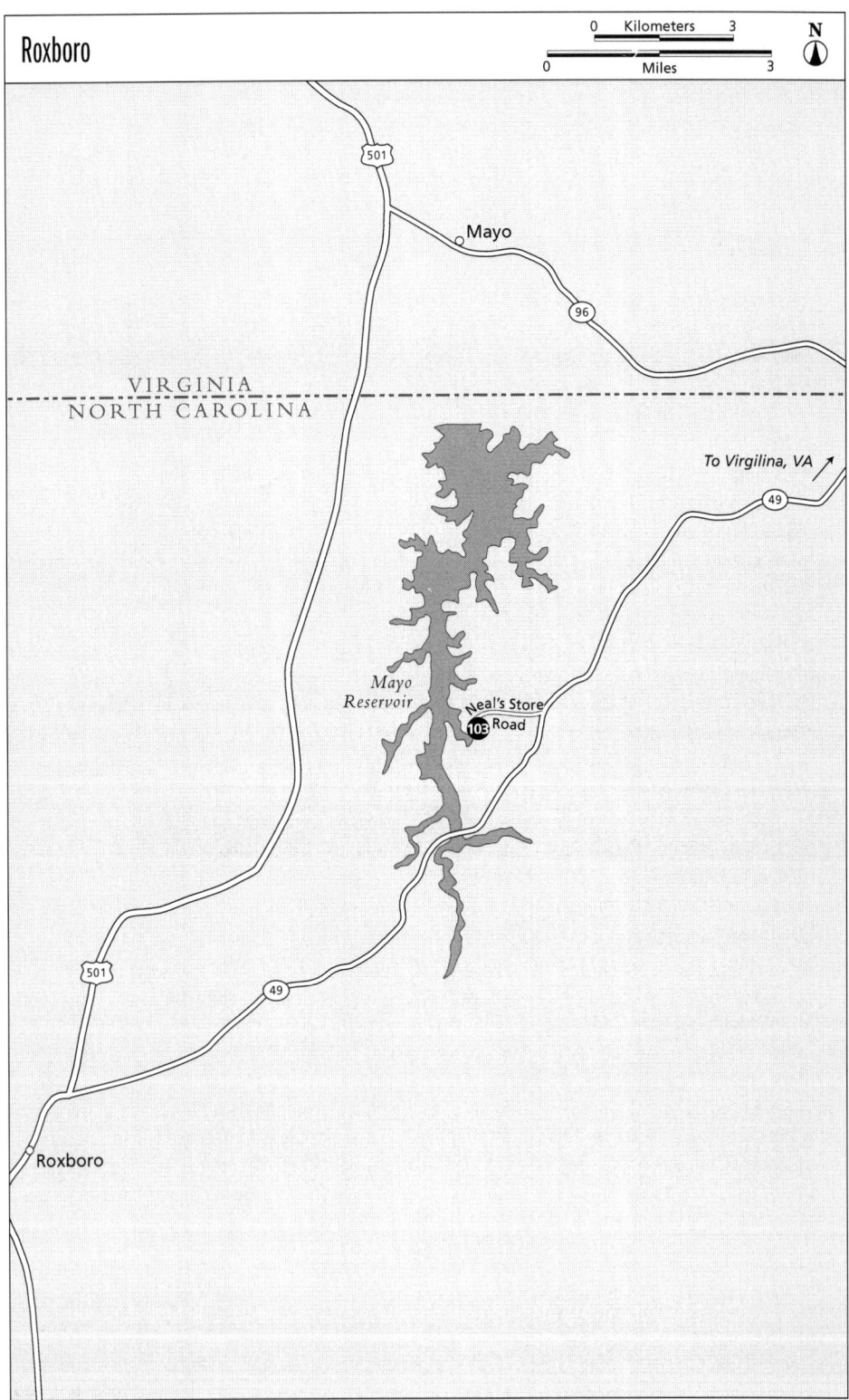

0   Kilometers   3

0   Miles   3

N

Mayo

VIRGINIA
NORTH CAROLINA

To Virgilina, VA

Mayo
Reservoir

Neal's Store
Road

Roxboro

Henderson

	Total Sites	Hookup Sites	Max. RV Length	Hookups	Toilets	Showers	Drinking Water	Dump Station	Recreation	Fee	Reservations
104 Kerr Lake Recreation Area: Hibernia	147	47	123'*	E	F	Y	Y	Y	H, S, F, B, L, P	$$-$$$	Y
104 Kerr Lake Recreation Area: Hibernia (Group)	1	0	n/a	N	F	Y	Y	Y*	H, S, F, B, L, P	$$$	Y
105 Kerr Lake Recreation Area: Henderson Point	74	45	123'*	E	F	Y	Y	Y	S, F, B, L, P	$$-$$$	Y
105 Kerr Lake Recreation Area: Henderson Point (Group)	1	0	n/a	N	F	Y	Y	Y*	S, F, B, L, P	$$$	Y
106 Kerr Lake Recreation Area: Nutbush	106	65	90'*	E	F	Y	Y	Y	F, B, L, P	$$-$$$	Y
107 Kerr Lake Recreation Area: Satterwhite (Group)	1	0	n/a	N	F	Y	Y	Y*	S, F, B, L, P	$$$	Y
108 Kerr Lake Recreation Area: J. C. Cooper	112	62	118'*	E	F	Y	Y	Y	H, S, F, B, L, P	$$-$$$	Y
109 Kerr Lake Recreation Area: Bullocksville	63	30	85'*	E, W	F	Y	Y	Y	H, F, B, L, P	$$-$$$	Y
110 Kerr Lake Recreation Area: County Line	71	36	115'*	E	F	Y	Y	Y	F, B, L, P	$$-$$$	Y
111 Kerr Lake Recreation Area: Kimball Point	79	49	90'*	E	F	Y	Y	Y	S, F, B, L, P	$$-$$$	Y

* See campground entry for specific information.

Kerr Lake State Recreation Area: Sites 104–111

With eight separate areas to camp along the shores of Kerr Lake, you are sure to find what you're looking for. Fishing, swimming, sailing, and boating are naturally highlights, but wildlife viewing and hiking are just as pleasurable throughout this wonderful recreation area. Stop at the ranger station off Satterwhite Point Road on the east side of the lake to obtain a map and get additional information specific to your needs. For more information visit their website at www.ncparks.gov/Visit/parks/kela/main.php. Maps are available online or at the visitor center, located off Satterwhite Point Road (exit 217 off I-85).

GPS coordinates for the visitor center: N36 26.425' / W78 22.039'

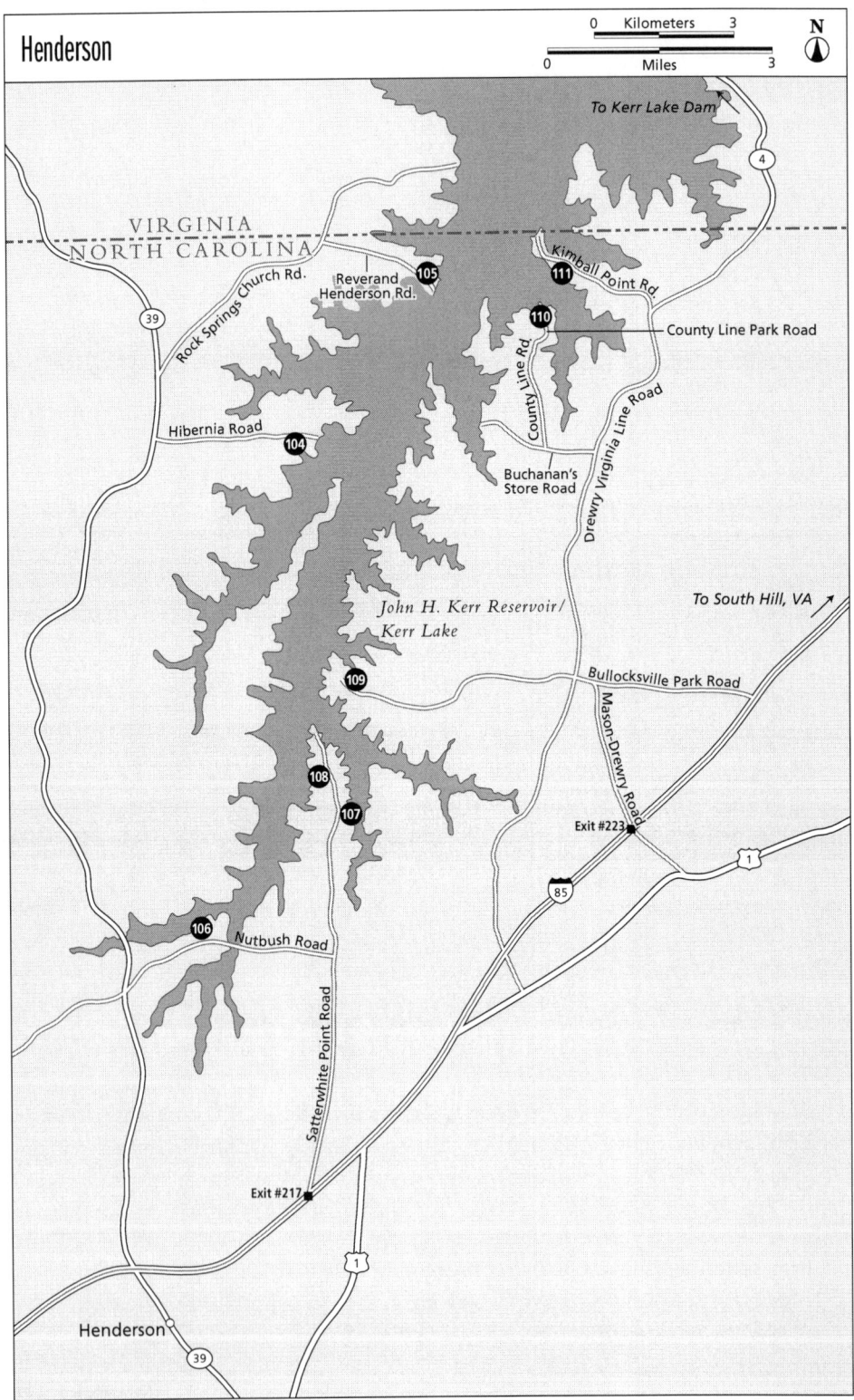

Henderson

104 Kerr Lake State Recreation Area: Hibernia Campground

Location: On the west side of Kerr Lake, off NC 39
Season: Apr–end of Oct
Sites: 147; also a single group campsite (reservations required) available that can accommodate up to 50 people
Maximum length: 123 feet
Facilities: Flush toilets, hot showers, electric, water spigots dispersed, fire rings, picnic tables, lantern holders, trash cans, dump station; pet friendly
Fee per night: $$–$$$
Management: North Carolina Department of Natural Resources
Contact: (252) 438-7791; www.ncparks.gov/Visit/parks/kela/main.php. For reservations call (877) 722-6762 or visit www.reserveamerica.com.
Finding the campground: From I-85 in Henderson, take exit 214 and drive north on NC 39 for 12.7 miles. Turn right onto Hibernia Road (SR 1347), and travel 1.9 miles to where the road dead-ends at the campground.

From the junction of NC 39 and the North Carolina–Virginia state line, drive south on NC 39 for approximately 3.4 miles. Turn left onto Hibernia Road (SR 1347), and follow directions above.
GPS coordinates: N36 30.294' / W78 22.569'
Maps: *DeLorme: North Carolina Atlas & Gazetteer:* Page 21 B6
About the campground: Hibernia juts well out into Kerr Lake, giving campers the perfect opportunity to view the lake from the comfort of their camp chair. With well-placed campsites and riprap lining the lakeshore, site after site is blessed with stunning waterfront views. Several picnic areas

A duck gracefully swims across Kerr Lake.

also sit near the edge of the lake, and a short hiking trail explores the forested inland before leading you to an old-time cemetery. If you have a boat, bring it along and take advantage of the twenty-four-hour boat ramp. There is more than ample parking for tons of cars with their boat trailers in tow. The full-service Steele Creek Marina, just south of Hibernia, has fuel pumps and mooring slips that are open year-round.

Although there's no swim "beach" per se, swimming is allowed at Hibernia, as is fishing. Prior to breaking out your rod and reel though, make sure you have a North Carolina state fishing license. The single group campsite is set well off the beaten path. Reservations are required for group camping.

105 Kerr Lake State Recreation Area: Henderson Point Campground

Location: On the west side of Kerr Lake, off NC 39
Season: Apr–Sept
Sites: 74; also 1 group campsite (reservations required) available that can accommodate up to 35 people
Maximum length: 123 feet
Facilities: Flush toilets, hot showers, water spigots dispersed, electric, fire rings, picnic tables, lantern holders, dump station; pet friendly
Fee per night: $$–$$$
Management: North Carolina Department of Natural Resources
Contact: (252) 438-7791; www.ncparks.gov/Visit/parks/kela/main.php. For reservations call (877) 722-6762 or visit www.reserveamerica.com.
Finding the campground: From I-85 in Henderson, take exit 214 and drive north on NC 39 for 13.5 miles. Turn right onto Rock Springs Church Road (SR 1356), and travel 2.9 miles. Turn right onto Reverend Henderson Road (SR 1359), and continue 1.4 miles to where the road dead-ends at the campground.

From the junction of NC 39 and the North Carolina–Virginia state line, drive south on NC 39 for approximately 2.6 miles. Turn left onto Rock Springs Church Road (SR 1356), and follow directions above.
GPS coordinates: N36 32.100' / W78 20.766'
Maps: *DeLorme: North Carolina Atlas & Gazetteer:* Page 21 A6
About the campground: Just south of the North Carolina–Virginia border lies Henderson Point, another well-designed campground within the Kerr Lake Recreation Area. Once again they've taken advantage of the lay of the land and given us several waterfront campsites. Along with lakeside camping, Henderson Point offers a swim beach, a playground, several picnic shelters, a fishing pier, and some very busy boat ramps. The open waters around Henderson Point make this a popular destination for the sailing community and anglers alike. The group campsite at Henderson Point is not as isolated as some of the others, but it's nice that it's just a short walk to the water. Reservations are required for group camping.

Deer thrive in Kerr Lake State Recreation Area.

106 Kerr Lake State Recreation Area: Nutbush Bridge Campground

Location: At the southern end of Kerr Lake, off Nutbush Road
Season: Year-round
Sites: 106
Maximum length: 90 feet
Facilities: Flush toilets, hot showers, electric, water spigots dispersed, fire rings, picnic tables, lantern holders, trash cans, dump station; pet friendly
Fee per night: $$–$$$
Management: North Carolina Department of Natural Resources
Contact: (252) 438-7791; www.ncparks.gov/Visit/parks/kela/main.php. For reservations call (877) 722-6762 or visit www.reserveamerica.com.
Finding the campground: From the north take I-85 south to exit 217, and drive north on Satterwhite Point Road (SR 1319) for 3 miles. Turn left onto Nutbush Road, and travel 1.7 miles to the entrance to the campground on your right and left on South and North Jack Wade Farm Road (SR 308).

From the south take I-85 north to exit 214, and drive north on NC 39 for approximately 4.3 miles. Turn right onto Nutbush Road, and travel 1.3 miles to the entrance to the campground on your right and left on South and North Jack Wade Farm Road (SR 308).

GPS coordinates: N36 24.663' / W78 23.944'
Maps: *DeLorme: North Carolina Atlas & Gazetteer:* Page 21 C5
About the campground: Although you can see the lake from many of the campsites at Nutbush Bridge, they really dropped the ball on privacy here. You get stupendous views of the sunset, but you also see everything that several of your neighbors are doing—and they you. If you're in an RV, this may not bother you so much, but if you're tent camping, head up the road to J. C. Cooper instead.

Amenities include a playground, a waterfront picnic shelter, and a few boat ramps that are open twenty-four hours. Unless you take a dip from your boat, you'll need to head over to Satterwhite Point for the nearest swim beach.

107 Kerr Lake State Recreation Area: Satterwhite Point Group Camp

Location: On the east side of Kerr Lake, off Satterwhite Point Road
Season: Apr–Oct
Sites: 1 group campsite that can accommodate up to 100 people (reservations required)
Maximum length: n/a; tents only
Facilities: Flush toilets, hot showers, water spigots dispersed, fire rings, picnic tables; pet friendly
Fee per night: $$$
Management: North Carolina Department of Natural Resources
Contact: (252) 438-7791; www.ncparks.gov/Visit/parks/kela/main.php. For reservations call (877) 722-6762 or visit www.reserveamerica.com.
Finding the campground: From the south, take I-85 north to exit 217, and drive north on Satterwhite Point Road (SR 1319) for 5 miles. Turn right into the campground.

From the north, take I-85 south to exit 220, and drive northwest on Flemingtown Road (SR 1368) for 1.8 miles. Turn left onto Anderson Creek Road (SR 1374), and travel 1.3 miles. Turn right onto Satterwhite Point Road (SR 1319), and continue 2 miles to a right turn into the campground.
GPS coordinates: N36 26.049' / W78 21.980'
Maps: *DeLorme: North Carolina Atlas & Gazetteer:* Page 21 C6
About the campground: Deer wander through the Satterwhite Point Group Camp on a nightly basis—when it's unoccupied, that is. If you can get your group to stay fairly quiet at dawn or dusk, you may spy a few deer yourselves. As far as location goes, Satterwhite has a great spot. There's an open field at the entrance, which is a great place to kick or toss a ball around or even get an organized game going. The campground is nestled alongside a cove in the lake. The contrast between the green water and the red clay of the shoreline is quite picturesque. There are plenty of flat spots to pitch a tent within easy view of the water, and primitive fire rings are located here and there right along the lake's edge.

You can swim, fish, or launch a canoe right from your campsite. Or if you have a motorized boat, head up the road about 0.5 mile and you'll find a paved boat ramp as well. The Satterwhite Point day-use area is also just 0.5 mile up the road, and there's a large swim beach, field upon field of open area, more waterfront picnic areas, a playground, and a nature trail. This is a wonderful place to simply sit and watch the sunset. Reservations are required.

108 Kerr Lake State Recreation Area: J. C. Cooper Campground

Location: On the east side of the Kerr Lake, off Satterwhite Point Road
Season: Year-round
Sites: 112
Maximum length: 118 feet
Facilities: Flush toilets, hot showers, electric, water spigots dispersed, fire rings, picnic tables, lantern holders, dump station; pet friendly
Fee per night: $$–$$$
Management: North Carolina Department of Natural Resources
Contact: (252) 438-7791; www.ncparks.gov/Visit/parks/kela/main.php. For reservations call (877) 722-6762 or visit www.reserveamerica.com.
Finding the campground: From the south take I-85 north to exit 217, and drive north on Satterwhite Point Road (SR 1319) for 5.5 miles. Turn left onto Shoreline Drive, and travel 0.1 mile. Turn left onto J. C. Cooper Lane, and travel 0.4 mile to the first campground loop on your right. Continue another 0.4 mile to the next campground loop.

From the north take I-85 south to exit 220, and drive northwest on Flemingtown Road (SR 1368) for 1.8 miles. Turn left onto Anderson Creek Road (SR 1374), and travel 1.3 miles. Turn right onto Satterwhite Point Road (SR 1319), and continue for 2.5 miles. Turn left onto Shoreline Drive, and follow directions above.
GPS coordinates: N36 26.485' / W78 22.119'
Maps: *DeLorme: North Carolina Atlas & Gazetteer:* Page 21 B6
About the campground: Location, location, location. This is paradise. Just about every site in the J. C. Cooper Campground has a waterfront view. As the sun sets at Satterwhite Point, the deer come out in droves, and a variety of colors bounce off the calm reflection on the lake. There are picnic areas tucked away in little coves along the lake's edge. A playground for the little ones and a boat launch for the adults are designated for campers only.

The campground sits just south of the Satterwhite Point day-use area, which gives you easy access to more playgrounds, open fields, an enormous swim beach, picnic shelters, and hiking trails. Without a doubt, J. C. Cooper is my favorite place to stay whenever I visit the Kerr Lake Recreation Area.

109 Kerr Lake State Recreation Area: Bullocksville Campground

Location: On the east side of Kerr Lake, off Bullocksville Park Road (SR 1366)
Season: Apr–Sept
Sites: 63
Maximum length: 85 feet
Facilities: Flush toilets, hot showers, electric, water spigots dispersed, fire rings, picnic tables, lantern holders, dump station; pet friendly

Fee per night: $$–$$$
Management: North Carolina Department of Natural Resources
Contact: (252) 438-7791; www.ncparks.gov/Visit/parks/kela/main.php. For reservations call (877) 722-6762 or visit www.reserveamerica.com.
Finding the campground: Take exit 233 off I-85, and drive north on Mason-Drewry Road (SR 1237) for 2.2 miles to the Drewry Crossroads. Go straight through the crossroads onto Bullocksville Park Road (SR 1366), and travel 3.1 miles to where the road dead-ends at the campground.

From the junction of Drewry Virginia Line Road and the North Carolina–Virginia state line, drive south on Drewry Virginia Line Road for 6.9 miles. Turn right onto Bullocksville Park Road (SR 1366), and follow directions above.
GPS coordinates: N36 27.471' / W78 21.794'
Maps: *DeLorme: North Carolina Atlas & Gazetteer:* Page 21 B6
About the campground: Bullocksville Campground is located halfway up the eastern coast of Kerr Lake. Like many of the campgrounds in this recreation area, Bullocksville has picnic shelters and a playground, and several of the campsites offer waterfront views. A single paved boat ramp gives you direct access to the lake, and the Satterwhite Point Marina is very close via boat. There are two short hiking trails, one of which leads to a lovely little fishing pier. But what really stands out at Bullocksville is the large ball field you pass on your way into the campground. It's a great place to get a game of kickball or Wiffle ball together and is even big enough for the real thing. That's right, you could easily play a game of baseball on this ball field.

110 Kerr Lake State Recreation Area: County Line Campground

Location: On the east side of Kerr Lake, off County Line Park Road (SR 1242)
Season: Apr–Sept
Sites: 71
Maximum length: 115 feet
Facilities: Flush toilets, hot showers, electric, water spigots dispersed, fire rings, picnic tables, dump station; pet friendly
Fee per night: $$–$$$
Management: North Carolina Department of Natural Resources
Contact: (252) 438-7791; www.ncparks.gov/Visit/parks/kela/main.php. For reservations call (877) 722-6762 or visit www.reserveamerica.com.
Finding the campground: Take exit 223 off I-85, and drive north on Mason-Drewry Road (SR 1237) for 2.2 miles to the Drewry Crossroads. Turn right at the crossroads onto Drewry Virginia Line Road, and travel 3 miles. Turn left onto Buchanan's Store Road (SR 1202) at the sign for County Line Park, and travel 0.6 mile. Turn right onto County Line Road (SR 1361), and travel 1.1 miles to a stop sign. Turn right at the stop sign onto County Line Park Road (SR 1242), and follow it for 0.4 mile to where the road dead-ends at the campground entrance.

From the junction of Drewry Virginia Line Road and the North Carolina–Virginia state line, drive south on Drewry Virginia Line Road for 3.9 miles. Turn right onto Buchanan's Store Road (SR 1202), and follow directions above.

GPS coordinates: N36 31.463' / W78 18.984'

Maps: *DeLorme: North Carolina Atlas & Gazetteer:* Page 21 B6

About the campground: Once again Kerr Lake has dressed to impress! They've really outdone themselves with County Line. The campsites give you perfect lakeside views, as well as privacy. This combination is something you rarely find in a campground. There are wooded picnic areas right next to the shore, with charcoal grills placed in between the pines. A playground for the young ones sits in the middle of the campground, and a very busy boat ramp is open twenty-four hours a day. The open waters surrounding County Line makes this a popular sailing destination as well. The fact that you get the water and complete privacy makes County Line one of my favorite campgrounds in the region.

111 Kerr Lake State Recreation Area: Kimball Point Campground

Location: On the east side of Kerr Lake, just south of the North Carolina–Virginia state line

Season: Apr–Oct

Sites: 79

Maximum length: 90 feet

Facilities: Flush toilets, hot showers, water spigots dispersed, electric, fire rings, picnic tables, dump station; pet friendly

Fee per night: $$–$$$

Management: North Carolina Department of Natural Resources

Contact: (252) 438-7791; www.ncparks.gov/Visit/parks/kela/main.php. For reservations call (877) 722-6762 or visit www.reserveamerica.com.

Finding the campground: Take exit 223 off I-85, and drive north on Mason-Drewry Road (SR 1237) for 2.2 miles to the Drewry Crossroads. Turn right at the crossroads onto Drewry Virginia Line Road and travel for 5.1 miles. Turn left onto Kimball Point Road (SR 1204), and travel 1.3 miles to where the road dead-ends at the entrance to the campground.

From the junction of Drewry Virginia Line Road and the North Carolina–Virginia state line, drive south on Drewry Virginia Line Road for 1.8 miles. Turn right onto Kimball Point Road (SR 1204), and follow directions above.

GPS coordinates: N36 32.191' / W78 18.604'

Maps: *DeLorme: North Carolina Atlas & Gazetteer:* Page 21 A6

About the campground: Less than 2 miles south of the North Carolina–Virginia state line, you will find Kimball Point Campground. Kimball Point juts out into Kerr Lake on a narrow peninsula, and the campground takes full advantage of its aquatic surroundings. Once again, many of the campsites offer waterfront views. As with the design of each campground in the recreation area, there is a playground in the middle and picnic areas and shelters near the water's edge. Although there is not a swim "beach" per se, swimming is permitted at Kimball Point. A single boat ramp graces the property, and the open waters near Kimball Point are popular with the sailing community.

Roanoke Rapids

	Total Sites	Hookup Sites	Max. RV Length	Hookups	Toilets	Showers	Drinking Water	Dump Station	Recreation	Fee	Reservations
112 Medoc Mountain State Park	34	12	50'	E	F	Y	Y	Y	H, R, F, B*, L*, P	$$$	Y
112 Medoc Mountain State Park (Group)	4	0	n/a	N	F	Y	Y	Y*	H, R, F, B*, L*, P	$$$	Y

* See campground entry for specific information.

112   Medoc Mountain State Park

Location: 1541 Medoc State Park Rd,, Hollister; about 21 miles southwest of Roanoke Rapids and about 23 miles north of Rocky Mount
Season: Year-round; closed Christmas Day; group camping closed Dec 1–Mar 15
Sites: 34; also 4 group campsites available that can accommodate up to 35 people each
Maximum length: 50 feet
Facilities: Flush toilets, hot showers, water spigots dispersed, electric, fire rings, picnic tables, lantern holders, trash cans, dump station; pet friendly
Fee per night: $$$
Management: North Carolina Department of Natural Resources
Contact: (252) 586-6588; www.ncparks.gov/Visit/parks/memo/main.php. For reservations call (877) 722-6762 or visit www.reserveamerica.com.
Finding the campground: From the junction of NC 561 and NC 4 near Hollister, drive east on NC 561/NC 4 for 0.8 mile. Turn right onto Medoc State Park Road (SR 1322) at the sign for MEDOC MOUNTAIN STATE PARK, and travel 1.9 miles. Turn left onto Main Park Road (SR 1347), and travel 0.2 mile. Turn right onto Camping Area Road, and continue less than 0.1 mile to a fork. The right fork leads to the Family Campground; the left fork leads to the Group Campground.
    Take exit 160 off I-95, and travel west on NC 561 for 10 miles. Turn left onto Medoc State Park Road (SR 1322), and follow directions above.
    From the junction of NC 561 and NC 48 in Brinkleyville, drive west on NC 561/NC 4 for 2.3 miles. Turn left onto Medoc State Park Road (SR 1322), and follow directions above.
GPS coordinates: Family campground: N36 14.803' / W77 53.548'; group campground: N36 14.805' / W77 53.640'
Maps: *DeLorme: North Carolina Atlas & Gazetteer:* Page 22 D2–E2
About the campground: The campground at Medoc Mountain has large campsites set among easy rolling-hill terrain. The sites are pretty wide open to one another, but you will get a little more privacy in spring and summer than you will in wintertime.

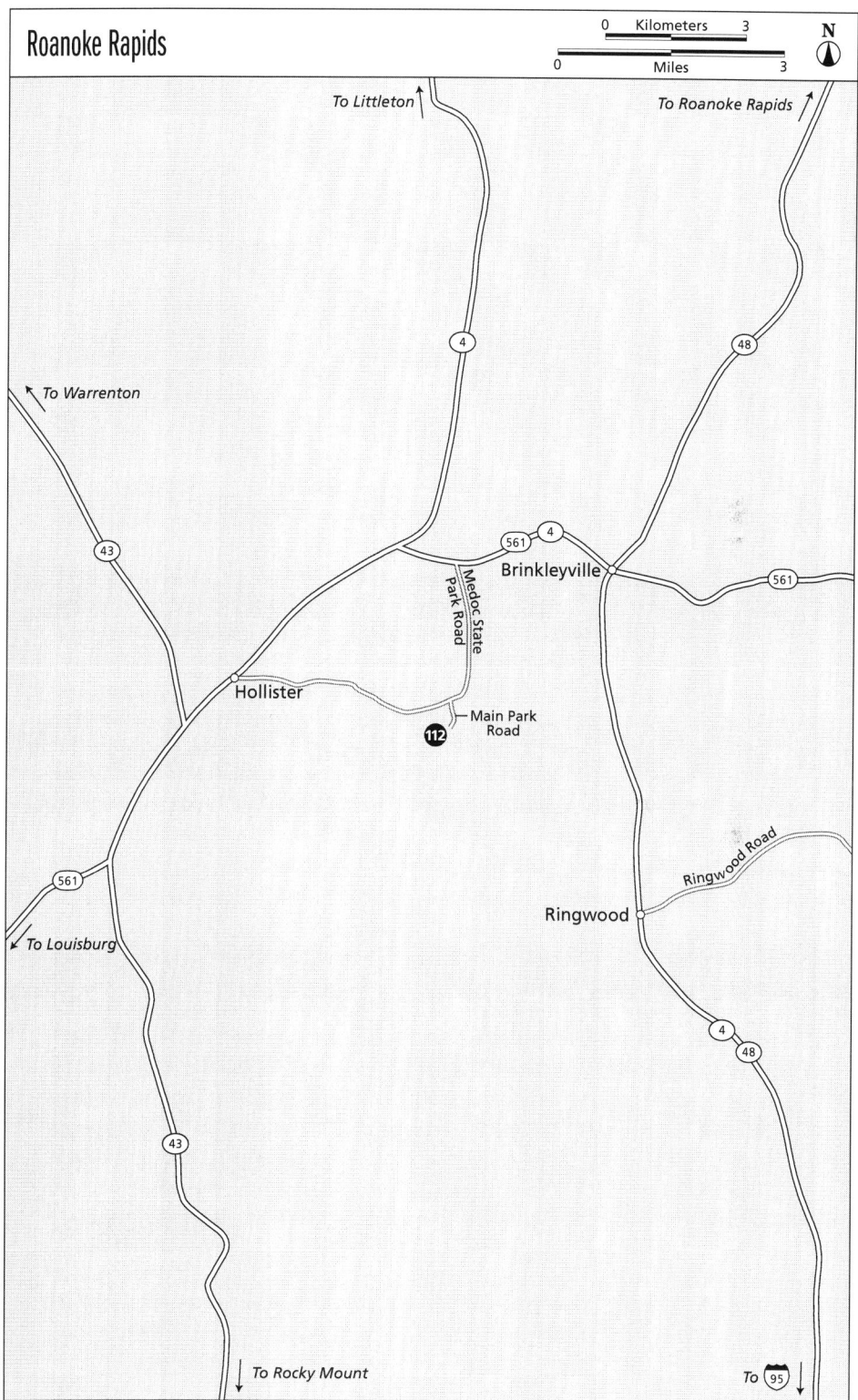

Roanoke Rapids

0 Kilometers 3
0 Miles 3

N

To Littleton

To Roanoke Rapids

To Warrenton

4

48

43

561 4

Brinkleyville

561

Medoc State Park Road

Hollister

Main Park Road

112

561

Ringwood Road

Ringwood

To Louisburg

4

48

43

To Rocky Mount

To 95

Rolls of hay are a common site in the Piedmont.

The park has a large trail system, with more than 10 miles of hiking trails, over 10 miles of bridle trails, and a paddle trail that follows Little Fishing Creek right through the park. Little Fishing Creek is known for its clean water and is home to many species of aquatic life, including the Neuse River waterdog (*Necturis lewisi*). The waterdog is a fairly large salamander that can grow up to 11 inches long and is only found within the Tar and Neuse River basins. These spotted salamanders can easily be identified by the red "ears" that stand out like flags from their head.

From mustangs running wild on the beach to historic island villages, the coastal region of North Carolina is full of diversity. You can hang glide from Jockey's Ridge or paddle to a camping platform along the Perquimans or Pasquotank River. Pitch your tent on the sands of the Atlantic Ocean as you fall asleep to the sound of the waves lapping on the shore, or head deep into the Croatan National Forest. Where else can you see alligators in one lake and thousands of white tundra swans floating on another?

The outdoor opportunities here are limitless. Whether you choose to climb to the top of a lighthouse, four-wheel-drive on the beach, go birding, hike or bike, the coast of North Carolina has it all.

The Currituck Lighthouse towers above the northern edge of the Outer Banks.

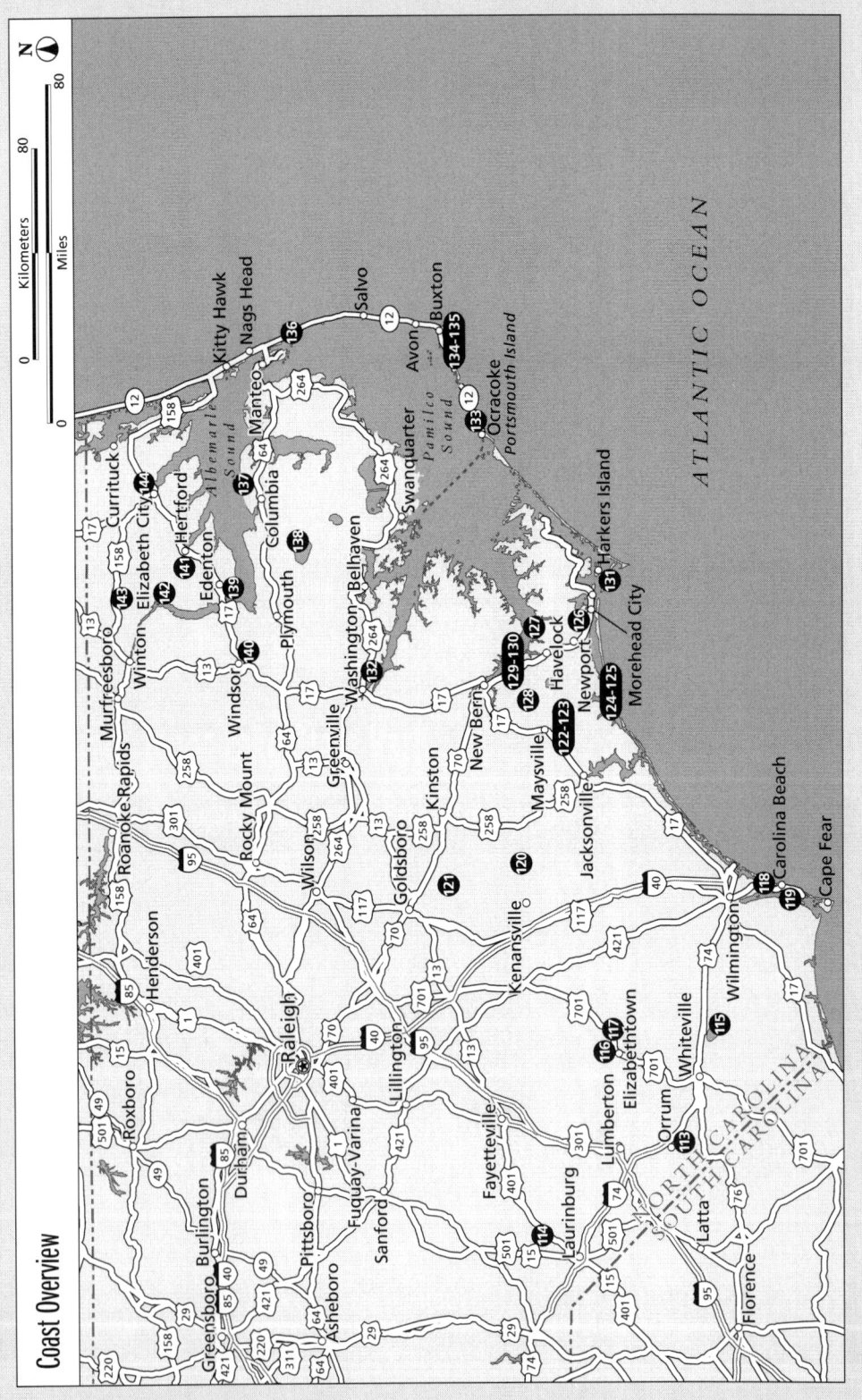

Coast Overview

N

Kilometers
0 — 80
Miles
0 — 80

ATLANTIC OCEAN

Albemarle Sound

Pamlico Sound

NORTH CAROLINA
SOUTH CAROLINA

Kitty Hawk
Nags Head
Salvo
Avon
Buxton
Ocracoke
Portsmouth Island
Manteo
Columbia
Swanquarter
Belhaven
Washington
Harkers Island
Morehead City
Newport
Havelock
New Bern
Maysville
Kinston
Jacksonville
Kenansville
Goldsboro
Wilson
Greenville
Windsor
Plymouth
Edenton
Hertford
Elizabeth City
Currituck
Winton
Murfreesboro
Roanoke Rapids
Rocky Mount
Henderson
Roxboro
Greensboro
Burlington
Durham
Raleigh
Pittsboro
Asheboro
Sanford
Fuquay-Varina
Lillington
Fayetteville
Laurinburg
Lumberton
Elizabethtown
Whiteville
Orrum
Latta
Florence
Wilmington
Carolina Beach
Cape Fear

Swansboro

Laurinburg to Whiteville, Elizabethtown

	Total Sites	Hookup Sites	Max. RV Length	Hookups	Toilets	Showers	Drinking Water	Dump Station	Recreation	Fee	Reservations
113 Lumber River State Park: Princess Ann	9	0	n/a	N	F	N	Y	N	H, F, B, L, P	$$	Y
113 Lumber River State Park: Princess Ann (Group)	2	0	n/a	N	F	N	Y	N	H, F, B, L, P	$$–$$$	Y
114 Lumber River State Park: Chalk Banks	14	0	70'	N	V	N	Y	N	H, F, B, L, P	$$	Y
114 Lumber River State Park: Chalk Banks (Group)	1	0	n/a	N	V	N	Y	N	H, F, B, L, P	$$–$$$	Y
115 Lake Waccamaw State Park	4	0	n/a	N	V	N	N	N	H, S, F, B, L, P	$$–$$$	Y
116 Jones Lake State Park	20	1	40'	E, W	F	Y	Y	N	H, S, F, B, L, P	$$	Y
116 Jones Lake State Park (Group)	1	0	n/a	N	F	Y	Y	N	H, S, F, B, L, P	$$$	Y
117 Singletary Lake State Park (Group)	*	0	n/a	N	F	Y	Y	N	H, S, F, B, L	$$	Y

* See campground entry for specific information.

113 Lumber River State Park: Princess Ann Access

Location: 2819 Princess Ann Rd., Orrum; about 19 miles southeast of Lumberton and 24 miles west of Whiteville

Season: Year-round; closed Christmas Day

Sites: 9, including 1 wheelchair-accessible site; 2 group campsites (reservations required) also available that can accommodate up to 20 people each

Maximum length: n/a; tents only

Facilities: Flush toilets, water spigots dispersed, fire rings, picnic tables, lantern holders, trash cans; pet friendly

Fee per night: $$

Management: North Carolina Department of Natural Resources

Contact: (910) 628-4564; www.ncparks.gov/Visit/parks/luri/main.php. For reservations call (877) 722-6762 or visit www.reserveamerica.com.

Finding the campground: From the junction of I-95 and US 74 near Lumberton, drive east on US 74 for 11.4 miles. Turn right onto unmarked Creek Road (SR 2225) at the sign for LUMBER RIVER STATE PARK, and travel 1.7 miles to a stop sign in the town of Orrum at NC 130. Continue straight

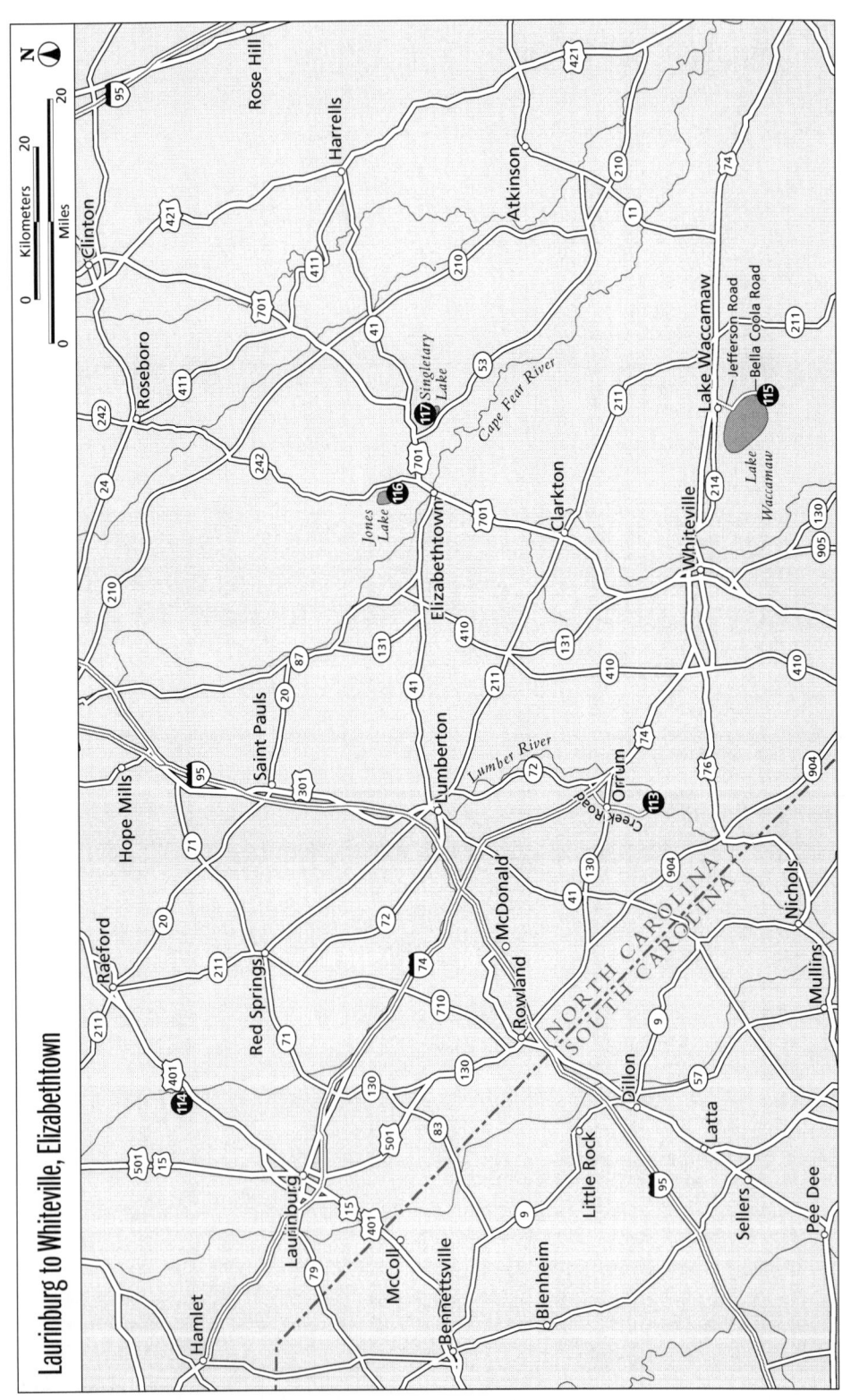

Laurinburg to Whiteville, Elizabethtown

across this intersection, and continue following Creek Road for another 3.6 miles. Turn left onto Princess Ann Road (SR 2246) at the sign for Lumber River State Park, and travel 2 miles to the entrance to the park on the left. Enter the park, and follow the road back around to the right for 0.1 mile to the parking lot with the boat ramp and trailhead to the campground.

From the junction of NC 130 and US 74 near Orrum, drive west on NC 130 for 2.3 miles. Turn left onto Creek Road (SR 2225), and travel 3.6 miles. Turn left onto Princess Ann Road (SR 2246) at the sign for Lumber River State Park, and follow directions above.

GPS coordinates: N34 23.279' / W79 00.086'

Maps: *DeLorme: North Carolina Atlas & Gazetteer:* Page 82 B4

About the campground: Nine hike-in campsites await you here. A short walk of less than 0.1 mile leads you to these wonderful wooded campsites. Most of the sites are set back and away from the river, but two sit side by side, right along the river's edge. The downside of these two riverside sites is that the river is on one side of the campsite and a hiking trail on the other, so you don't have much privacy at these two. The remaining campsites are tucked away in a nice little secluded area of the forest. Piles of firewood can be found scattered between the sites, so you don't have to cart that along.

There's a boat ramp just outside the campground, so bring your canoe or kayak along to enjoy this wild and scenic river. The park has limited hiking trails, so if you plan to explore Princess Ann, the best way to do so is by boat.

114 Lumber River State Park: Chalk Banks Access

Location: About 12.5 miles northeast of Laurinburg and 8.5 miles southwest of Raeford
Season: Year-round, Thurs–Sun only; closed Christmas Day
Sites: 14, including 1 wheelchair-accessible site; also 1 group campsite (reservations required) available
Maximum length: 75 feet
Facilities: Vault toilets, water spigots dispersed, fire rings, picnic tables, lantern holders, trash cans; pet friendly
Fee per night: $$
Management: North Carolina Department of Natural Resources
Contact: (910) 628-4564; www.ncparks.gov/Visit/parks/luri/main.php. For reservations call (877) 722-6762 or visit www.reserveamerica.com.
Finding the campground: From US 74 near Laurinburg, take exit 183 to US 401 (Wargam Road). Follow US 401 north for 12.6 miles to the entrance to Lumber River State Park: Chalk Banks on your left. From the gate, travel 1 mile on the main park road to the campground entrance on your right.
GPS coordinates: N34 53.929' / W79 21.301'
Maps: *DeLorme: North Carolina Atlas & Gazetteer:* Page 73 B8
About the campground: As you settle into your camp chair following a busy workweek or after a long day of hiking, the sounds of the crickets and frogs begin to lull you. Your tension eases as the glow of the flame flickers, mesmerizes. Then you hear in the distance the rustle of a raccoon or a series of hoots from the great horned owl. This is why you are here; this is what you came for.

Welcome to Lumber River: Chalk Banks. That's the experience you are in for at this remote corner of the state park, near the headwaters of the Lumber River. The park has a canoe/kayak launch, mountain bike and hiking trails, and a large picnic area along the banks of the river. Be aware that this portion of the state park is only open Thursday through Sunday.

115 Lake Waccamaw State Park

Location: 1866 State Park Dr., Lake Waccamaw; about 18 miles east of Whiteville and 40 miles west of Wilmington
Season: Year-round; closed Christmas Day
Sites: 4 group campsites that can accommodate up to 30 people each; individual campers welcome to use the sites as well
Maximum length: n/a; tents only
Facilities: Vault toilets, picnic tables, fire rings, grills; pet friendly
Fee per night: $$–$$$
Management: North Carolina Department of Natural Resources

A young American alligator cruises the canal near Lake Waccamaw State Park.

Turtles line the banks of the canal near Lake Waccamaw State Park.

Contact: (910) 646-4748; www.ncparks.gov/Visit/parks/lawa/main.php. For reservations call (877) 722-6762 or visit www.reserveamerica.com.

Finding the campground: From the town of Whiteville, drive east on US 74 for approximately 12 miles. Turn right onto unmarked Chauncey Town Road at the sign for Lake Waccamaw, and travel 0.5 mile to a stop sign at NC 214. Turn left onto NC 214 and drive east for 2.3 miles. Turn right onto Jefferson Road (SR 1757) at the sign for Lake Waccamaw State Park, and continue for 1.2 miles to where the road makes a sharp turn to the right. Go left at this sharp turn onto Bella Coola Road (SR 1947) at the sign for Lake Waccamaw State Park, and continue for 2.6 miles to Lake Waccamaw State Park on your left. Follow the main park road for 1.9 miles to where it dead-ends at the trailhead and parking for the campground.

GPS coordinates: N34 15.585' / W78 28.609'

Maps: *DeLorme: North Carolina Atlas & Gazetteer:* Page 84 D1

About the campground: Alligators in North Carolina! Well who'd have thought? As you make the approach to Lake Waccamaw State Park, turtles line the banks of the canal along Bella Coosa Road by the dozen. If you're lucky, the occasional gator will greet you as well. The park seems untouched, primal. There are hiking trails and a fishing pier, and the four primitive campsites are just that, primitive. The sites are hike-in only and require anywhere from a 0.25- to 0.5-mile hike to reach them. While they are designated as group campsites, individual families are welcome to camp here as well. Two of the four sites rest on the shores of Lake Waccamaw, and as the wind howls off the lake in the evening, it stirs the embers of your campfire.

Lake Waccamaw is a classic example of what is known as a Carolina bay. A bay is an elliptical- or oval-shaped natural depression that for some unexplained reason is situated in a northwest to southeast orientation. Hundreds of these bays can be found within the state's coastal region.

The park requests that you collect wood on site for burning rather than bring in your own firewood. Sadly, a nonnative beetle is killing off the common red bay trees, and one of the ways this invasive species is being introduced to the area is by people bringing in their own firewood. This one small act can help preserve the area's natural habitat.

116 Jones Lake State Park

Location: 4117 Highway 242 N, Elizabethtown; about 3 miles north of Elizabethtown and 21 miles south of Roseboro
Season: Year-round; closed Christmas Day
Sites: 20; also 1 group site (reservations required) that can accommodate up to 35 people
Maximum length: 60 feet
Facilities: Flush toilets, hot showers, water spigots dispersed, fire rings, picnic tables, trash cans; pet friendly
Fee per night: $$$
Management: North Carolina Department of Natural Resources
Contact: (910) 588-4550; www.ncparks.gov/Visit/parks/jone/main.php. For reservations call (877) 722-6762 or visit www.reserveamerica.com.
Finding the campground: From the junction of NC 242/NC 53 and US 701 in Elizabethtown, drive north on NC 242/NC 53 and immediately turn right onto NC 242. Follow NC 242 north for 2.7 miles to the park entrance on the left.

From the junction of NC 242 and NC 210 near Roseboro, drive south on NC 242 for approximately 14.6 miles to the park entrance on the right.
GPS coordinates: N34 40.830' / W78 35.868'
Maps: *DeLorme: North Carolina Atlas & Gazetteer:* Page 75 E7
About the campground: It appears as though a brush fire ran through the campground, removing all the underbrush and leaving the base of the trees charred. As a result, the campsites are not very shaded, or private. But what the campground lacks in privacy, it makes up for with activities.

With only 224 acres, this small state park packs a punch. If you prefer to stay on dry land, there is a large picnic area with grills built in, a volleyball court, and 6 miles of hiking trails. If you prefer the water, there's a great swimming area with a lovely sand beach, a fishing pier, and a boat launch. Motorized boats are allowed but are limited to boats with a 10 horsepower motor or less. Canoes and kayaks are always welcome. At its deepest point, Lake Jones is only 9 feet deep. Fed solely by rainwater, the lake remains acidic; as a result, only twelve species of fish thrive here.

117 Singletary Lake State Park Group Camp

Location: 6707 Highway 53 East, Kelly; about 10 miles southeast of Elizabethtown
Season: Year-round; closed Christmas Day
Sites: 2 group camping areas (reservations required) available for nonprofit organizations
Maximum length: n/a; cabins only
Facilities: Cabins with communal bunk areas, flush toilets, hot showers, large mess hall with fireplace, community fire ring, charcoal grills
Fee per night: $$$
Management: North Carolina Department of Natural Resources
Contact: (910) 669-2928; www.ncparks.gov/Visit/parks/sila/main.php
Finding the campground: From the junction of NC 53 and US 701 near Elizabethtown and White Lake, drive east on NC 53 for 6.7 miles. Turn left into Singletary Lake State Park.

From the junction of NC 53 and NC 210 North near Kelly, drive northwest on NC 53 for approximately 15 miles. Turn right into Singletary Lake State Park.
GPS coordinates: N34 34.974' / W78 26.990'
Maps: *DeLorme: North Carolina Atlas & Gazetteer:* Page 76 F1
About the campground: While the state park system calls this group "camping," it is not actually camping. You don't come in, pick your site, and set up a tent. Instead there are two separate areas with several cabins in each area. Some of the cabins are like army barracks, with beds lined up in a row and lockers in them. Others are smaller and have several sets of bunk beds ready to go. There are community bathhouses and a large mess hall with a beautiful fireplace. Both camps are wheelchair accessible. The property sits right on Singletary Lake, and there are plenty of activities to keep your group entertained for days. There's a swim area, a fishing pier, and a canoe launch with canoes on the premises for you to use. A basketball net, volleyball court, and horseshoe pits are all within walking distance of the cabins. If this isn't enough, the nearby town of White Lake also has a golf course, a water park, and a small go-kart track. Advance reservations are required.

Wilmington

	Total Sites	Hookup Sites	Max. RV Length	Hookups	Toilets	Showers	Drinking Water	Dump Station	Recreation	Fee	Reservations
118 Carolina Beach State Park	83	0	None	N	F	Y	Y	Y	H, F, B, L, P	$$$	Y
118 Carolina Beach State Park (Group)	2	0	n/a	N	V	N	N	N	H, F, B, L, P	$$-$$$	Y
119 Freeman Park (Primitive Camping)	*	0	n/a	N	V	N	N	N	S, F, B, O, Surf	$$$	N*

* See campground entry for specific information.

118 Carolina Beach State Park

Location: 1010 State Park Rd., Carolina Beach; about 10 miles south of Wilmington in the town of Carolina Beach
Season: Year-round; closed Christmas Day
Sites: 83, including 2 wheelchair-accessible sites; 2 group camping areas (advance reservations required) also available that can accommodate up to 25 and 35 people, respectively
Maximum length: 48 feet
Facilities: Flush toilets, hot showers, water spigots dispersed, fire rings, picnic tables, lantern holders, dump station; pet friendly
Fee per night: $$$
Management: North Carolina Department of Natural Resources
Contact: (910) 458-8206; www.ncparks.gov/Visit/parks/cabe/main.php. For reservations call (877) 722-6762 or visit www.reserveamerica.com.
Finding the campground: From the junction of US 421 and NC 132 near Wilmington, drive south on US 421 for 6.6 miles. Turn right onto Dow Road (soon after crossing the bridge over the Intracoastal Waterway) at the sign for Carolina Beach State Park, and continue 0.2 mile to the park entrance on your right.
    From Southport take the Southport Ferry to Fort Fisher (approximately 35-minute ride). Once at Fort Fisher, drive north on US 421 for approximately 7.4 miles. Turn left onto Dow Road (before crossing the bridge over the Intracoastal Waterway) at the sign for Carolina Beach State Park. After turning onto Dow Road, follow directions above.
GPS coordinates: N34 02.826' / W77 54.405'
Maps: *DeLorme: North Carolina Atlas & Gazetteer:* Page 85 F6
About the campground: Carolina Beach State Park has the best of both worlds. Miles of hiking trails lead through the forest over rolling, hilly terrain. The sandy banks of Snows Cut offer amazing waterfront views, and the beach is just minutes away. All this, combined with perfectly spaced, very private wooded campsites, makes Carolina Beach one of my favorite campgrounds in the coastal

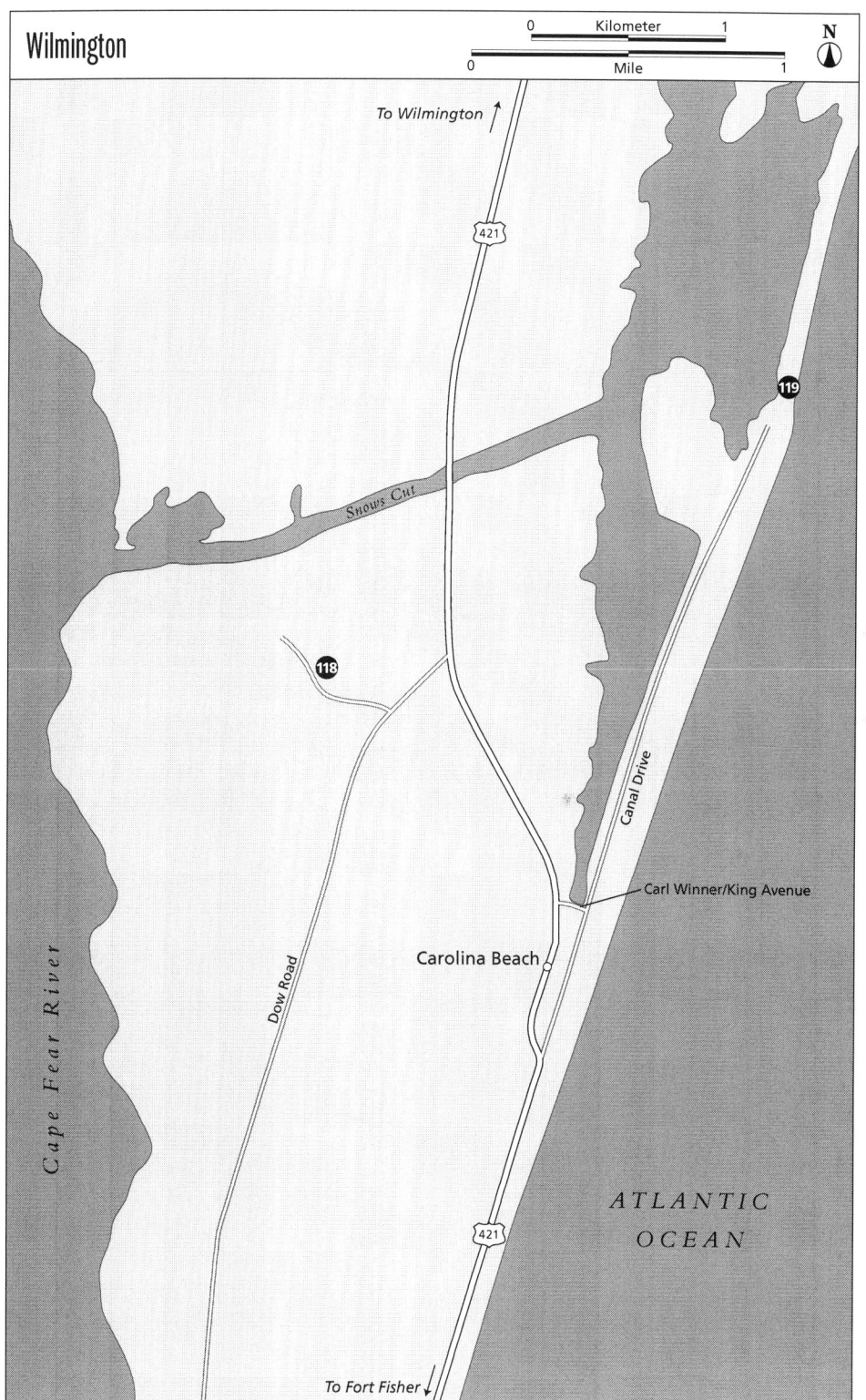

Wilmington

To Wilmington

421

Snows Cut

119

118

Canal Drive

Dow Road

Carl Winner/King Avenue

Carolina Beach

Cape Fear River

ATLANTIC

OCEAN

421

To Fort Fisher

Downed trees line the banks of Snows Cut.

region. But be forewarned; there is no beachfront camping here. To do that you need to head down the road to Freeman Park.

The group camping areas are primitive camping only, and you must hike in about 0.25 mile to reach the sites. Advanced reservations are required.

Be sure to tread lightly as you explore all that Carolina Beach has to offer. The park is home to the Venus flytrap (*Dionaea muscipula*), a unique carnivorous plant that feeds primarily on insects and arachnids.

If you are coming from the south, please call (800) BY-FERRY (800-293-3779) to confirm the ferry schedule or if you have any additional questions. It's about a thirty-five-minute ferry ride from Southport to Fort Fisher.

119 Freeman Park Primitive Camping

Location: About 10 miles south of Wilmington in the town of Carolina Beach
Season: Year-round, weather permitting
Sites: Designated area where camping is permitted but no set campsites
Maximum length: n/a; tents only
Facilities: Vault toilets, trash cans; pet friendly
Fee per night: $$$
Management: Town of Carolina Beach Parks and Recreation Department
Contact: (910) 458-2977; www.carolinabeach.org/site_new/pages/freeman_park.html
Finding the campground: From the junction of US 421 and NC 132 near Wilmington, drive south on US 421 for 7.4 miles. Turn left at the stoplight onto unmarked Carl Winner Avenue/King Avenue, and travel less than 0.1 mile to where it dead-ends at Canal Drive. Turn left onto Canal Drive, and follow it for 1.6 miles to where it dead-ends at the beach. Drive north on the beach; camping is allowed at the far north end of the beach.

From Southport take the Southport Ferry to Fort Fisher (approximately 35-minute ride). Once at Fort Fisher, drive north on US 421 for approximately 6.6 miles. Turn right at the stoplight onto unmarked Carl Winner Avenue/King Avenue, and follow directions above.
GPS coordinates: N34 03.599' / W77 52.822'
Maps: *DeLorme: North Carolina Atlas & Gazetteer:* Page 85 F6
About the campground: The great little harbor town of Carolina Beach has a small wharf, fishing charters, and some of the best beachfront camping you can find in the state. Simply buy your permit, hop in your four-wheel-drive vehicle (required), and go. When I say beachfront, I mean beachfront. You drive on the hard-packed sands of the beach, find a spot to set up your tent (first come, first served), and literally go to sleep to the sound of the waves falling on the shore. All your worries drift away with the constant ocean breeze.

There are no fire pits provided, and open fires are prohibited in the sand itself, so, if you want to enjoy a campfire you must bring your own portable fire pit. Remember that the tides will change, so be sure to pitch your tent and park your car above the high-water mark. There's a "jiffy john" provided, and that's it. So be sure to bring lots of fresh water for drinking, cooking, etc. Camping passes can be purchased at several vendors in town. Call the contact number above to find out where.

Sand dunes line the beach at Freeman Park.

	Total Sites	Hookup Sites	Max. RV Length	Hookups	Toilets	Showers	Drinking Water	Dump Station	Recreation	Fee	Reservations
120 Cabin Lake Park	16	13	67'	E, W	F	Y	Y	Y	H, S, F, B, L, P	$$$	Y
121 Cliffs of the Neuse State Park	35	0	50'	N	F	Y	Y	Y	H, S, F, B, L, P	$$$	Y
121 Cliffs of the Neuse State Park (Group)	4	0	n/a	N	V	N	Y	N	H, S, F, B, L, P	$$-$$$	Y

120 Cabin Lake Park Campground

Location: 220 Cabin Lake Rd., Pink Hill; about 5 miles north of Beulaville and about 15 miles east of Kenansville

Season: Year-round

Sites: 13; also 3 group tent-camping areas that can be reserved by groups or individuals

Maximum length: 67 feet

Facilities: *RV sites:* flush toilets, hot showers, water spigots shared between sites, electric, fire rings, picnic tables, lantern holders, trash cans, dump station

Group tent camping: flush toilets, hot showers, picnic tables, charcoal grills, trash cans, community fire rings

Fee per night: $$$

Management: Duplin County Department of Parks and Recreation

Contact: (910) 298-3648; www.duplincountync.com/governmentOffices/parksRecreation.html

Finding the campground: From the junction of NC 111 and NC 241 in Beulaville, drive north on NC 111 for 4.4 miles. Turn right onto Cabin Lake Road (SR 1746), and continue for 0.4 mile to the campground.

From the junction of NC 111 and NC 11 near Pink Hill, drive south on NC 111 for 5.8 miles. Turn left onto Cabin Lake Road (SR 1746), and continue for 0.4 mile to the campground.

GPS coordinates: N34 58.861' / W77 47.958'

Maps: *DeLorme: North Carolina Atlas & Gazetteer:* Page 77 A7

About the campground: By far the best feature of Cabin Lake Park is the lake itself. The park has canoes and paddleboats for rent by the hour, or you can bring your own and use the boat ramp. There's a nice sandy swim beach, a fishing pier, playgrounds for the little ones, and a picnic area.

You can see the lake from the campground, but it's not as though you have lakefront campsites. While there is some tree cover, the sites are close together, and there's no privacy. On top of this, Cabin Lake sits in the middle of cow country, so there's a slight smell of the nearby dairy farms wafting through the air at times. The tent camping area also has some tree cover, but the sites are really just a picnic table here and there, the occasional charcoal grill, and a community fire pit. They offer no privacy and are designed to be group campsites. However, individuals and

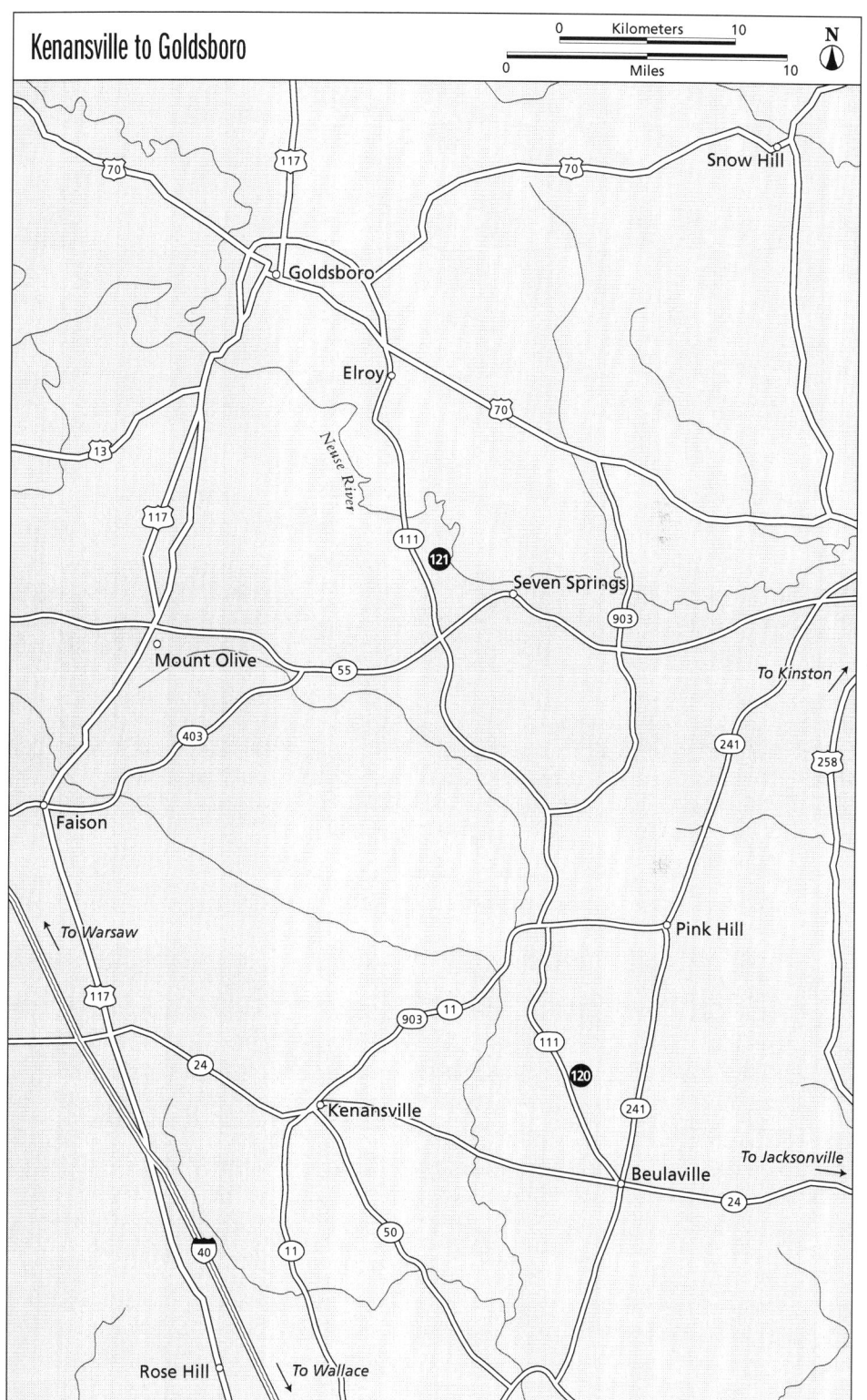

Kenansville to Goldsboro

0 Kilometers 10
0 Miles 10

N

Snow Hill

70

117

70

Goldsboro

Elroy

70

13

Neuse River

117

111

121

Seven Springs

903

To Kinston

Mount Olive

55

403

241

258

Faison

To Warsaw

Pink Hill

241

117

903 11

24

111

120

Kenansville

To Jacksonville

241

Beulaville

24

40

50

11

Rose Hill

To Wallace

Dairy farms are abundant near Cabin Lake Park.

families are welcome to pitch a tent and camp here as well. While reservations are not required, they are recommended, as the tent sites frequently fill up with local scout troops.

121 Cliffs of the Neuse State Park

Location: 345-A Park Entrance Rd., Seven Springs; about 11 miles southeast of Goldsboro and about 5 miles northwest of Seven Springs
Season: Year-round; closed Christmas Day
Sites: 35, including 1 wheelchair-accessible site; also 4 group campsites (reservations required) available that can accommodate up to 35 people each
Maximum length: 50 feet
Facilities: Flush toilets, hot showers, water spigots dispersed, fire rings, picnic tables, dump station, ice and firewood for sale; pet friendly
Fee per night: $$–$$$
Management: North Carolina Department of Natural Resources

Contact: (919) 778-6234; www.ncparks.gov/Visit/parks/clne/main.php. For reservations call (877) 722-6762 or visit www.reserveamerica.com.

Finding the campground: From the junction of NC 111 and NC 55 near Seven Springs, drive north on NC 111 for 2.3 miles. Turn right onto Park Entrance Road (SR 1743) at the sign for Cliffs of the Neuse State Park, and travel 0.5 mile to the park entrance straight ahead of you.

From the junction of NC 111 and US 70 near Goldsboro, drive south on NC 111 for 8.3 miles. Turn left onto Park Entrance Road (SR 1743), and follow directions above.

GPS coordinates: N35 14.425' / W77 53.268'

Maps: *DeLorme: North Carolina Atlas & Gazetteer:* Page 64 E2

About the campground: With hiking trails that lead down to the river and cliffside overlooks that give you a bird's-eye view from above, Cliffs of the Neuse is quite a pleasant park. There's a lovely lake in which you can swim, and you can rent canoes and paddleboats by the hour. The campsites are wooded and well spaced.

The only drawback is that there's a US Air Force Base just up the road, so you can occasionally hear the thunderous roar of the jet planes overhead. Aside from that one drawback, this is a great place to camp and among my favorites in the coastal region.

Jacksonville to Havelock

	Total Sites	Hookup Sites	Max. RV Length	Hookups	Toilets	Showers	Drinking Water	Dump Station	Recreation	Fee	Reservations
122 Dixon Fields (Dispersed)	*	0	n/a	N	V	N	N	N	F, B, L*, P	No fee	N
123 Long Point (Dispersed)	2	0	n/a	N	V	N	N	N	F, B, L*, P	No fee	N
124 Hammocks Beach State Park	14	0	n/a	N	F	Y	Y	N	S, F, B, L, P	$$	Y*
124 Hammocks Beach State Park (Group)	2	0	n/a	N	F	Y	Y	N	S, F, B, L, P	$$-$$$	Y*
125 Cedar Point	39	39	50'	E	F	Y	Y	Y	H, F, B, L, P	$$	Y
126 Oyster Point	16	0	50'	N	V	N	Y	N	H, F, B, L*	$	N
127 Siddie Fields (Dispersed)	*	0	n/a	N	N	N	N	N	S, F, B, L*, P	No fee	N
128 Catfish Lake (Dispersed)	2	0	n/a	N	N	N	N	N	S, F, B, L*	No fee	N
129 Neuse River	41	14	50'	E, W	F	Y	Y	Y	H, M, S, C, P	$$	N
130 Fisher's Landing (Dispersed)	*	0	n/a	N	V	N	Y	N	S, F, P	No fee	N

* See campground entry for specific information.

122 Dixon Fields Dispersed Camping

Location: About 5.5 miles south of Maysville and about 16 miles north of Cape Carteret
Season: Year-round
Sites: No set number of designated campsites
Maximum length: n/a; tents only
Facilities: Vault toilet, community primitive fire ring, *no* potable water; pet friendly
Fee per night: None
Management: Croatan National Forest—Croatan Ranger District
Contact: (252) 638-5628
Finding the campground: From the junction of NC 58 and NC 24 in Cape Carteret, drive west on NC 58 for 14.5 miles. Turn left onto Highway 58 Loop Road (SR 1102), and follow it for 0.3 mile. Turn right onto Dixon Field Road (FR 3057), and continue for 1.4 miles to where it dead-ends at Dixon Fields.

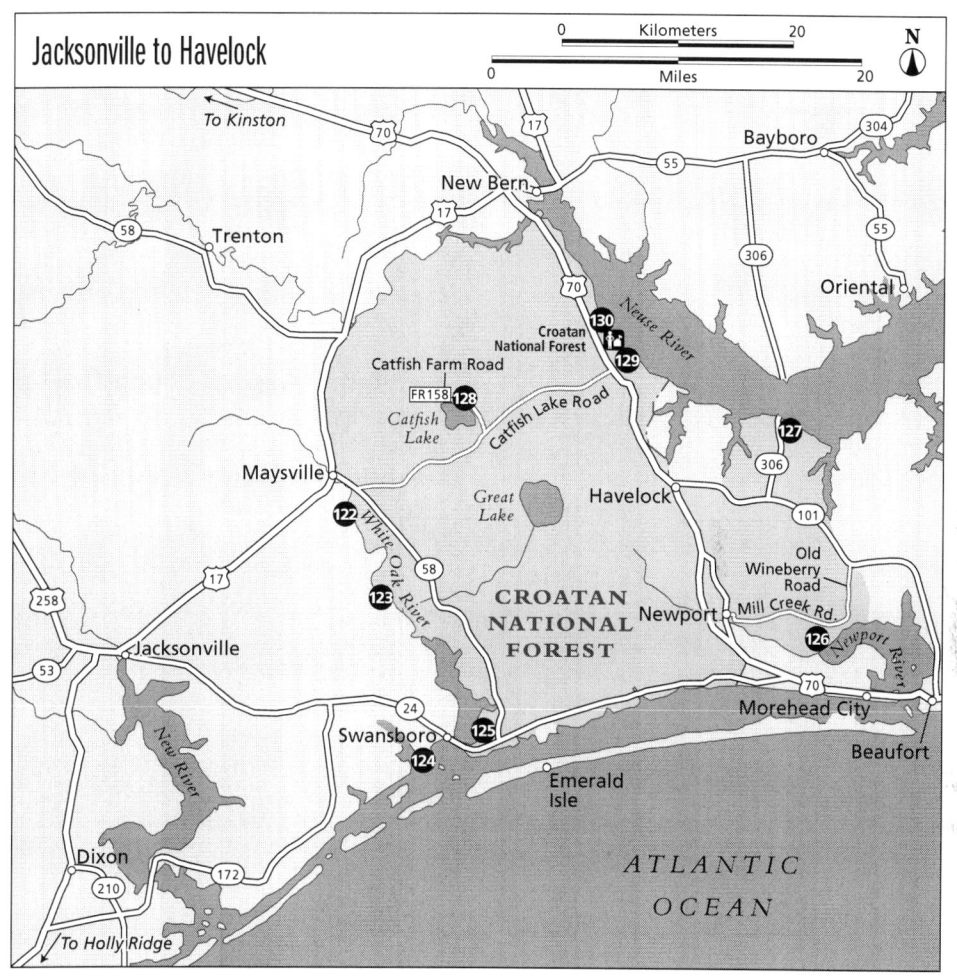

From the junction of NC 58 and US 17 in Maysville, drive east on NC 58 for 3.8 miles. Turn right onto Highway 58 Loop Road (SR 1102), and follow directions above.

GPS coordinates: N34 51.360' / W77 12.613'

Maps: *DeLorme: North Carolina Atlas & Gazetteer:* Page 78 C4

About the campground: This is as primitive as it gets. A single open camping area with a primitive fire ring in the middle makes up the Dixon Fields dispersed camping area. The area is unique, as the camp "sites" sit right next to the swampy White Oak River. With cypress trees and saw palmetto, it's unlike any other camping area within the Croatan. A narrow hiking trail runs alongside the river, and I recommend that you bring some bug spray along—whether you're going for a hike or simply sitting by the fire.

123 Long Point Dispersed Camping

Location: About 10 miles south of Maysville and about 13 miles north of Cape Carteret
Season: Year-round
Sites: 2
Maximum length: n/a; tents only
Facilities: Vault toilet, fire rings, picnic tables, lantern holders, *no* potable water; pet friendly
Fee per night: None
Management: Croatan National Forest–Croatan Ranger District
Contact: (252) 638-5628; www.fs.usda.gov/recarea/nfsnc/recreation/camping-cabins/recarea/?recid=48480&actid=34
Finding the campground: From the junction of NC 58 and NC 24 in Cape Carteret, drive west on NC 58 for 11 miles. Turn left onto FR 120 at the sign for Long Point Landing, and travel straight back for 2.3 miles (be sure to stay left at the fork at 1.2 miles where FR 146 goes off to the right and FR 120 continues straight ahead) to the end of the road at Long Point.

From the junction of NC 58 and US 17 in Maysville, drive east on NC 58 for 7.3 miles. Turn right onto FR 120, and follow directions above.
GPS coordinates: N34 47.886' / W77 10.686'
Maps: *DeLorme: North Carolina Atlas & Gazetteer:* Page 79 D5
About the campground: You're in for a big surprise. When you hear the term dispersed camping in the Croatan, it usually refers to an open field with a picnic table here or a fire ring there. Not at Long Point. Here you have two perfectly groomed campsites that look as though they were plucked right out of the Neuse River Campground and placed alongside a wide and wonderful portion of the White Oak River. Like night and day, the river transforms from the swampland you see at Dixon Fields to the fresh, clean-cut banks that line the river at Long Point. This area is part of the White Oak River Paddle Trail, and there's a paddle trail map at the entrance and a canoe/kayak launch right next to the campsites.

Remember, there are only two campsites here, so arrive early if you want to secure your spot, especially on the weekends. Also, there is no drinking water on site, so bring plenty along for drinking, cooking, bathing, and such. *NOTE:* Never bathe in any natural water source unless you are using biodegradable soap. Leave no trace.

124 Hammocks Beach State Park Primitive Camping

Location: 1572 Hammocks Beach Rd., Swansboro; about 5 miles west of Cape Carteret and about 15 miles east of Jacksonville
Season: Year-round; closed Christmas Day. Although the campground is open to the public year-round, the ferry system operates seasonally Apr–Oct. If you plan to visit the campground Nov–Mar, you must get to Bear Island via private boat or water taxi.
Sites: 14; also 2 group camping areas available that can accommodate up to 12 and 24 people, respectively (reservations required for all sites)
Maximum length: n/a; tents only

Although four-wheel driving is allowed on many beaches along the coast of North Carolina, it's prohibited on Bear Island.

Facilities: Flush toilets, outdoor showers, water fountains, picnic tables, concession stand with snacks open seasonally; no water available on the island Nov–Mar; no open fires allowed except for grills that you pack in. No pets are allowed on the ferry, but if you arrive by private boat, pets are allowed at the campsites.

Fee per night: $$

Management: North Carolina Department of Natural Resources

Contact: (910) 326-4881 or (910) 326-1861; www.ncparks.gov/Visit/parks/habe/main.php. For reservations call (877) 722-6762 or visit www.reserveamerica.com.

Finding the campground: From the junction of NC 24 and NC 58 in Cape Carteret, drive west on NC 24 for 5.1 miles. Turn left onto Hammocks Beach Road (SR 1511), and travel 2 miles to the entrance to the park on your right.

From the junction of NC 24 and NC 172 in Hubert, drive east on NC 24 for approximately 5.2 miles. Turn right onto Hammocks Beach Road, and follow directions above.

GPS coordinates: N34 40.263' / W77 08.604'

Maps: *DeLorme: North Carolina Atlas & Gazetteer:* Page 79 E5

About the campground: The camping at Hammocks Beach State Park is hard earned, but worth the effort. That's because there is no camping on the mainland park premises. Instead, the Hammocks Beach camping facilities are in a remote location out in the Atlantic Ocean on Bear Island. A seasonal passenger ferry leaves daily from the park, carting people and their gear out to the island. After crossing Cow's Channel, you arrive at Bear Island, but you now have to hike 0.5 mile across the island to get to the campsites. Be sure to wear sandals or shoes. The sandy trail can often get desert hot, as can the campsites.

Although some sites catch a great ocean breeze, all are completely exposed to the sun, so be prepared; drink lots of water, and use plenty of sunscreen. There is running water on the island (Mar–Nov only), so you can refill your water bottles, and a concession stand is open during the day in season.

The ferry schedule changes daily, so contact the park for exact times and more information. Anyone can access Bear Island via private boat or water taxi, but if you plan on camping here, advance reservations are required.

No pets are allowed on the ferry, but pets are allowed on the island, so if you want to bring Fido along, do so via private boat. Also, *please* keep the heat in mind for your pets too. There is no shade, and the sand can get extremely hot on their pads. If you still opt to bring your pooch, be sure to have *lots* of water available for him at all times. Dogs can overheat very easily.

125 Cedar Point Campground

Location: In the town of Cape Carteret, about 20 miles east of Jacksonville
Season: Year-round
Sites: 39
Maximum length: 50 feet
Facilities: Flush toilets, hot showers, water spigots dispersed, electric, fire rings, picnic tables, lantern holders, dump station; pet friendly
Fee per night: $$

A great white egret fishes along the banks of the White Oak River at Cedar Point.

Management: Croatan National Forest—Croatan Ranger District

Contact: (252) 638-5628; www.fs.usda.gov/recarea/nfsnc/recreation/camping-cabins/recarea/?recid=48470&actid=29. For reservations call (877) 444-6777 or visit www.recreation.gov.

Finding the campground: From the junction of NC 58 and NC 24 in Cape Carteret, drive north on NC 58 for 0.7 mile. Turn left onto VFW Road, and travel 0.5 mile to the entrance to Cedar Point Recreation Area. Turn left into the recreation area, and continue 1.1 miles to the campground entrance on your left.

GPS coordinates: N34 41.569/'W77 05.047'

Maps: *DeLorme: North Carolina Atlas & Gazetteer:* Page 79 E5

About the campground: If you look at a map, it appears as though Cedar Point Campground should offer waterfront camping. Well, the map is deceiving. Cedar Point itself is on the water, but unfortunately the campground is nowhere near the water. It's fairly wooded, and the sites are spaced out a bit, but there is no underbrush, so you don't have a ton of privacy.

What the campground lacks, the recreation area makes up for. It has a picnic ground, hiking trails, paddle trails, and a boat launch. Wildlife is plentiful, and you are sure to enjoy the area whether you explore it by land or by water. I recommend bringing bug repellent and binoculars to get the most out of your visit. Birders flock to the area to view a wide variety of species.

126 Oyster Point Campground

Location: About 9 miles east of Newport and about 15 miles northwest of Beaufort

Season: Year-round

Sites: 16

Maximum length: 50 feet

Facilities: Vault toilets, water spigots dispersed, fire rings, picnic tables, lantern holders; pet friendly

Fee per night: $

Management: Croatan National Forest—Croatan Ranger District

Contact: (252) 638-5628; www.fs.usda.gov/recarea/nfsnc/recreation/camping-cabins/recarea/?recid=48474&actid=29

Finding the campground: From the junction of US 70 and NC 24 near Newport, drive north on US 70 for 3.7 miles. Turn right onto East Chatham Street, and continue toward Newport for 1.7 miles. Turn right onto Main Street, and travel just over 0.1 mile to a right turn onto Orange Street (Orange Street becomes Mill Creek Road). Follow this for 6.1 miles, turning right onto FR 181 at the sign for OYSTER POINT AND DUNCAN LANDING. Travel 1 mile on FR 181 to the end at the entrance to the Oyster Point Campground on your right.

From the junction of NC 101 and US 70 in Beaufort, drive west on NC 101 for approximately 10.5 miles. Turn left onto Old Wineberry Road at the sign for OYSTER POINT/DUNCAN LANDING, and continue 3.7 miles (be sure to stay right at the fork at about 2 miles) to a stop sign at Mill Creek Road. Turn right, and follow Mill Creek Road for 0.2 mile. Turn left onto FR 181 at the sign for OYSTER POINT/DUNCAN LANDING, and continue 1 mile to where it ends at the entrance to the campground on your right.

GPS coordinates: N34 45.655' / W76 45.718'

Maps: *DeLorme: North Carolina Atlas & Gazetteer:* Page 79 D8

About the campground: It appears as though a brush fire or a controlled burn ran through the campground. On one side of the campground, the sites sit amid the charred remains of the pine trees. The sites on the other side rest alongside the Intracoastal Waterway. Although the campground is a few hundred feet from the water, the fire removed all the underbrush, giving way to a clear view of the waterway. Unfortunately this lack of underbrush also takes away some of your privacy.

There's a canoe/kayak launch on the property, and the southern terminus of the 20-mile Neusiok Trail sits just outside the campground entrance. You may also want to check out Walkers Millpond as you head west on Mill Creek Road. It's quite a sight, much like the Merchants Millpond in the far northern reaches of the coastal region.

Cypress trees line the water's edge near Oyster Point Campground.

127 Siddie Fields Dispersed Camping

Location: About 11 miles northeast of Havelock
Season: Year-round
Sites: Open field; no set number of designated campsites
Maximum length: n/a; tents only
Facilities: Charcoal grills, benches, trash cans, limited number of community fire rings, *no* bathroom, *no* potable water; pet friendly
Fee per night: None
Management: Croatan National Forest—Croatan Ranger District
Contact: (252) 638-5628; www.fs.usda.gov/recarea/nfsnc/recreation/camping-cabins/recarea/?recid=48484&actid=34
Finding the campground: From the NC 101 and US 70 in Havelock, drive east on NC 101 (Fontana Boulevard) for 7.2 miles. Turn left onto Temples Point Road (SR 1711), and travel 2 miles.

Turn left onto Pine Cliff Road (SR 1762), and continue for 1.5 miles. Turn left onto FR 167, and travel 1 mile to where the road dead-ends at Siddie Fields.

GPS coordinates: N34 55.769' / W76 47.494'

Maps: *DeLorme: North Carolina Atlas & Gazetteer:* Page 79 B8

About the campground: Peaceful! If you don't mind digging a cat hole for your sanitary needs, Siddie Fields is for you. The dispersed camping area comprises a small open field with a bench here and there, charcoal grills, and a community fire ring. The grassy field sits right on the banks of the Neuse River as it flows out to Pamlico Sound.

Set your tent up wherever you choose and then take a dip, or launch your canoe or kayak and go for a paddle. This is primitive camping, so come prepared. There is no drinking water on site, and there's also no bathroom—not even a vault toilet. Remember: If you dig a cat hole, be sure that it's at least 200 feet from any natural water source.

128 Catfish Lake Dispersed Camping

Location: About 10 miles east of Maysville and about 15 miles northwest of Havelock

Season: Year-round

Sites: 2

Maximum length: n/a; tents only

Facilities: Primitive fire rings, *no* bathrooms, *no* potable water; pet friendly

Fee per night: None

Management: Croatan National Forest—Croatan Ranger District

Contact: (252) 638-5628; www.fs.usda.gov/recarea/nfsnc/recreation/camping-cabins/recarea/?recid=48488&actid=34

Finding the campground: From the junction of US 70 and NC 101 in Havelock, drive north on US 70 for 7.2 miles. Turn left onto Catfish Lake Road (SR 1100) at the small white church, and travel 7.4 miles. Turn right onto unmarked FR 158 (Catfish Farm Road), and continue 1.2 miles to a T. The left leads 0.1 mile to the first primitive camping area. Go right, continuing on FR 158 for another 0.9 mile to the second primitive camping area on your left alongside the lake.

From the junction of NC 58 and US 17 in Maysville, drive east on NC 58 for approximately 2.2 miles. Turn left onto Catfish Lake Road (FR 1100), and travel approximately 8.2 miles. Turn left onto FR 158, and follow directions above.

GPS coordinates: Primitive campsite 1: N34 56.151' / W77 05.802'

Primitive campsite 2: N34 56.618' / W77 06.658'

Maps: *DeLorme: North Carolina Atlas & Gazetteer:* Page 79 B5

A snow-white deer stands out, tall and proud, in Croatan National Forest.

About the campground: It's a far stretch to call this dispersed camping. Actually there are two open muddy areas where you could launch a small boat. These are the two spots that are suitable for camping. A primitive fire ring sits beside the lake at each of these sites, and that is it—no drinking water, no picnic table, no vault toilet. Keep this in mind as you are packing your gear.

The sunset views are amazing, but be sure to bring bug repellent along. Although it's pretty sizable, Catfish Lake is shallow throughout and is therefore only suitable for canoes, kayaks, and flat-bottom boats.

129 Neuse River Campground (Flanners Beach)

Location: Flanners Beach, about 7 miles north of Havelock and 10 miles south of New Bern
Season: Mar 1–Nov 30
Sites: 41
Maximum length: 50 feet
Facilities: Flush toilets, hot showers, water spigots dispersed, fire rings, picnic tables, lantern holders, dump station; pet friendly
Fee per night: $$
Management: Croatan National Forest—Croatan Ranger District
Contact: (252) 638-5628; www.fs.usda.gov/recarea/nfsnc/recreation/camping-cabins/recarea/?recid=48472&actid=29
Finding the campground: From the junction of US 70 and NC 101 in Havelock, drive north on US 70 for 6.8 miles. Turn right onto Flanners Beach Road (SR 1107), and travel 1.1 miles to the entrance to the Neuse River Recreation Area. Continue another 0.4 mile to a right turn into the campground.

From the junction of US 70 and US 17 near New Bern, drive south on US 70 for 9.9 miles. Turn left onto Flanners Beach Road (SR 1107), and follow directions above.
GPS coordinates: N34 58.909' / W76 56.929'
Maps: *DeLorme: North Carolina Atlas & Gazetteer:* Page 79 A7
About the campground: Historically known as Flanners Beach, Neuse River Campground sees a lot of traffic, and understandably so. The forty-one campsites are all within easy reach of the Neuse River. There's a lovely picnic area and a sandy beach with a swim area, and a paved path for walking or biking runs throughout the park.

As you will see by the mounds and mounds of downed trees, a tornado and a hurricane tore through the park in 2011, stripping the campsites of their privacy. The only other downside to this campground is the bugs. Even in February—on a cool, foggy night with a soft, steady breeze blowing off the river—the mosquitoes are plentiful. Be sure to bring lots of bug repellent or a citronella tiki torch or two to fend them off.

130 Fishers Landing Dispersed Camping

Location: Riverdale, about 9 miles north of Havelock, and about 8 miles south of New Bern
Season: Year-round
Sites: Open field; no set number of designated campsites

A tent camper sets up near the banks of the Neuse River at the Neuse River Campground.

Maximum length: n/a; tents only
Facilities: Vault toilet, water spigot, a handful of picnic tables, a few fire rings dispersed
Fee per night: None
Management: Croatan National Forest—Croatan Ranger District
Contact: (252) 638-5628; www.fs.usda.gov/recarea/nfsnc/recreation/camping-cabins/recarea/?recid=49348&actid=34
Finding the campground: From the junction of US 70 and NC 101 in Havelock, drive north on US 70 for 9.3 miles. Turn right onto SR 1159 (the first right after passing the Croatan National Forest Ranger Station). Immediately turn right again, and then make an immediate left onto the dirt FR 141. Continue 0.5 mile to where FR 141 dead-ends at Fishers Landing camping area.

From the junction of US 70 and US 17 near New Bern, drive south on US 70 for approximately 7.4 miles. Turn left onto SR 1159 (0.5 mile north of the Croatan National Forest Ranger Station), and follow directions above.
GPS coordinates: N35 00.015' / W76 58.607'
Maps: *DeLorme: North Carolina Atlas & Gazetteer:* Page 79 A6
About the campground: Perched high above the banks of the Neuse River, Fishers Landing is a great place to pitch your tent and enjoy the breeze as it feeds the fire. This large, open grassy field was the site of a Civil War battle.

Fishers Landing is a perfect place to sit and relax with a good book. Several picnic tables and fire rings are available, and a cement staircase leads down to a pristine sandy beach. Take a dip, or just sun yourself. If you like to paddle, be sure to bring some portage wheels so that you can cart your canoe or kayak down to the water's edge and explore the river from within.

Beaufort to Harkers Island

	Total Sites	Hookup Sites	Max. RV Length	Hookups	Toilets	Showers	Drinking Water	Dump Station	Recreation	Fee	Reservations
131 Cape Lookout	*	0	n/a	N	V	N	N	N	H, S, F, B, O	No fee	Y*

* See campground entry for specific information.

131 Cape Lookout National Seashore: Cape Lookout Primitive Camping

Location: Cape Lookout is accessed by boat only; passenger ferries leave daily from Harkers Island, and vehicle ferries leave daily from Davis and Atlantic—weather permitting.
Season: Year-round. Ferries run weather permitting, so be sure to call ahead, especially in the winter months, Dec–Mar.
Sites: No designated campsites; camping is on a first-come, first served-basis; cabin rentals (advance reservations required) also available
Maximum length: n/a; tents only
Facilities: Vault toilets, *no* potable water
Fee per night: None for camping; cabin rentals: $$$

The Cape Lookout Lighthouse can be seen off in the distance from the visitor center on Harkers Island.

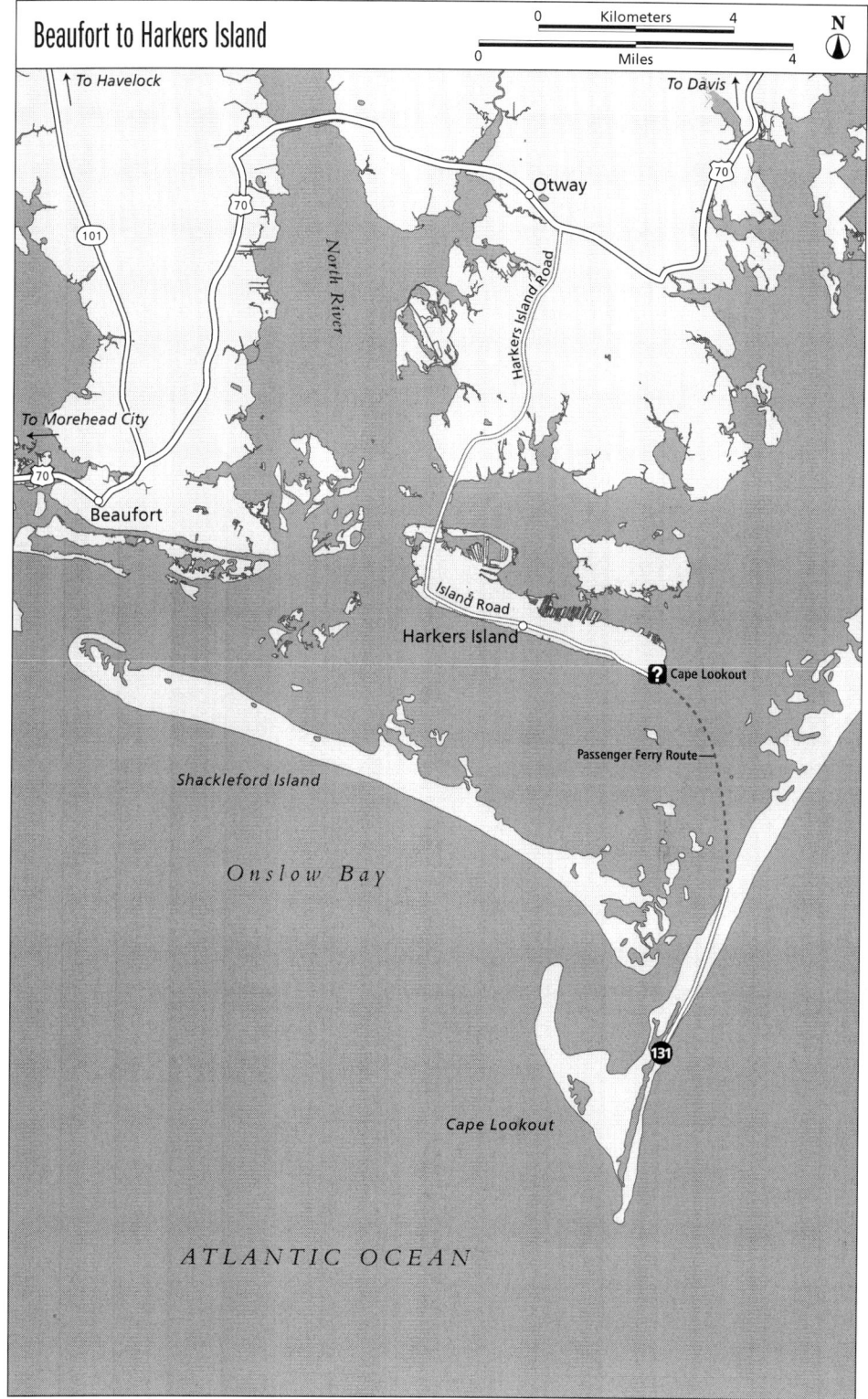

Beaufort to Harkers Island

Wild horses can be seen grazing along the beach on Shackleford Island.

Management: National Park Service—Cape Lookout National Seashore
Contact: (252) 728-2250; www.nps.gov/calo/index.htm; www.nps.gov/calo/planyourvisit/
upload/camping2007.pdf. For cabin reservations call (877) 444-6777 or visit www
.recreation.gov.
Finding the campground: From the junction of US 70 and NC 101 in Beaufort, drive northeast
on US 70 for approximately 9.5 miles (through the town of Otway). Turn right onto Harkers Island
Road (SR 1332), and travel approximately 4.5 miles onto Harkers Island. Once on Harkers Island,
Harkers Island Road becomes Island Road (SR 1335). Follow Island Road for another 4.5 miles to
where the road dead-ends at the Cape Lookout National Seashore Visitor Center on your left.
GPS coordinates: Visitor center: N34 41.094' / W76 31.643'; Cape Lookout: N34 38.144' /
W76 30.832'
Maps: *DeLorme: North Carolina Atlas & Gazetteer:* Page 80 F3
About the campground: Once again, the National Park Service has outdone itself. But this time
it's with simplicity and by sheer location. At the far southern tip of the barrier islands is Cape
Lookout. This splendid, undeveloped island has a lighthouse, an abundance of birdlife, and miles
of shoreline you can explore on foot or in your four-wheel-drive vehicle. Neighboring Shackleford
Island, home to herds of wild horses and historic Portsmouth Village, is just a quick boat ride away.

Camping is allowed anywhere on the beach, within the rules provided by the NPS. You can
access Cape Lookout with your own private boat or take the ferry over. Ferries are completely
weather dependent, so be sure to call ahead to confirm that the ferries are running, especially
from December through March. There is no drinking water provided, so be sure to bring plenty
along with you, as well as all the food, firewood, sunscreen, etc., you require.

Washington

	Total Sites	Hookup Sites	Max. RV Length	Hookups	Toilets	Showers	Drinking Water	Dump Station	Recreation	Fee	Reservations
132 Goose Creek State Park	12*	0	n/a*	N	V	N	Y	N	H, S, F, B, L*, P	$$	Y
132 Goose Creek State Park (Group)	1	0	n/a	N	V	N	Y	N	H, S, F, B, L*, P	$$-$$$	Y

* See campground entry for specific information.

132 Goose Creek State Park

Location: 2190 Camp Leach Rd., Washington; about 10 miles southeast of Washington and about 8 miles west of Bath
Season: Year-round; closed Christmas Day; group camping area open mid-Mar–late Nov
Sites: 12, including 2 wheelchair-accessible sites; also 1 group camping area (reservations required) that can accommodate up to 30
Maximum length: n/a; tents only
Facilities: Vault toilets, water spigots dispersed, fire rings, picnic tables, lantern holders, *no* showers; pet friendly
Fee per night: $$
Management: North Carolina Department of Natural Resources
Contact: (252) 923-2191; www.ncparks.gov/Visit/parks/gocr/main.php. For reservations call (877) 722-6762.
Finding the campground: From the junction of US 264 and NC 32 at Douglas Crossroads, drive east on US 264 for 2.7 miles. Turn right onto Camp Leach Road (SR 1334) at the sign for GOOSE CREEK STATE PARK, and travel 2.2 miles to the entrance to the park on your right.
　　From the junction of US 264 and NC 92 in Jessama, drive west on US 264 for less than 0.25 mile. Turn left onto Camp Leach Road (SR 1334), and follow directions above.
GPS coordinates: N35 28.690' / W76 54.098'
Maps: *DeLorme: North Carolina Atlas & Gazetteer:* Page 66 B3
About the campground: A tree-lined drive leads you through the swamp on your way through Goose Creek State Park. The park is nearly surrounded by water and rests upon a peninsula along the Pamlico River. Bordered by Flatty and Goose Creeks, recreational activities include swimming, fishing, and boating. There's a boat launch and paddle trails, but the launch site is for canoes and kayaks only. Hiking trails traverse the area, often with raised boardwalks to keep your feet dry. As you explore the swampy, wooded terrain, cypress trees tower overhead, and waterfowl silently tiptoe across the water.
　　The campground is designed for tent campers, and although a few sites may fit a small pop-up camper, the campground is not suitable for RVs.

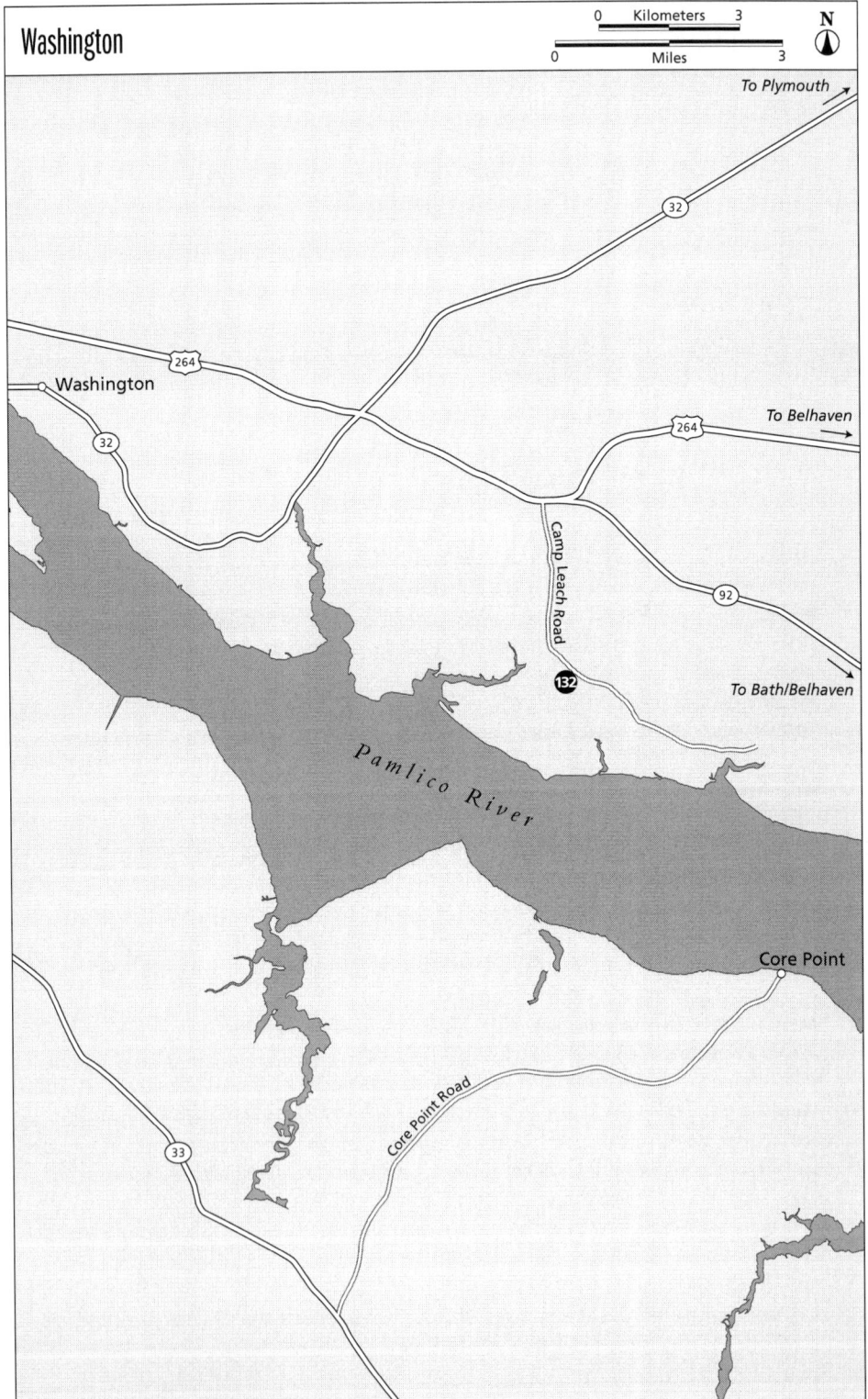

Washington

0 Kilometers 3
0 Miles 3

N

To Plymouth

32

264

Washington

32

264

To Belhaven

Camp Leach Road

92

132

To Bath/Belhaven

Pamlico River

Core Point

33

Core Point Road

	Total Sites	Hookup Sites	Max. RV Length	Hookups	Toilets	Showers	Drinking Water	Dump Station	Recreation	Fee	Reservations
133 Ocracoke	136	0	40'	N	Y	Y	Y	Y	H, S, F, O	$$$	Y
134 Frisco	127	0	40'	N	Y	Y	Y	N	H, S, F, O	$$$	N
135 Cape Point	202	0	40'	N	Y	Y	Y	Y	H, S, F, O	$$$	N
136 Oregon Inlet	121	0	40'	N	Y	Y	Y	Y	H, S, F, O	$$$	N

133 Cape Hatteras National Seashore: Ocracoke Campground

Location: 4352 Irvin Garrish Hwy. Ocracoke; about 4 miles east of Ocracoke Village and about 9.5 miles west of the Hatteras-Ocracoke ferry port

Season: Apr–Oct; exact dates vary each year

Sites: 136

Maximum length: 40 feet

Facilities: Flush toilets, showers, water spigots dispersed, charcoal grills, picnic tables, dump station; pet friendly

Fee per night: $$$

Management: National Park Service–Cape Hatteras National Seashore

Contact: (252) 473-2111; www.nps.gov/caha/planyourvisit/campgrounds.htm. For reservations call (877) 444-6777 or visit www.recreation.gov.

Finding the campground: From Swanquarter take the Swanquarter–Ocracoke Ferry to the village of Ocracoke (about a 2.5-hour ferry ride). Once you get off the ferry, drive east on NC 12 (Irvin Garrish Highway) for 4.3 miles to the entrance to the campground on your right.

From Hatteras Island take the Hatteras-Ocracoke Ferry (about a 35-minute ferry ride). Once you get off the ferry, drive west on NC 12 for 9.5 miles to the entrance to the campground on your left.

GPS coordinates: N35 07.546' / W75 55.329'

Maps: *DeLorme: North Carolina Atlas & Gazetteer:* Page 68 F4

About the campground: Ocracoke Campground is located at the south end of the Outer Banks. The campground sits on the west side of the dunes, so you can't see the ocean, but you can hear it in the night. The sites are wide open, with no tree cover and no privacy. However, you can enjoy the beach, the village, the dunes, the ponies, and the history here and won't be disappointed. The island has a charming village with great restaurants, quaint shops, and a lighthouse. The lighthouse sits just blocks away from Springer's Point, a maritime forest and nature preserve. The forest has hiking trails and is said to be the place where the pirate Blackbeard met his demise. Farther north on the island, you can visit the Ocracoke ponies. These "wild" mustangs are actually kept in

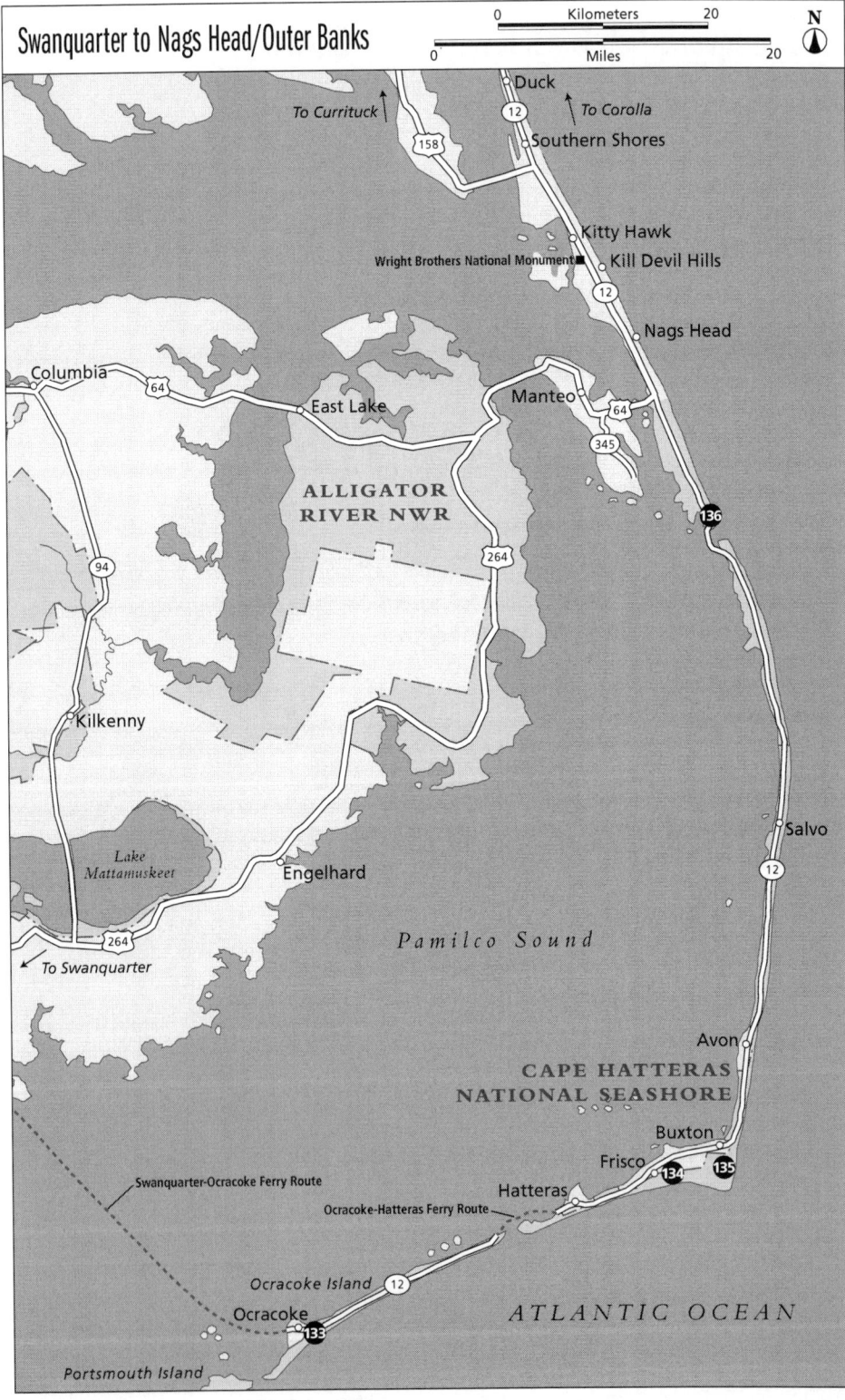

Swanquarter to Nags Head/Outer Banks

Kilometers 0 — 20
Miles 0 — 20

N

To Currituck
Duck
To Corolla
158
Southern Shores
12
Kitty Hawk
Wright Brothers National Monument ■
Kill Devil Hills
12
Nags Head
Columbia
64
East Lake
Manteo
64
345
ALLIGATOR
RIVER NWR
264
136
94
Kilkenny
Salvo
12
Lake
Mattamuskeet
Engelhard
264
To Swanquarter
Pamlico Sound
Avon
CAPE HATTERAS
NATIONAL SEASHORE
Buxton
Frisco
134
135
Swanquarter-Ocracoke Ferry Route
Ocracoke-Hatteras Ferry Route
Hatteras
Ocracoke Island
12
ATLANTIC OCEAN
Ocracoke
133
Portsmouth Island

The still waters off Ocracoke Village reflect the colors of sunset.

captivity for their own protection. They are an endangered species—direct descendents of those ridden by the Spaniards hundreds of years ago.

Sit on the beach with a good book, or obtain a permit from the national park headquarters and take your four-wheel-drive vehicle for a spin on the sands. Be sure to let some air out of your tires and drop their pressure to around 15 to 18 pounds per square inch before you go four-wheeling on any of the beaches or you may get stuck in some of the softer sand.

Although NC 12 runs through the island, no roads lead to Ocracoke, so you must take a ferry to get there. Ferries depart from Cedar Island, Swanquarter, and Hatteras Island on a daily basis. To check on the ferry schedule and fees, make a reservation, or get any other information, contact the ferry system directly at (800) 293-3779 or visit www.ncdot.gov/ferry.

134 Cape Hatteras National Seashore: Frisco Campground

Location: 53415 Billy Mitchell Rd., Frisco; on the south end of Hatteras Island, about 6 miles east of the Hatteras-Ocracoke Ferry Port, 7 miles west of Buxton, and about 57 miles south of Nags Head
Season: Apr–Oct, exact dates vary each year
Sites: 127
Maximum length: 40 feet
Facilities: Flush toilets, showers, water spigots dispersed, charcoal grills, picnic tables; pet friendly
Fee per night: $$$
Management: National Park Service–Cape Hatteras National Seashore
Contact: (252) 473-2111; www.nps.gov/caha/planyourvisit/campgrounds.htm
Finding the campground: From Ocracoke Island take the Hatteras-Ocracoke Ferry (about a 35-minute ferry ride). Once you get off the ferry, drive east on NC 12 for 5.3 miles. Turn right onto Billy Mitchell Road at the sign for the Airstrip and Campground, and travel 1 mile to where it dead-ends at the entrance to the campground.

Off-road driving is one of the many activities you can enjoy during your stay at Frisco.

From Buxton drive west on NC 12 for approximately 6 miles. Turn left onto Billy Mitchell Road at the sign for the AIRSTRIP AND CAMPGROUND, and follow directions above.

GPS coordinates: N35 14.076' / W75 36.544'

Maps: *DeLorme: North Carolina Atlas & Gazetteer:* Page 69 E7

About the campground: Frisco is by far my favorite campground on the Outer Banks. The campsites are nestled among the large rolling hills of the sand dunes. Although they are not right on the beach, you can clearly see the ocean from a select few sites that sit high upon the dunes, and the sound of the waves provides a constant song of solace, serenading you all night long.

The town of Frisco is rich with Native American history and offers plenty of action. You can obtain a permit to drive on the beach (four-wheel-drive vehicles only) or visit the nearby Cape Hatteras Lighthouse. Head just outside the campground and rent a pontoon boat or kayak, or try your hand at kiteboarding. Another great feature is Frisco's nearby pet-boarding facility, since it's difficult to take your pup paddling, etc.; check out the OBX Pet Boarding Kennel.

135 Cape Hatteras National Seashore: Cape Point Campground

Location: 46700 Lighthouse Rd., Buxton; on the south end of Hatteras Island in the village of Buxton; about 12 miles east of the Hatteras-Ocracoke Ferry Port and about 50 miles south of Nags Head

The sun sets beside the Wright Brothers National Monument.

Bodie Lighthouse is one of many lighthouses along the Outer Banks of North Carolina.

Season: May–Sept; exact dates vary each year

Sites: 202

Maximum length: 40 feet

Facilities: Flush toilets, showers, water spigots dispersed, charcoal grills, picnic tables, dump station; pet friendly

Fee per night: $$$

Management: National Park Service—Cape Hatteras National Seashore

Contact: (252) 473-2111; www.nps.gov/caha/planyourvisit/campgrounds.htm

Finding the campground: From Buxton drive south onto Lighthouse Road at the sign for the campground. Follow the road through the park, past the lighthouse, until you've gone 2.3 miles. Turn right onto an unmarked road at the sign for the campground, and continue to the campground entrance.

From Ocracoke Island take the Hatteras-Ocracoke Ferry (about a 35-minute ferry ride). Once you get off the ferry, drive east on NC 12 for 11.9 miles. Turn right onto Lighthouse Road at the sign for the campground, and follow directions above.

GPS coordinates: N35 14.139' / W75 32.022'

Maps: *DeLorme: North Carolina Atlas & Gazetteer:* Page 69 E8

About the campground: Cape Hatteras is better known for its lighthouse than its campground. The world-famous Hatteras Lighthouse you see today has stood tall and proud since it was built in 1870. The lighthouse has not always stood where it sits today, however. Up until 1999 it was perched on the shoreline of the Atlantic, overlooking the sands below. Because of erosion, the National Park Service decided to move it a little over 0.5 mile inland from its original location. At 208 feet, the Hatteras Lighthouse is the tallest lighthouse in the United States, and for a small fee you can climb to the top. While the lighthouse is definitely a highlight, the area also has hiking trails, lots of wildlife, plenty of birding opportunities, a picnic area, and of course the beach.

The campground is nothing to write home about, with row upon row of campsites all lined up next to one another. Cape Point Campground is probably enjoyed more by RV campers, who can go inside for privacy and cool air, than it is by tent campers, especially since the ground tends to stay damp following rain. I personally prefer camping down at Frisco and coming up to Buxton as a day trip to enjoy the best of both worlds.

136 Cape Hatteras National Seashore: Oregon Inlet Campground

Location: NC 12, Nags Head; at the south end of Bodie Island, about 11 miles south of Nags Head and about 15 miles north of Rodanthe

Season: Apr–Oct; exact dates vary each year

Sites: 120; 1 group camping area

Maximum length: 40 feet

Facilities: Flush toilets, showers, water spigots dispersed, charcoal grills, picnic tables, dump station; pet friendly

Fee per night: $$$

Management: National Park Service—Cape Hatteras National Seashore

Wild Corolla mustangs feed along the sand dunes of the Currituck National Wildlife Refuge.

Contact: (252) 473-2111; www.nps.gov/caha/planyourvisit/campgrounds.htm. To reserve the group campsite, call (252) 441-0882. For Kitty Hawk Kites call (877) 359-8447; for Beach Jeeps call (252) 453-6141.

Finding the campground: From the junction of NC 12 and US 64 near Nags Head, drive south on NC 12 for 7.9 miles to the entrance to the campground on your left.

GPS coordinates: N35 48.030' / W75 32.743'

Maps: *DeLorme: North Carolina Atlas & Gazetteer:* Page 49 D8

About the campground: Oregon Inlet Campground lies at the northern end of the Cape Hatteras National Seashore. The campground itself is so-so. The campsites sit on the west side of the sand dunes, so you can't see the ocean, and there's little tree cover or brush. Don't expect too much privacy, and be prepared for the heat during the summer months.

Oregon Inlet is all about location. Head south to Pea Island and you can see herds of deer grazing along the dunes or spy the remains of the *Oriental* shipwreck. As you head north the Bodie Lighthouse is just a few miles away, or you can continue up the coast to Jockey's Ridge State Park. You can't camp here, but Jockey's Ridge is the tallest natural sand dune on the eastern coastline and is home to Kitty Hawk Kites, a hang-gliding school where you can take lessons and learn the foundations of this daring sport.

Up the coast you pass through the lovely town of Duck and then arrive at the Currituck Lighthouse. The grand finale of the Outer Banks, and just thirty minutes north of Oregon Inlet Campground, is the Currituck National Wildlife Refuge. The refuge is home to the wild Corolla mustangs, an endangered species that roams freely among the sand dunes. Take a guided tour to see these descendents of Spanish horses with Beach Jeeps of Corolla, or rent a jeep from them and do your own four-wheel driving in search of the herds.

Jockey's Ridge is the tallest natural sand dune system in the eastern United States.

Columbia to Plymouth

	Total Sites	Hookup Sites	Max. RV Length	Hookups	Toilets	Showers	Drinking Water	Dump Station	Recreation	Fee	Reservations
137 Hidden Lake (Canoe Camping)	1	0	n/a	N	N	N	N	N	H, F, B, L*	$$$	Y*
138 Pettigrew State Park	13	0	50'	N	F*	Y*	Y	N	H, S, F, B, L, P	$$–$$$	Y
138 Pettigrew State Park (Group)	1	0	n/a	N	V	N	Y	N	H, S, F, B, L, P	$$–$$$	Y

* See campground entry for specific information.

137 Hidden Lake Canoe Camping

Location: Along Albemarle Sound, about 13 miles northeast of Columbia and about 26 miles northwest of Manns Harbor
Season: Year-round
Sites: 1 (reservations required)
Maximum length: n/a; tents only
Facilities: Wooden camping platform, *no* bathrooms, *no* potable water, *no* fires allowed
Fee per night: $$$
Management: The Conservation Fund–Palmetto-Peartree Preserve
Contact: (252) 792-3790; www.roanokeriverpartners.org/RiverCamping_HiddenLake.htm; www.palmettopeartree.org
Finding the campground: From the junction of US 64 and NC 94 in Columbia, drive east on US 64 for 7.2 miles. Turn left onto Old Highway 64 (SR 1229) at the sign for PALMETTO-PEARTREE PRESERVE, and travel 2 miles. Turn left onto SR 1221 at the sign for PALMETTO-PEARTREE PRESERVE, and continue 1.9 miles to the end of the road at a stop sign. Go left here onto SR 1209 (Soundside Road), and follow it for 0.8 mile. Turn right onto Loop Road (SR 1220), and travel 0.7 mile. Turn right onto an unmarked road that runs alongside a small canal, and continue for 0.3 mile. Turn right onto another unmarked road that leads 0.1 mile to the canoe launch on Albemarle Sound.

From the junction of US 64 and NC 264 near Manns Harbor, drive west on US 64 for approximately 19.4 miles. Turn right onto Old Highway 64, and travel 3 miles. Turn right onto SR 1221 at the sign for PALMETTO-PEARTREE PRESERVE, and follow directions above.
GPS coordinates: N35 59.364' / W76 07.916'
Maps: *DeLorme: North Carolina Atlas & Gazetteer: Page 48 B2*
About the campground: The aptly named Hidden Lake sits on the south side of Albemarle Sound amid the Palmetto-Peartree Preserve. A single, well-maintained wooden camping platform is located on the eastern edge of the lake, and the campsite can only be reached via canoe or kayak. The paddle route takes you along the southern shoreline of Albemarle Sound before leading

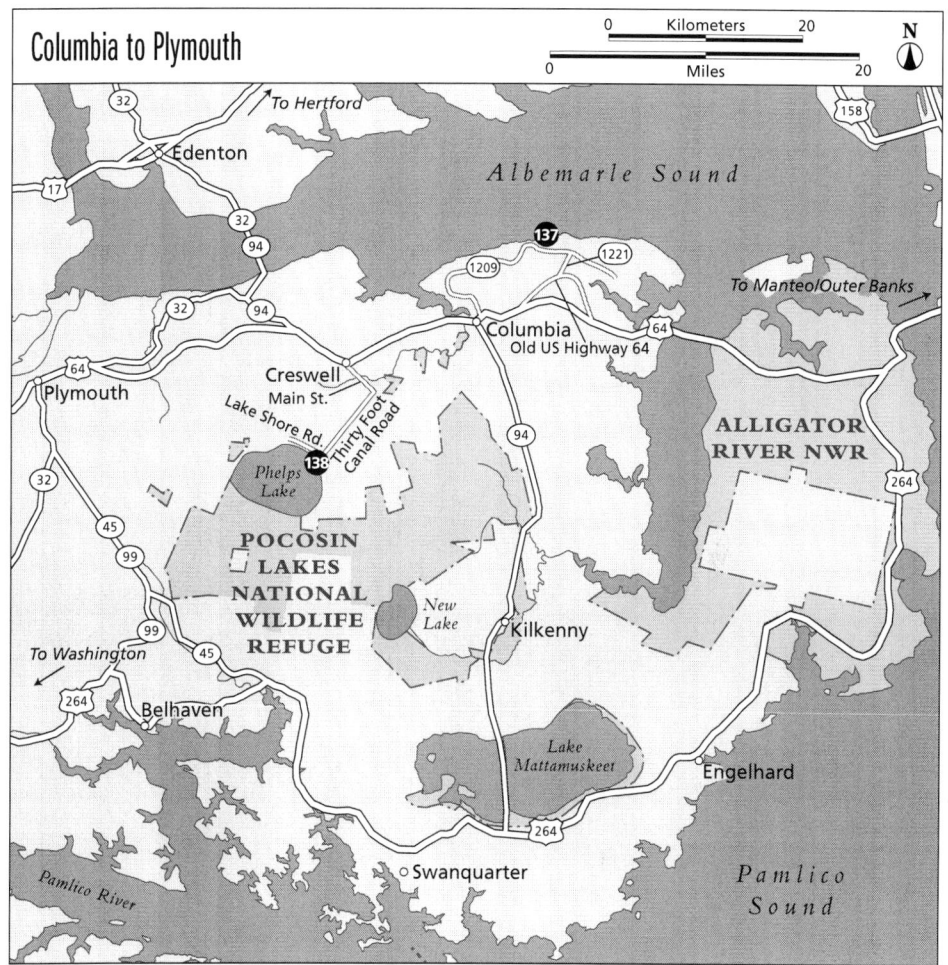

0   Kilometers   20

0   Miles   20

N

32

To Hertford

Edenton

158

17

Albemarle Sound

32

94

137

1209

1221

32

94

To Manteo/Outer Banks

Columbia
Old US Highway 64

64

64

Plymouth

Creswell
Main St.

Lake Shore Rd.

Thirty Foot Canal Road

94

ALLIGATOR
RIVER NWR

32

Phelps
Lake

138

264

45

POCOSIN
LAKES
NATIONAL
WILDLIFE
REFUGE

New
Lake

99

Kilkenny

99

To Washington

45

264

Belhaven

Lake
Mattamuskeet

Engelhard

264

Swanquarter

Pamlico River

Pamlico
Sound

you inland along a channel for about 0.25 mile to Hidden Lake. There's a sign at the entrance to the channel; pay attention, or you could miss the turnoff.

For maps and detailed information on the area, camping, and the paddle trail, visit the websites listed above. I have included hiking on the recreation list because hiking trails run throughout the Palmetto-Peartree Preserve, but you cannot hike to the camping platform. There are no campfires allowed on the platform and no bathroom facilities, so you may want to bring a portable toilet. Reservations are required and can be made using the contact number above.

Stunning sunsets can be viewed from the boat launch at Pettigrew State Park.

138 Pettigrew State Park

Location: 2252 Lake Shore Rd., Creswell; about 17 miles southwest of Columbia and about 30 miles southeast of Plymouth
Season: Year-round; closed Christmas Day
Sites: 13; 1 group camping area also available that can accommodate up to 24 people
Maximum length: 50 feet
Facilities: Flush toilets, hot showers, water spigots dispersed, fire rings, picnic tables, lantern holders, trash cans; pet friendly. *NOTE:* The bathhouse is closed Nov 1–Mar 15. During this time, vault toilets are available and there are *no* showers.
Fee per night: $$–$$$
Management: North Carolina Department of Natural Resources
Contact: (252) 797-4475; www.ncparks.gov/Visit/parks/pett/main.php. For reservations call (877) 722-6762 or visit www.reserveamerica.com.
Finding the campground: From Columbia drive west on US 64 for approximately 7 miles. Take exit 558 at the sign for Pᴇᴛᴛɪɢʀᴇᴡ Sᴛᴀᴛᴇ Pᴀʀᴋ, and head toward Creswell for 0.5 mile. Turn left onto Main

White tundra swans flock to Phelps Lake by the thousands every winter.

Street (SR 1142), and follow it for 1.8 miles. Turn right onto Thirty Foot Canal Road (SR 1160) at the sign for Pettigrew State Park, and continue for 3.8 miles to a stop sign at Cherry Road. Continue straight across the intersection and travel for another 4.5 miles. Turn left onto Lake Shore Road; the entrance to Pettigrew State Park is immediately on your right. *NOTE:* Main Street in Creswell becomes Spruill Bridge Road.

From Plymouth drive east on US 64 to exit 558 at the sign for Pettigrew State Park, and follow directions above.

GPS coordinates: N35 47.453' / W76 24.527'

Maps: *DeLorme: North Carolina Atlas & Gazetteer:* Page 47 D8

About the campground: What a fabulous state park this is. Resting along the banks of Phelps Lake, Pettigrew is on the small side, but it has a lot to offer for its size. There are hiking trails; a picnic area; several massive, state-champion trees; and the historic Somerset Place right next door. But the highlight by far is Phelps Lake. A fishing pier, canoe rentals, a boat ramp, and a swim area allow you to enjoy this wonderful lake firsthand.

Spectacular sunsets greet you each evening, and in winter thousands of great white tundra swans migrate to the area, making the lake their winter haven. This is a birders dream, and the birdlife is certainly not limited to the swans. Woodpeckers, cardinals, bluebirds, and chickadees make their home here as well. One of the great pleasures of camping is waking up to the sounds of birds singing, so you are in for a treat at Pettigrew. The campsites seem to be right next to one another but in truth they are nestled amid the trees, giving you all the privacy you need. Grab your binoculars and your fishing pole, and enjoy your stay.

Edenton to Windsor

	Total Sites	Hookup Sites	Max. RV Length	Hookups	Toilets	Showers	Drinking Water	Dump Station	Recreation	Fee	Reservations
139 John's Island (Canoe)	5	0	n/a	N	N	N	N	N	F, B, L	$$$	Y*
140 Windsor Campground	15	11	50'	E, W	Y*	Y*	Y	N	F, B, L	$	N

* See campground entry for specific information.

139 John's Island Canoe Camping

Location: The camping platforms are along the banks of Pembroke Creek in the town of Edenton and can only be accessed by boat. Three boat launch sites are described below.
Season: Year-round
Sites: 5 (reservations required)
Maximum length: n/a; tents only
Facilities: Wooden camping platforms, *no* bathrooms, *no* potable water, *no* fires allowed
Fee per night: $$$
Management: Chowan County Department of Parks and Recreation
Contact: (252) 482-8595; www.roanokeriverpartners.org/RiverCamping_JohnsIsland.htm; www.pathsofchowan.org/platformji.html

Bayside Marina Access

Finding the launch site: 802 Queen St., Edenton. Take exit 224 off US 17, and follow Queen Street (US 17 Business) east for 2 miles to Bayside Marina on your left.
GPS coordinates: N36 03.442' / W76 37.796'

Edenton Marina Access

Finding the launch site: 621 Queen St., Edenton. Take exit 224 off US 17, and follow Queen Street (US 17 Business) east for 2.4 miles to Edenton Marina on your right.
GPS coordinates: N36 03.569' / W76 37.395'

Colonial Waterfront Park Access

Finding the launch site: 510 South Broad St., Edenton. Take exit 224 off US 17, and follow Queen Street (US 17 Business) east for 3.4 miles. Turn right onto Broad Street, and travel 0.2 mile to where it ends at Colonial Waterfront Park.
GPS coordinates: N36 03.381' / W76 36.599'
Maps: *DeLorme: North Carolina Atlas & Gazetteer:* Page 47 A6

Edenton to Windsor

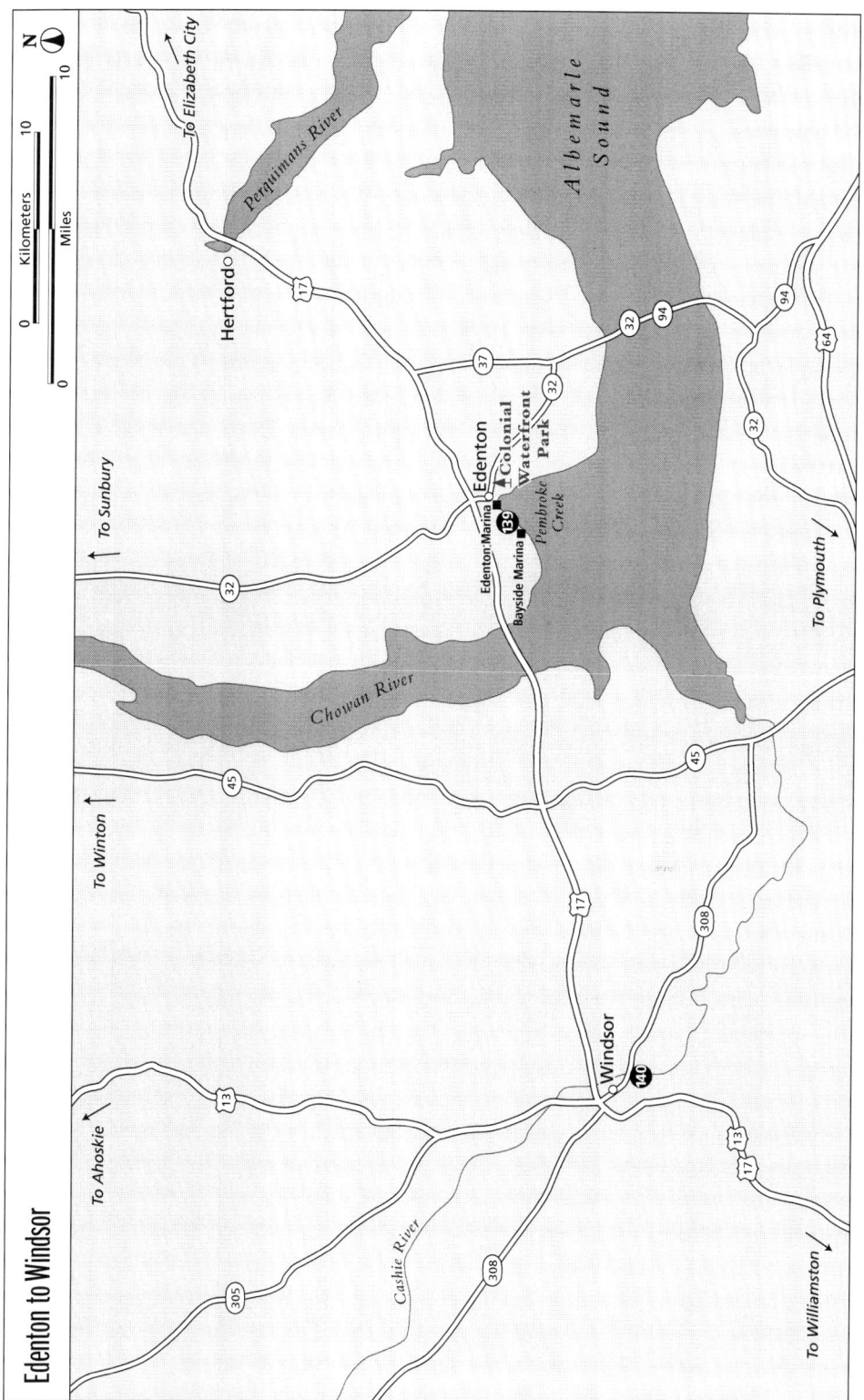

Cannons once protected the shores of downtown Edenton.

About the campground: This is privacy at its best. The camping platforms at John's Island offer complete seclusion, hidden amid the tall cypress trees and thick underbrush, yet only minutes from downtown Edenton. The platforms are part of the 5-mile Pembroke Creek Paddle Trail and are on the northern edge of John's Island, which juts out into Edenton Bay and acts as a natural barrier to protect the town from the elements.

The platforms can be accessed by canoe, kayak, or motorized boats. I have provided three easy access launch points for canoes and kayaks. If you have a motorized boat, you can use the boat launches at either Bayside or Edenton Marina. Both of these places have ample overnight parking for your vehicle and trailer. There's a nominal fee to use the ramps at Bayside and Edenton Marinas, but they have the best parking options, and you don't have to paddle across the windy Edenton Bay if you put in here.

Campfires are not allowed on any of the camping platforms, and remember to bring a portable toilet as well. The websites above contain a wealth of information on John's Island and all the camping platforms in this area. Advance reservations are required.

A pair of geese fly over the Cashie River near Windsor.

140 Windsor Campground

Location: East Elm Street, Windsor
Season: Year-round
Sites: 15
Maximum length: 50 feet
Facilities: Flush toilets, hot showers (bathhouse closed in winter), electric, water spigots, charcoal grills, picnic tables, trash cans; pet friendly
Fee per night: $
Management: Town of Windsor
Contact: (252) 794-3121
Finding the campground: From the junction of US 17/NC 308 West and NC 308 East (Cooper Hill Road) in Windsor, drive west on US 17/NC 308 (South King Street) for 0.8 mile. Turn left onto East Elm Street, and continue 0.3 mile to a fork at the entrance to the park. The right leads to a public boat launch site; the left leads directly into the campground.

From the junction of US 17/NC 308 and US 17 South (West Water Street) in Windsor, drive east on US 17/NC 308 (South King Street) for 0.3 mile. Turn right onto East Elm Street, and follow directions above.

GPS coordinates: N35 59.134' / W76 56.415'

Maps: *DeLorme: North Carolina Atlas & Gazetteer:* Page 46 B3

About the campground: Windsor Campground rests along the headwaters of the Cashie River on the outskirts of the town of Windsor. One tiny loop makes up the campground. Eleven RV sites sit on the outside of the loop, and a small open grassy area in the middle has four tent campsites. Although there's not much privacy here, the price is unbeatable, especially when you can park your RV and have a water and electric hookup. There's a public boat ramp right next door, so you also have easy access to the Cashie River.

The town of Windsor has deep historical roots and was placed on the National Register of Historic Places in 1991. Take a drive down King Street to see some of the wonderful historical architecture, head to the river center in downtown, or visit the town's petting zoo.

	Total Sites	Hookup Sites	Max. RV Length	Hookups	Toilets	Showers	Drinking Water	Dump Station	Recreation	Fee	Reservations
141 Paths of Perquimans (Canoe)	7	0	n/a	N	V	N	N	N	F, B, L	$$$	Y*
142 Holladay Island (Canoe)	5	0	n/a	N	N	N	N	N	F, B, L	$$$	Y*
143 Merchants Millpond State Park	44	0	68'*	N	F	Y	Y	N	H, F, B, L*, P	$$-$$$	Y

* See campground entry for specific information.

141 Paths of Perquimans Canoe Camping

Location: Camping platforms located along the Perquimans River, with several different canoe/boat launch sites open to the public
Season: Year-round
Sites: 7; 2 double platforms, and 1 triple platform (reservations required for all sites)
Maximum length: n/a; tent only
Facilities: Elevated platforms along the river, vault toilet, *no* potable water, *no* fires allowed
Fee per night: $$$
Management: Perquimans County Recreation Department
Contact: (252) 426-5695; www.pathsofperquimans.org; www.albemarlercd.org/Paddle_Trails.asp

Hertford Town Hall Access

Finding the launch site: From the junction of US 17 Business (Church Street) and US 17/NC 37 in Hertford (just before crossing the bridge over the Perquimans River), drive north on Church Street for 0.9 mile. Turn left onto Grubb Street, and travel less than 0.1 mile. Turn right onto Punch Alley; you will see the boat launch directly in front of you, behind the Hertford Town Hall.
GPS coordinates: N36 11.462' / W76 27.991'

Winfall Park Access

Finding the launch site: From the junction of US 17 Business and NC 37 near Hertford, drive north on NC 37 for 0.4 mile. Turn left onto Major Street, and travel 0.1 mile to the end. Turn left into Winfall Park.
GPS coordinates: N36 12.440' / W76 27.981'

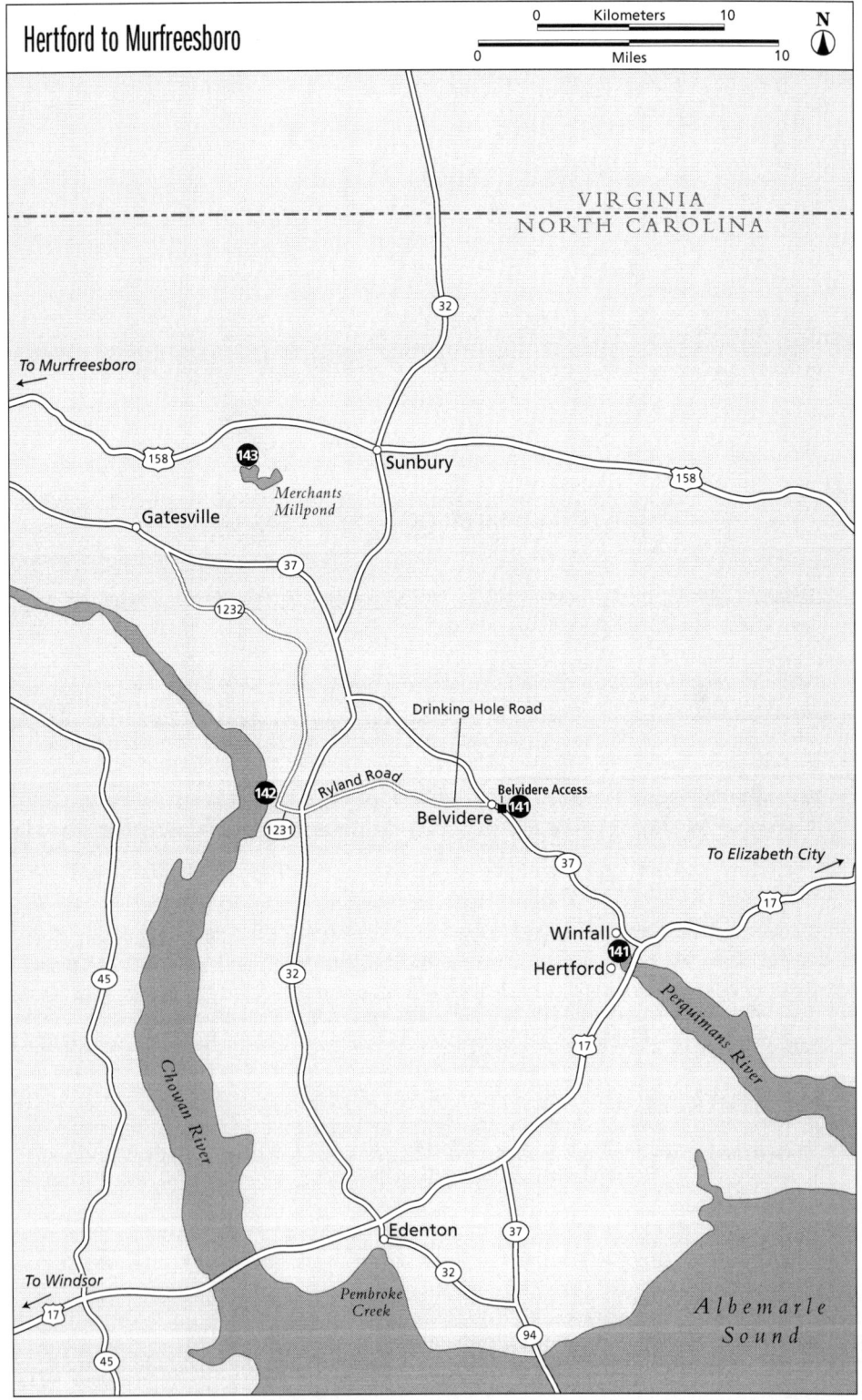

0   Kilometers   10

0   Miles   10

N

VIRGINIA
NORTH CAROLINA

32

To Murfreesboro

158

143

Sunbury

158

Merchants
Millpond

Gatesville

37

1232

Drinking Hole Road

Ryland Road

Belvidere Access

142

141

Belvidere

1231

37

To Elizabeth City

17

Winfall

141

Hertford

17

45

32

17

Chowan River

Perquimans River

Edenton

37

To Windsor

17

32

45

Pembroke
Creek

94

Albemarle
Sound

A pelican enjoys the freedom of flight over Albemarle Sound.

Belvidere Access

Finding the launch site: From the junction of US 17 Business and NC 37 near Hertford, drive north on NC 37 for 7.7 miles to the Belvidere access point, immediately after you cross the bridge over the Perquimans River.

GPS coordinates: N36 16.098' / W76 32.745'

Maps: *DeLorme: North Carolina Atlas & Gazetteer:* Page 25 E7–E6

About the campground: Seven wooden camping platforms await as you head out to explore the waterways of the Perquimans River. Each is a 16×24-foot elevated wooden platform, where you can pitch your tent and spend the night under the stars. The sites are located along the Perquimans River Trail and the Mill Creek Paddle Trail as they wind through the northeast coastal region.

Rich in history, the town of Hertford is one of the earliest settlement areas in North Carolina. With Victorian homes lining the streets, take a drive and step back in time. Or hop on your bike and ride along the very first bike trail in the state. For a wealth of information about the paddle trails and the area in general, visit the websites above. Reservations are required and can be made by calling the phone number above.

142 Holladay Island Canoe Camping

Location: Holladay Island is located along the Chowan River at the northern end of Chowan County near Cannon's Ferry and is only accessible by boat. The boat launch is about 15 miles north of Edenton and about 15 miles northwest of Hertford.
Season: Year-round
Sites: 5 (reservations required)
Maximum length: n/a; tents only
Facilities: Wooden camping platforms, vault toilet, *no* potable water, *no* fires allowed
Fee per night: $$$
Management: Edenton-Chowan Department of Parks and Recreation
Contact: (252) 482-8595 or (252) 221-4901; www.roanokeriverpartners.org/RiverCamping_HolladayIsland.htm
Finding the campground: From the junction of NC 32 (Virginia Road) and NC 37 South near Sign Pine, drive south on NC 32 for 4.5 miles. Turn right onto Cannon's Ferry Road (SR 1231), and travel 1.1 miles to the boat launch on your left at the corner of SR 1231 and SR 1232 in Cannon's Ferry.

From the junction of NC 32 (Virginia Road) and US 17 in Edenton, drive north on NC 32 for approximately 14.2 miles. Turn left onto Cannon's Ferry Road (SR 1231), and follow directions above.
GPS coordinates: Canoe launch: N36 16.231' / W76 40.346'; motorized boat launch: N36 16.080' / W76 40.249'
Maps: *DeLorme: North Carolina Atlas & Gazetteer:* Page 25 D5–E5
About the campground: In the middle of the Chowan River lies Holladay Island, named for Thomas Holladay, who first owned the island back in 1730. There are five campsites on the island, but Holladay Island is unique. A cypress swamp makes up the "island," and the "campground" is really several elevated wooden platforms to keep you and your gear out of the swampland.

On the south end of the island, there is a cluster of three platforms connected by boardwalks. This is a great option if you have a larger group of people who want to explore the Chowan from within. The two remaining platforms are individuals, set off by themselves amid the towering trees. Each platform is 16 × 24 feet, and the county has provided a vault toilet, so you do not have to bring your own portable toilet.

The boat launch listed above is only suitable for canoes and kayaks. Motorized boats are welcome to camp at Holladay Island as well, and a boat ramp for them is located less than 0.2 mile southeast on Cannon's Ferry Road (SR 1231), before reaching the canoe launch.

143 Merchants Millpond State Park

Location: 176 Millpond Rd., Gatesville; about 30 miles northeast of Ahoskie and about 30 miles northwest of Hertford
Season: Year-round; closed Christmas Day
Sites: 20; individual and group backpack sites and individual and group canoe-to sites also available

Mikey overlooks the Cypress trees scattered throughout Merchants Millpond.

Maximum length: 68 feet
Facilities: Flush toilets, hot showers, water spigots dispersed, fire rings, picnic tables, trash cans, firewood for sale; pet friendly
Fee per night: $$–$$$
Management: North Carolina Department of Natural Resources
Contact: (252) 357-1191; www.ncparks.gov/Visit/parks/memi/main.php. For reservations call (877) 722-6762 or visit www.reserveamerica.com.
Finding the campground: From the junction of US 158 and NC 32 in Sunbury, drive west on US 158 for 4.7 miles. Turn left into Merchants Millpond State Park, and follow the road back 0.4 mile to where it dead-ends at the campground. To reach the visitor center, go back out to NC 158, and drive west for 0.3 mile. Turn left onto Millpond Road (SR 1403), and travel 0.8 mile to the main entrance to the park on your left.

From the junction of US 158 and NC 37 at Eleanors Crossroads, drive east on US 158 for 4 miles. Turn right into Merchants Millpond State Park, and follow directions above.
GPS coordinates: N36 26.625' / W76 41.702'
Maps: *DeLorme: North Carolina Atlas & Gazetteer:* Page 25 B5–C5

About the campground: Merchants Millpond State Park is a tent camper's haven. There's a fabulous family campground, and backcountry camping is also available and can be reached either by foot or canoe. Every campsite in the family campground is wooded and very private. It's almost as though they designed the campground with tent campers in mind, although it's suitable for RVs up to 68 feet as well. There's a picnic area, a canoe launch, and canoe and kayak rentals. Firewood is available for sale on the honor system. Miles of hiking trails lead through amazing, diverse terrain as you explore the Merchants Millpond, Lassiter Swamp, and the rolling hills that surround them.

Elizabeth City

	Total Sites	Hookup Sites	Max. RV Length	Hookups	Toilets	Showers	Drinking Water	Dump Station	Recreation	Fee	Reservations
144 Pasquotank River (Canoe)	4	0	n/a	N	N	N	N	N	F, B, L	$$$	Y

144 Pasquotank River Canoe Camping

Location: Camping platforms located along the Pasquotank River, with several different canoe/boat launch site options
Season: Year-round
Sites: 4 (reservations required)
Maximum length: n/a; tents only
Facilities: Wooden camping platforms, *no* bathrooms, *no* potable water, *no* fires allowed
Fee per night: $$
Management: Pasquotank County/Elizabeth City Parks & Recreation
Contact: (252) 335-2897; www.albemarlercd.org/Paddle_Trails.asp. For reservations call (252) 337-6600.

Waterfront Park Access

Finding the launch site: From the junction of US 17 and US 158 in downtown Elizabeth City, drive east on US 158 for 0.2 mile. Turn right onto South Water Street (just before crossing the bridge over the Pasquotank River), and continue 0.25 mile to Waterfront Park on your left.
GPS coordinates: N36 17.796' / W76 13.113'

Lamb's Marina Access

Finding the launch site: From the junction of US 17 and US 158 in downtown Elizabeth City, drive east on US 158 for 3.2 miles to Lamb's Marina on your left.
From the junction of US 158 and NC 343 in Camden, drive west on US 158 for 0.5 mile to Lamb's Marina on your right.
GPS coordinates: N36 19.289' / W76 10.576'

Sawyer Creek Access

Finding the launch site: From the junction of NC 343 and US 158 in Camden, drive north on NC 343 for 0.5 mile to a left turn into the Sawyer Creek Access area.

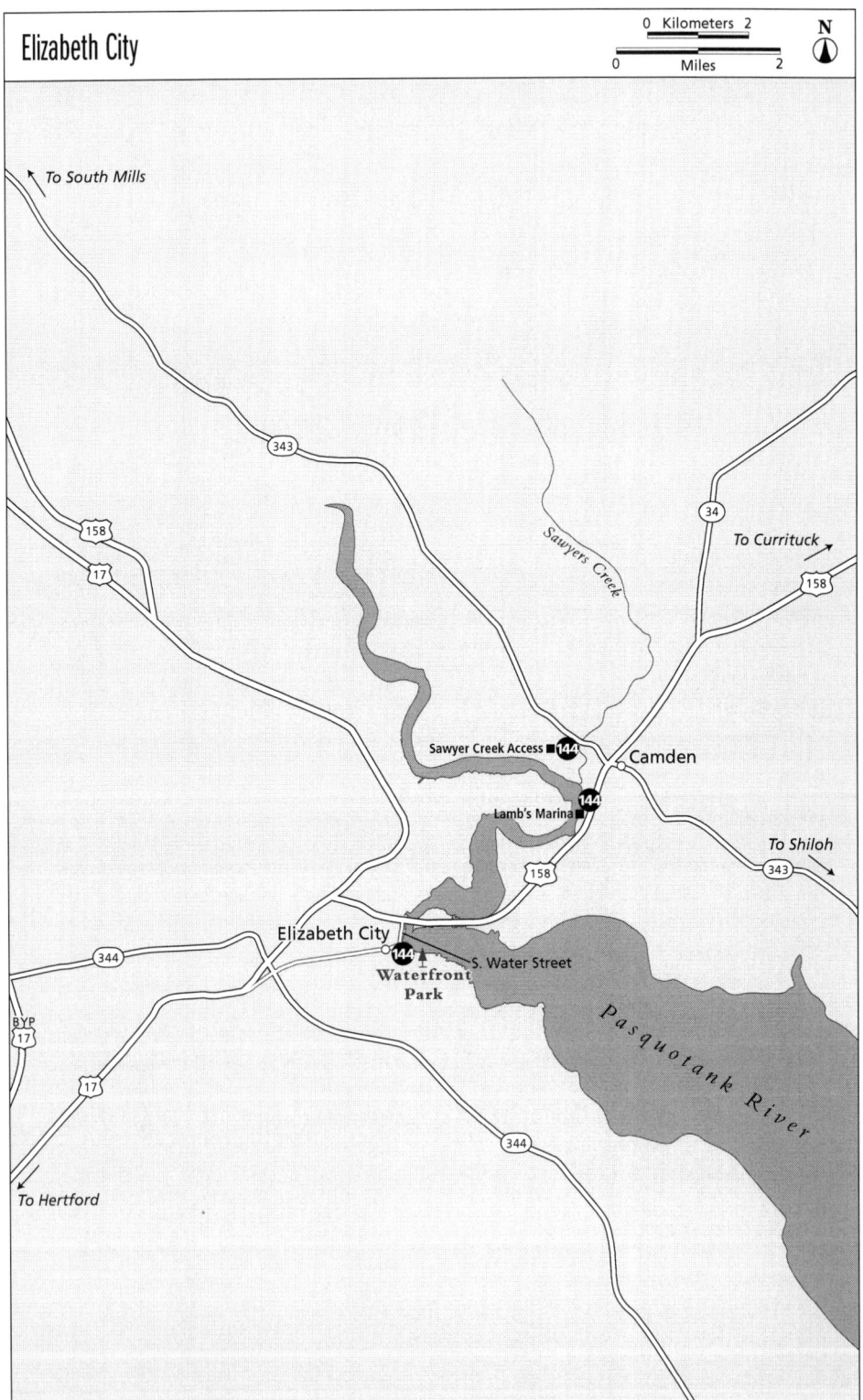

Elizabeth City

From the junction of NC 343 and US 17 near Johnsons Corner, drive south on NC 343 for approximately 12.8 miles to a right turn into the Sawyer Creek Access area.

GPS coordinates: N36 19.905' / W76 10.785'

Maps: *DeLorme: North Carolina Atlas & Gazetteer:* Page 26 D1

About the campground: The Pasquotank River Trail stretches 21 miles northwest from Elizabeth City and has two separate camping areas. The Goat Island and Northside areas both have double camping platforms, meaning each area has two separate wooden camping platforms connected by a boardwalk—perfect for a small group of paddlers to enjoy some isolated riverside camping with a little bit of privacy from each other as well.

The platforms are 16×24 feet, and as an added bonus, both camping areas also have an enclosed area for you to use your own portable toilet in privacy. There are no facilities whatsoever, so be sure to bring all your food, water, and supplies along with you. Also, as with any canoe camping, pack your gear in dry bags, because the bottom of any canoe always ends up with just enough water to get your gear wet if you leave it unprotected.

Index

About the Author

Melissa Watson is a professional fire-fighter who has been camping, hiking, mountain biking, and photographing waterfalls and wildlife in North Carolina for more than twenty years. From deep in the mountains to the foothills of the Piedmont and stretching all the way to the far reaches of the Outer Banks, she continually explores new territory with a map and compass in hand and a pack on her back. Melissa is also the author of *Hiking Waterfalls in North Carolina* and *Hiking Waterfalls in Georgia and South Carolina* (both from FalconGuides).